THE HAND HOLDING THE BRUSH

ROBERT STACEY

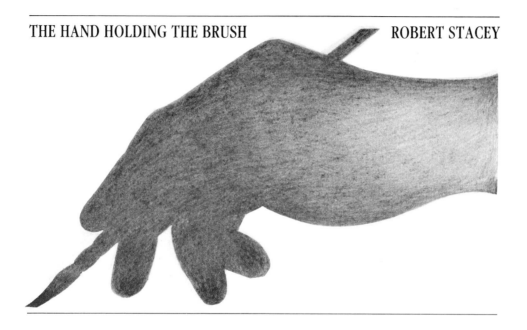

ISBN 0-920872-31-X

The London Regional Art Gallery
wishes to express sincere appreciation
to the many lenders, both private and
public, whose generous cooperation
has made this exhibition possible. Also
to the National Museums of Canada
for research and production grants,
and to the Canada Council, the
Ontario Arts Council, the Ministry of
Citizenship and Culture and the City
of London, for additional funding
support.

London Regional Art Gallery
421 Ridout Street North,
London, Canada N6A 5H4

THE HAND HOLDING THE BRUSH

Self Portraits by Canadian Artists

ROBERT STACEY

Front Cover: Caven Atkins: *Self Portrait*
(1939) (detail)
Collection: Art Gallery of Windsor

Back Cover: Ernest Lindner: *Sketching*
(1975)
Watercolour (54.6 × 74.3 cm)
Collection: The Artist, Saskatoon
Photo: T.E. Moore, Toronto

Photography Credits

Credits

Most photographs of works in public institutions were obtained directly from the photo-services departments of these public galleries, museums or archives; otherwise, photography credits are included with individual catalogue entries and figure captions. In certain instances, sources for photographs used as figures were not obtainable. Attempts were made to contact all copyright-holders and owners for permission to reproduce images, and apologies are hereby tendered to individuals and/or institutions not properly credited because of lack of information as to present whereabouts of works included as supplementary illustrations to text and catalogue entries.

Guest Curator	Robert Stacey
Exhibition Co-ordinator	Paddy O'Brien
Assistant Co-ordinator	Lee Clark
Bibliographies	Carol Lowrey
Special Photography	T. E. Moore
Reader	Dr. Ross Woodman
Catalogue Design	V. John Lee Communications Graphics Inc.
Production	Rene Demers
Word-Processors	Becky Boughner Sharon Gignac
Signage Designer	Robert Ballantine
Printing	The Hearn/Kelly Printing Company Limited
Typesetting	Compeer Typographic Services Limited

Guest-Curator Acknowledgements

Without the patience, forebearance and hard work of Paddy O'Brien, Chief Curator of the London Regional Art Gallery, and her assistant, Lee Clark, this exhibition and catalogue would not have been possible. My thanks also to Matthew Teitelbaum for advice and assistance. I am grateful to Brenda Wallace, Director of the London Regional Art Gallery, for inviting me to guest-curate this show. The industry and enthusiasm of the entire Gallery staff are much appreciated.

Among outside colleagues, I am especially indebted for information and encouragement to Jim Burant, Picture Division, Public Archives of Canada; Charles C. Hill, Curator, Post-Confederation Canadian Art, National Gallery of Canada; Dennis Reid, Curator, Historical Canadian Art, Art Gallery of Ontario; and the late Dr. J. Russell Harper. Carol Lowrey, of the Art Gallery of Ontario's E.P. Taylor Library, provided invaluable bibliographical assistance, and answered many other queries. Photographs and helpful data were also supplied by Anita Aarons, Art Gallery at Harbourfront, and Marjorie Lismer Bridges.

The photo-services departments of numerous public galleries, museums, archives and libraries provided prints on short notice; my apologies to their overworked staffs for my many frequent and urgent requests.

Special thanks are owed, of course, not only to the collectors and institutions which generously have loaned works, but to the artists who participated by contributing facts, photographs, and suggestions, and to their dealers, agents, or descendents, for similar courtesies. To Maggie, for enduring yet another Winter Campaign, my beholdenness is, as usual, immeasurable.

Robert Stacey
Guest Curator

Foreword

The production of a major travelling exhibition is always a very complex process of research, selection, fundraising, writing and publication – to say nothing of the myriad details of coordination that must be attended to over a long period of time. Consequently, there is a matching degree of excitement and satisfaction when everything comes together and the exhibition is actually hanging on the walls. It is particularly true when the content of the show deals with the exploration of an aspect of Canadian art that has not previously been examined in any great depth. *The Hand Holding the Brush* is just such a theme, and I am pleased to congratulate our guest curator, Robert Stacy, for allowing us to become aware of the intensely interesting subject of self-portraiture in both its historic and contemporary aspects. The manner in which an artist perceives his or her own visage inevitably enables us to approach each revelation with a psychological awareness not always of immediate concern when looking at their non-autobiographical work and, as such, permits a high degree of a special kind of insight which is unusually rewarding.

While our guest-curator's research requirements have been thoroughly investigated, he has unfortunately been governed by constraints of time due to the Gallery's early 1983 closing, as well as other gallery-related financial problems. It was unfortunate, too, that their condition of previous commitments prevented the inclusion of several key works. A few of them would have more vividly exemplified Mr. Stacey's research objectives. However, what is clearly evident as a result of his chosen area of pursuit is that he now has more than sufficient exciting material on which to build another exhibition at a future date on this almost unexplored topic in Canadian art history. Continued investigation could permit scholars and viewers whose concern is portraiture and/or self-portraiture to see an expanded selection of work designed to reinforce the curator's premise on which the present exhibition *The Hand Holding the Brush* was founded – that there definitely exists a strong tradition of portrait painting in Canada, and that it must be celebrated and acknowledged as it has been in other western countries. I would like to think that it would not be presumptuous to suggest that this exhibition could lead to the establishment of a national portrait gallery in Canada at some future date.

On behalf of the London Regional Art Gallery, and the other institutions participating in the tour, I would like to express sincere appreciation to all those who have lent work from their collections in order to make this exhibition possible. Their generosity and support is quite outstanding. We also deeply appreciate the financial assistance of the National Museums of Canada, the Canada Council and the Ontario Arts Council, which has enabled our gallery to assemble this important exhibition.

Brenda Wallace
Director

Itinerary

November 4, 1983–January 8, 1984	London Regional Art Gallery
January 20–March 4, 1984	Macdonald Stewart Art Centre, Guelph
March 19–April 29, 1984	Art Gallery of Hamilton
May 14–June 24, 1984	McCord Museum, Montréal
July 9–August 19, 1984	Beaverbrook Art Gallery, Fredericton
September 3–October 14, 1984	Mount Saint Vincent University Art Gallery, Halifax
October 29–December 16, 1984	Agnes Etherington Art Centre, Kingston

NOTE

All catalogue entries followed by an asterisk (*) were shown only at London Regional Art Gallery (4 November 1983 – 8 January 1984). Works excluded from tour were deemed to be in too fragile a condition or too cumbersome to travel for the duration of a year-long tour.

INTRODUCTION

I Preamble

"A portrait! What could be simpler and more complicated, more obvious and more profound?"
– Charles Baudelaire: "The Salon of 1859: Portraiture", *Art in Paris 1845-1862: Reviews of Salons and Other Exhibitions.*
Translated by Jonathan Mayne (London: Phaidon Press, 1965), p. 189.

"How do you do a self-portrait that doesn't show yourself drawing?"
– Margaret Keith, verbal query to the author, 21/10/1982.

The title of this exhibition, *"The Hand Holding the Brush"*, is taken from W. G. Constable's *The Painter's Workshop.* In the chapter on "Preliminaries to Making a Painting" in that guide to the techniques and *apparati* of the masters, Constable notes that

> Every portrait painter at some time paints his own portrait, usually more than once, and for so doing uses a mirror. This, of course, reverses everything, and care has to be taken if the painter is right-handed that he is not represented as left-handed, or vice versa, while *the hand holding the brush* [my italics] may have to be painted from memory, or by adaptation from the free hand. It has therefore been suggested that sometimes a second mirror may have been used to overcome this difficulty . . . Incidentally, it is not always easy, in the case of an artist whose features are not known, to tell a self-portrait from a portrait of another painter. The arrangement of the hands is usually the best clue, since in the case of a self-portrait this will be such that the hand holding the brush is always free.[1]

I came across this passage while preparing a preliminary proposal for an exhibition to be devoted — so I then intended — to the twin subjects of self-portraits and portraits-of-artists; my determination to use the phrase "the hand holding the brush" as a title was confirmed in November 1982, two months before I was to begin the guest-curating of a show predicated on the premise that most *Canadian* artists had produced at least one self-portrait. Work on a catalogue-editing project had sent me to Europe, and I was taking the opportunity provided by airline tickets that allowed for four "free" stops *en route* to visit Florence — my major objective being the Uffizi and, if admission might be arranged, a tour of the Vasari Corridor, home of the greatest single collection of historical self-portraits in existence. The question quoted above as a second epigraph seemed to clinch the matter; for although all self-portraits do not belong to the category of *portraits d'apparat*, a sufficient number of the familiar and unfamiliar instances hung in that long and narrow covered passage spanning the Arno (originally a private gallery whereby the Medici could make their elevated way from the Pitti Palace to the offices of state across the river) suggested that, for artists preoccupied by the quandary of self-definition, the implements of their calling represent considerably more than convenient props in their pictures of themselves and their colleagues. The brush in the hand becomes a sacred wand, indentifying the artist as a member of a secret sodality of descendants of Apelles and disciples of St. Luke, the patron saint of painters, doctors, and butchers.

Imagine, then, how struck I was, a month hence, on a last weekend in Paris before flying back to a Toronto winter (and the complications of curating a show dedicated to a hitherto little-discussed and grossly under-documented aspect of Canadian art), by the unexpected experience of wandering into so modest and unassuming an exhibition and yet so utterly charming an exhibition as that which then was on view in the Grand Palais: the *Donation J. H. Lartigue* photographic collection. It was the illustrated admission-ticket to this happy event that jerked me into alertness: there (Fig. 1), on a folding stool, sits a *plein air* painter; to his right, a large horizontal mirror reflects his head, torso, right arm, and the canvas on which he is working. To the left, directly before him, stands his easel and canvas, to which his brush-wielding hand was caught by the photographer in the process of applying pigment to what appears to be background foliage. Sketched in with white chalk (?) is the artist's right arm and hand, transformed by the magic of lateral inversion into the painting-subject's left. The triad of images implies infinity: for what the painted painter paints is the painting he "sees" in the mirror, and mirrors mirroring mirrors do so to the

Fig. 1 Grand Palais, Paris, admission ticket, 1982

10

Fig. 1

vanishing-point. I get dizzy just trying to describe what is going on in this artifactual photograph of a factual art-act taking place in the two-dimensional time-space continuum of the moment preserved. Here is a paradoxical parable to beguile the analytical skills of such non-Euclidean geometrists of mazes and looking-glasses as Lewis Carroll, Jorge Luis Borges, Vladimir Nabokov, John Barth, and Roland Barthes. And while Barthes never had occasion to dissect Lartigue's bemusing dance of frozen gestures in *Camera Lucida*, he did offer this miniature assay of Gustave Courbet's monumental self-portrait of 1845-1855, *L'Atelier* (Musée du Louvre, Paris):

it is a complete allegory. Shut up in a room, the artist is painting a landscape he does not see, turning his back to his (naked) model, who is watching him paint. In other words, the painter establishes himself in a space carefully emptied of any gaze but his own. Now, all art which has only two dimensions, that

of the work and that of the spectator, can create only a platitude since it is no more than the capture of a shop-window spectacle by a painter-voyeur. Depth is born only at the moment the spectacle itself slowly turns its shadow toward man and begins to look at him.[2]

I had stumbled upon the Lartigue by accident on my way to the huge Fantin-Latour exhibition installed on the same premises (it later travelled to Ottawa, one of its curators being a Canadian in the employ of the National Gallery of Canada). Small wonder, then, that my head should have been so full of the subject of self-portraiture by the end of that crowded day. The core of the latter show was that too-long-neglected *intimatiste* master's remarkable series of *autoportraits* and conversation-pieces commemorating fellow painters and writers. Emerging from the Grand Palais, I experienced an access of mingled joy and despair. Would I be able, back home, to discover anything at once so allusive and elusive, so

profoundly ambiguous and ambigu-ously profound as these two contrasting instances of intense French self-consciousness — a self-consciousness so refreshingly insouciant as to suggest some plane of cosmic awareness beyond the ken of the remainder of lumpen civilization? Having made my pre-liminary survey — for that is all this exhibition pretends to be — I have formed the opinion (subject to change, on persuasion by further evidence) that Canada's artists have yet to approach the complications and contradictions inherent in the genre from the objectified perspectives of phenomen-ology, metaphysics, symbolism, even of structuralism — a fortunate failure, some might protest, — and have only begun to engage the history of the self-portrait in a liberally creative and imaginative manner. On the other hand, *not* to have come wholly to terms with so obvious and subtle, so demanding and commanding a form of expression as the self-portrait is to be able to contemplate the prospect of one day discovering an artist capable of meeting its diverse challenges. The talent already exists in this country; the will or the audience for its potential's fulfilment may yet be lacking. In the meantime, one has to make sense of what one has found — or of what finds one.

Some months after my return, and after I had given up on being able to borrow a considerable array of the most significant French-Canadian self-portraits, for reasons I outline elsewhere in this introduction, I received by mail a photocopy of a scholarly article on a painter at least one example of whose self-portrait output I still entertained the vain dream of obtaining for ''*The Hand*

Holding the Brush'': Zacharie Vincent (1815-1886), the extraordinary primitive from Lorette, Québec, whose aboriginal name, ''Telariolin'', signifies ''*sans mélange*'' or ''*non divisé*''.[3] A stickler for the purity of his Huron Indian blood, Vincent nonetheless adapted his decorative aptitudes to the painting of portraits and landscapes with the white man's implements, and in a style that endeavoured (with refreshing unsuccess) to combine flat patterning with representational three-dimension-ality. Reproduced in the article were no fewer than eight self-portraits in oils, oil pastels, graphite, and char-coal, along with two sharply similar photographs of the artist as an old man. One of these, in the Archives nationales du Québec, shows the painter seated at his easel, his eyes to the camera, his right, brush-holding hand poised before a half-length portrait of a male Amerindian in headdress and ornamented with the regalia that are prominently featured in Vincent's self-portraits (Fig. 2). In this concession to the usurper's technological wizardry, the aborigine has agreed to be recorded wearing what looks like a smock and trousers. But the portrait on which he is working — probably a lost member of the series of versions of himself wearing a feathered headdress and sporting the Queen Victoria treaty medallion and silver breastplate ironically symbolic of the tradeoff of native lands and rights for the *quondam* security of reservation status — is of a chief resplendent in native finery (wampum, gorget, calumet and arm-bands). Compare this mech-anically produced yet elegiac image with the self-portrait (Fig. 3) entitled *Zacharie Vincent Telari-o-lin, chef huron et son portrait peint par*

Fig. 2 Zacharie Vincent (1812–1886)
Anonymous photographer
Archives nationales du Québec, collection
initiale

Fig. 3 Zacharie Vincent (1812–1886)
*Zacharie Vincent Telai-o-lin, chef huron et
son portrait peint par lui-meme*
Graphite on paper (65.3 x 49.5 cm.)
Musée du Québec, Québec
Photo: Patrick Altman

Fig. 2

Fig. 3

lui-même. The face and pose strongly suggest that Vincent relied on the photograph for the details he incorporates in the pencil drawing, reducing, however, in the manner of naive artists (and Picasso), the proportions of the body in order to emphasize the tragically noble head. Notice, too, that in portraying himself Vincent edited out the humble rags his conquerers imposed upon him, and replaced them with a variant on the costume visible in the portrait he was captured working on by the unknown photographer. The self-portrait he represents himself painting is shown, like the painter-painting-the-painter, in a sitting position, right arm raised (but with painting-hand this time not yet sketched in); bare-headed in the photograph, Vincent confronts us in this double self-portrait crowned with a feather bonnet and headband. The waists of both protagonists are encircled by *ceintures flechées*. In the photo, he appears to be working out-of-doors; a realist, Vincent portrays himself engaged in what any portraitist knows is an indoor activity. Placed together, photograph and drawing threnodically resonate. There is so much *loss* implicit in their contents, and so much that awaits discovery, that I have adopted them as icons emblematic of the echo-fraught, image-within-image, paranomical variety of enigma that is self-portraiture.

A more contemporary equivalent — one that links up also with Lartigue's portrait of a painter painting a self-portrait painting a self-portrait (etc., *ad infinitum*) — came to my attention toward the end of the curatorial exercise, when all the available places in the show had been filled and it was too late to make any

further additions to an exhibition already too large to be able to travel in its entirety: a serial photographic construction of 1983 by the Montréal artist Sorel Cohen, entitled *An Extended and Continuous Metaphor.*[4] On the grounds that the work was not to be included in the show, Cohen refused to permit a photograph of one of the triptyches in this complex arrangement of multiple-exposures to be reproduced here as an illustration. I was informed by her that the work is "not a self-portrait" and "not *about* self-portraiture" — something that could be said of many of the pieces in this show, and indeed of the show itself. The theme under scrutiny is twofold: the process of artmaking and the self-image of the artist in our society. The self-portrait is a device whereby artists can testify to their own persistence in pursuing the hopeless but exhilirating calling of art. Portraiture is frequently trivial, self-portraiture rarely so. Indeed, many a bad self-portrait tells us more about painting and the relation of the painter to his subject-matter (and to art history) than many a good portrait of a second party can do. Not all the works in "*The Hand Holding the Brush*" are of the highest quality, nor were my choices always reflections of personal preference. The selections were made to attempt to demonstrate, through a wide spectrum of examples, the various approaches to self-definition and self-commemoration taken by a relatively representative cross-section of Canadian visual artists. It is to the struggle undergone in their creation — and in remaining artists in the face of staggering odds — that this exhibition is dedicated.

Such richly meditative and mediated

self-portraiture as the examples cited above may yet be anomalous in Canadian art, the conditions for circumspectly innovative extensions of the possibilities of the mode or medium remaining inimical to portraiture of any variety. So one may be driven to concede — except that, more often by serendipity than by deliberate searching, instances of the kind to which I allude continue sporadically to emerge from the underbrush of mediocrity and sameness. The personal tone of these remarks may be attributed to the fact that self-portraiture is itself an inherently personal artform. "*The Hand Holding the Brush*" is less a final report than a communiqué dispatched from some undetermined point in the course of a perhaps endless quest-in-progress. I have no final conclusions to offer at this juncture, but trust that the material presented will help the viewer to arrive at the formulation of individual questions, if not the framing of far-reaching and universally applicable answers. A context is first required before an understanding of meanings can be contemplated.

11

II A Bit of History

"The history of portrait-art as running parallel with the history of biography, and that of the self-portrait parallel with the history of autobiography: that is what we would expect."
  – Max J. Friedlander, "Something of the Principles and History of Portraiture", *Landscape, Portrait, Still Life* . . .
  Translated by R. F. C. Hull (Oxford: Bruno Cassirer, 1949), p. 231.

"In a sense painting, like poetry, is about one's own life; thus what is happening is happening to *me*; thus, in a way, *I* am important. There is a connection with the device of the narrator so often used by Joseph Conrad."
  – Alex Colville, letter to Robert Stacey, 1 April 1983.

The question of where self-portraiture finds its beginning is a vexed one: no matter how deeply one delves into the history and pre-history of the human image-making instinct, there will be (so it appears) a precedent to any example that one isolates as possessing the essential qualities of a likeness of the image-maker. According to Ludwig Goldscheider, the earliest known self-portrait is in the tomb of Ptah-hotep, near Sakkara, "in the realm of the great Pyramids": the sculptor represents himself, *circa* 2650 B.C., as a kneeling witness of the activities he depicts in relief: wrestling, hunting, a river-fight. Above this reposeful figure, writes Goldscheider, "the only one at rest amid so much movement, and the earliest self-portrait in the world, appears the name of the artist: Ni-ankh-Ptah."[5] I have no idea whether present-day Egyptologists accept this attribution, or concur with Goldscheider that the next recorded self-portrait is of an Egyptian painter depicted on a fragment of limestone dated *circa* 1300 B.C., in the Cairo Museum. Pliny is the source of the information that the Greek sculptor Phidias included an image of himself (prophetic of Ghiberti's introduction of his own visage twice into his bronze doors for the Baptistry

in Florence, completed in 1424 and 1452) in the gigantic gold-and-ivory statue of Athena that was erected inside the Parthenon in 438 B.C.

It was not until the twelfth and thirteenth centuries A.D., however, that the sculptors responsible for the decoration of medieval churches and cathedrals began to delineate themselves as crowd-members ("*assistenza*") at ceremonies and processions as pilgrims, as spectators at the arrival of the Magi at the manger in Bethlehem, or as witnesses of the crucifixion. At a time it was unacceptable (indeed, inconceivable) for an artist-craftsman collaborating with fellow guild-members in an act of creative adoration to sign his name to a product of his hand, it was permissible for him to declare pride of accomplishment by secreting a self-image amid the choristers clustering in the wooden wings of a choir-stall, or by limning himself as one of the worshippers in a prayer-book illumination executed for a patron, who himself would typically be shown in the guise of a donor or as a supplicant before the Virgin or a saint.

In time, the artist was to wax so bold as to feel no qualms of modesty about representing himself as a participant in a frescoed pageant, or, as Jan van Eyck cunningly contrived to do in 1434,

inserting a miniature self-portrait in the convex mirror wherein are reflected from behind the wealthy Arnolfini and his bride, for whom the famous oil in the National Gallery, London, was painted. This latter tactic, of course, was to be reversed by Velazquez in his *Las Meninas*, of 1656 (Prado, Madrid), in which the painter appears as the dominant, stage-managing figure on the left. The subjects of his unseen portrait congregate to his right in the foreground, while the parents of the handmaiden-surrounded Infanta, Philip IV of Spain and his queen, are glimpsed in the black-framed mirror on the wall at the back of the room over which the otherwise "absent" royal couple presides — their point-of-view being that of the spectator on whom, by implication, Velazquez trains his aristocratic gaze. He alone, this self-portrait-within-a-portrait grandly declares, can look beyond the limits of picture-plane and frame to take the measure of the greater world. But long before the dubious benefits of patronage and regal approbation could allow an artist so to elevate himself to the status of more-than-courtier, painters and sculptors had to be content with less ostentatious means of thrusting themselves into the pictorial fore. Few

Fig. 4 Antonello da Messina (1430–1479)
Portrait of a Man (formerly entitled
Self-Portrait) (c. 1475)
Oil on wood (35.6 x 25.4 cm)
National Gallery, London, England

Fig. 4

self-portraits dating from the pre-Renaissance era take any other form than that of the artist re-enacting, in contemporary garb, the apocryphal office of St. Luke. Ludwig Goldscheider explains this seemingly presumptuous identification of the religious painter with the Evangelist, who, according to legend, executed a portrait of the Virgin Mary:

> For this reason the painters in the middle ages chose him as their patron saint, and they and other artists and craftsmen joined in forming Guilds of St. Luke. And when these guilds dedicated a picture of the Virgin, their patron was generally represented in it, painting his picture of the Virgin and Child. In this motive of the Virgin with St. Luke, the painter found a pretext . . . for introducing

his own portrait; ''in mingled self-consciousness and piety'' he would invest the first Christian painter with his own features, and thus introduce himself into the picture as one of the chief actors in the scene. This form of self-portrait, as St. Luke, is restricted to the North.[6]

The iconographic leap from Rogier van der Weyden's portrayal of himself as *St. Luke painting the Virgin* (Boston Museum of Fine Arts) — ''the earliest picture of this kind'', according to Goldscheider, — was not a long one to Dürer's utterly unabashed depictions of himself as Christ in his manifestation of the Salvator Mundi, first in 1498 (Prado, Madrid), and again in circa 1505 (Alte Pinakothek, Munich). A great deal, however, had occurred in portraiture in the interval. Most significantly, the advent of the secular portrait had taken place, and it was the self-portrait as much as any other genre of figure-painting that had helped to engineer that humanistic transformation. In John Pope-Hennessy's words,

> In one sense the portrait in the Renaissance is no more than a watershed between the medieval portrait and the portrait as we know it now. Representationally it is the story of how eyes cease to be linear symbols and become instead the light-reflecting, light-perceiving organs we ourselves possess . . . The transition is reflected not only in the rendering of individual organs, but in their depiction in relation to each other as part of a coherent structural whole . . . The conquest of physical appearances is in turn bound up with a change in the function of the artist. In the earliest of the portraits

illustrated here [*i.e.*, Taddeo di Bartola's *Self-Portrait* as St. Thaddeus in his *Assumption of the Virgin* (Duomo, Montepulciano)] . . . he appears as an observer; his puzzled face peers out at us through the ground fog of a theocratic world. In the later [*i.e.*, Lorenzo Lotto's *Portrait of a Youth* (Accademia, Venice)] . . . he is an interpreter whose habit is to probe into the mind and for whom inspection connotes analysis.[7]

Initially, Pope-Hennessey observes, ''the role of the Renaissance portrait was commemorative; it was consciously directed to a future when the living would no longer be alive.''[8] The earliest Renaissance portraits likewise had a didactic bias and a hortatory as well as laudatory purpose, the object being that the sitter should be presented in such a light as to suggest the attainment of a near-saintlike spirituality. *Virtus* and virility, however, must also be conveyed; increasingly, the artist was enjoined to emphasize the lineaments and accoutrements of worldly wisdom and admiration-engendering success. The portrait gradually became the record of terrestrial achievements, whether military or financial, political or — in the case of the self-portrait — artistic.

The pictorial revolution instigated in Flanders by the Van Eycks, with their experiments in half-length or head-and-shoulders portraits-in-a-room, led the way eventually to the development of the ''psychological'' portrait: the attempted extrapolation, in a two-dimensional medium, of character from surface features, and of ''soul'' from character. The evocation of these abstractions from three-quarter-view

(later from full-frontal) heads was essayed through the play of light on the planes of faces depicted, as often as not, peering out of windows that look in on interior spaces. The planar structure of these spaces in turn served as the medium for the transition from shadow to brightness, against which contrasts the foreground figure was interposed. The Eyckian portrait-in-oils was introduced into Venice in 1475 by a Flemish-trained Sicilian, Antonella da Messina (1430?-1479) — ''the first Italian painter'', Pope-Hennessy informs us, ''for whom the independent portrait was an art form in its own right . . . Alone among Italian quattrocento painters he acknowledged frankly that the key to personality lay in the lips and eyes.''[9] (Fig. 4).

For self-portraiture the next major development was the invention by Leonardo (guided by his belief that the painter should portray ''the motions of the mind'') of the ''independent'' portrait. Leonard's discovery — as much a scientific as an aesthetic one — was that through the interactions of light and shadow could be communicated ''the mystery and uniqueness'' — Pope-Hennessy again — ''of the human personality.'' This concept was passed on through Leonardo's example to Raphael, who, ''more humanly inquisitive'' than da Vinci, adopted as the object of his attention ''not the human phenomenon but the individual man''. A Raphael portrait was therefore ''conceived as a psychologically truthful image based on conscious analysis of character.''[10] The inevitable application of these principles to self-portraiture had already been anticipated by Raphael's first master, Perugino, who inculcated in his pupil

"BEFORE AND AFTER": YOUNGER AND OLDER SELVES

A) Daniel Fowler (1810-1894)
Portrait of the Artist (c. 1868)
James Daniel Fowler, Kingston, Ontario

B) Daniel Fowler (1810-1894)
Self-Portrait 1886
National Gallery of Canada, Ottawa

A   B

C) George A. Reid (1860-1947)
Self-Portrait 1884
Art Gallery of Ontario, Toronto

D) George A. Reid (1860-1947)
Self-Portrait 1936
Ontario College of Art Archives, Toronto

C   D

14   the ethos of self-replication if not of self-analysis: one of Raphael's earliest surviving works is the famous self-portrait drawing of around 1500 (Ashmolean Museum, Oxford). The implied direction is that of *serial* self-depiction as an artistic as well as a psychological discipline. Although there are earlier self-portrait sequences, such as the profile medallions of Leon Battista Alberti, the first painter to make regular records of his appearance was Albrecht Dürer, of whom Pope-Hennessy notes that "there is no prior case of any painter applying himself over many years to the problem of self-portraiture."[11] Dürer's earliest contribution to the genre is his silverpoint of 1484, depicting himself at the age of thirteen (Albertina, Vienna).

Portraiture, by the time of Dürer's last self-portrait, that of *circa* 1505, was beginning, in Italy, to divide into two streams, which, it could be argued, have never again been rejoined. The question challenging the painter in the Venice of the early sixteenth century has been worded by Pope-Hennessy: should the portrait "portray the sitter . . . in a state of emotional involvement which shows up one aspect of the personality as a beam of light shows up the face" (Giorgione), or should it "represent the whole man, stripped of local contingencies and outside time, for the inspection of mankind?" (Titian).[12] It might be ventured that the private self-portrait, painted to flatter no patron and serving the purpose neither of self-aggrandizement nor of auto-erotic gratification, intended neither to beguile posterity nor to attract a lover, meant neither for sale nor for publication, does perform both of

these two seemingly irreconcilable offices. Up to now we have not had the opportunity to examine a wide range of Canadian self-portraiture, past and present, in order to determine whether any of our own painters, working though most have done in isolated obscurity, far from the lights and sounds of the great world, and bathed only in the faintest lingering glimmer of Renaissance glory, have managed to achieve this marriage of the universal and the individual, the inner and outer person.

It hardly need be reiterated that the art of portraiture has received little critical or historical attention in Canada (although the genre has been less widely ignored by painters and sculptors than some commentators would have us think). Reasons for this are not hard to come by. The most obvious is that there has been a decreasing public demand for either formal or intimate portraits since the arrival of photography to our shores in the 1840s. In the preceding century, and in fact throughout much of the nineteenth, there was a sizeable market for civic, legal, ecclesiastical, and military likenesses, as well as for such less grandiose and more private types of portraiture as the silhouette, the miniature, and the conversation-piece. We know scarcely more about the professional limners of these periods than we do about the cultural, economic and social forces that shaped the genre in its developing and consolidating phases. Sufficient attention has not yet been paid to the critical climate and the quality of the connoisseurship which alternately fostered and discouraged portraiture's progress both in Québec and in the British colonies-become-provinces. Has

the demise of the portrait in our own time resulted from the successful takeover by modernists of the art academies and the jettisoning of traditional courses from the curriculum, such as figure-drawing and painting from the draped and nude model? Will the revival of interest in these disciplines evinced by today's students, for whom non-referential abstractionism is a decadent form of decoration most at home in the boardrooms of multi-national corporations, lead to the concomitant rediscovery of portraiture as an acceptable mode of expression? I raise these questions elsewhere in this catalogue.

Preoccupation with the locating of portraiture within the national art-histories of European nations is long-standing; in the case of the United States, it took the occasion of the Bicentennial to divert the critical, curatorial and archival eye from landscape to the portrait: witness the appearance of *Portrait Painting in America: The Nineteenth Century*, edited by Ellen Miles (New York, 1977) and of *Modern Portraits: The Self and Others*, published by Wildenstein for the Department of Art and History and Archaeology, Columbia University, in 1976. Canada's Centennial in 1967 had a somewhat similar, though considerably less far-reaching and sustained, effect; if the portrait in itself was not singled out for exposure and celebration, then at least examples from the re-evaluated past were hung alongside landscapes in such occasion-marking exhibitions as the National Gallery of Canada's *Three Hundred Years of Canadian Art*, curated by R. H. Hubbard and J. R. Ostiguy, and the Montreal Museum of Fine Art's *The Painter and the New*

World, in which Canadian paintings were shown in conjunction with American ones.

As the list of general references at the back of this catalogue reveals, the 1970s and '80s have seen the publication of records of exhibitions documenting the phenomenon of the self-portrait not only in the United States, Great Britain, and Germany, but in Switzerland, Italy, and New Zealand(!). An indispensible survey of the subject, Siegmar Holsten's *Das Bild Der Künstlers: Selbstdarstellung* (Hamburg, 1980), is especially valuable not only for the manner in which the material is organized, but for its extensive bibliography. Specialized study has intensified since the end of World War II, to the extent that the self-portraits of individual artists are being treated to separate examinations: for instance, those of Jan and Hubert van Eyck (1949), Dürer (1951), Van Gogh (1964), Rembrandt (1967 and 1969), Courbet (1973), Egon Schiele (1974), Otto Dix (1975), and Jurgen Ovens (1976), are all listed by Holsten. To this collection of monographs should be added Jura Bruschweiler's *Ferdinand Hödler: Selbstbildnisse als Selbstbiographie* (Bern, 1979).

How does Canadian self-portraiture compare in terms of commentary and exposition? A glance at the paltry and padded bibliography tells all: no full-length studies, not a single treatise on the entire country's portrait-history, and (most damningly of all) no National Portrait Gallery catalogue (there being, of course, no National Portrait Gallery).[13] Those few and scattered exhibitions of relatively recent date that have been devoted to self-portraiture (or at least the portrayal of

E   F   G   H

artists), such as *Self-Portraits of Canadian Artists* (Montreal Museum of Fine Arts, 1964), *Artists Look at Themselves* (Memorial Art Centre, University of New Brunswick, 1965), *Portraits of Painters* (Woodstock Public Library and Art Gallery, 1973), *Portraits on Paper* (Morris Gallery, Toronto 1976), the multi-media *Self Images* (Shoestring Gallery, Saskatoon, 1982), and the juried *Self-Portraits by Women* and *Self-Portraits by Men* (Punchinello Gallery, Toronto, 1983), all lacked proper catalogues, being accompanied, at best, by simple handlists.

The self-portraits recently donated to the Uffizi at the behest of the Royal Canadian Academy do not represent Canadian art or Canadian self-portraiture (David Blackwood and York Wilson) at their peaks; indeed, the gesture — a misguided one, however, sincere — unfortunately suggests a publicity stunt, rather than (as it was intended to do) a considered effort to awaken the world to Canada's artistic existence. On the other hand, Canadian art's own self-image might be improved and clarified were a symbolic if not actual domestic version of the Vasari Corridor to be projected, for possible realization at least in visual-inventory-form.

Such comprehensive agglomerations as the international *autoritratti* treasury in Florence required a breed of patron endowed at once with a breadth of vision and a refinement of sensibility that have not yet made themselves manifest here in the form of a dynasty of patriotic philanthropes or of a *consistently* generous corporate sponsor. The Uffizi and its unique Collezione di Autoritratti are monuments to four connoisseurs

motivated by a sense of history and a desire to go down in it as the friends and supporters of artists: Cosimo I de'Medici, who commissioned Vasari to construct the passageway in 1565; Cardinal Leopold de'Medici, from whose bequest to the Uffizi in 1675 the self-portrait collection began to be assembled; Cosimo III, who in 1682 set aside a special gallery for the growing accumulation of ''*Ritratti di Pittori fatti di loro mano*''; and Grand Duke Pietro Leopoldo of Lorraine, who acquired Abbot Pazzi's collection in 1768 and opened the Uffizi to the public. The Vasari Corridor was not used for the exhibition of works of art until 1866; the Uffizi's Iconographical Collection (1,200 items) was displayed in it until World War II. After undergoing restoration, it re-opened in 1973 with a new grouping of paintings, among which are the 414 self-portraits on display from the Ponte Vecchio to beyond the church of Santa Felicita on the south bank of the Arno. The works are divided by region and also according to chronological criteria. In storage are over a thousand additional examples of the genre. In December 1981 the Uffizi celebrated the tri-centenary of the systematizing of the self-portrait collection by Cosimo III by mounting a special exhibition, *Autoritratti de Novecento per gli Uffizi.*

The earliest self-portraits in the Uffizi date from the Quattrocento, perhaps the most familiar of them being Raphael's refreshingly straightforward *Autorittrato* of 1506, painted, like Dürer's aforementioned silverpoint drawing, at the age of thirteen. Painting in New France begins with the arrival in Québec in 1664 of Abbé Hugues Pommier (1637-1686), who

taught at the Séminaire of that city until 1669; he established an archetypal Canadian behaviour-pattern by quarrelling with his employers and returning to France in a huff, convinced that his talents had been insufficiently appreciated. He was succeeded in the colony by Frère Luc (1614-1685), a pupil of Simon Vouet in Paris and a colleague of Poussin, Claude Lorrain and François Perrier. Before coming to Canada in 1670 with Jean Talon and a group of Récollet fathers bent on re-establishing the Order in the New World, Luc rose to the station of ''Painter to the King''. During his Québec sojourn of 1670-1671 he found time amid his architectural endeavours to depict several of the colony's leading religious figures, thus establishing votive portraiture as an art-form in early Canada second only to ecclesiastical painting and decoration.

Portraiture as an independent artform did not become rooted here until the late eighteenth century. As J. R. Harper and Robert Hubbard explain, before 1759, portraits — usually by European-trained immigrants or visitors, or by amateurs — tended to be ''of clerics or nuns, sometimes posthumously painted and quite often competent. Yet even these had religious overtones for they were constant reminders of the spiritual labours of the sitters. A few portraits of high officials and seigneurs were also painted but the great majority of the colonists had no recourse to the painter.'' However, they continue,

The character of Canadian painting in the English colonial period was largely due to the new importance assumed by the portrait. The

traditional likenesses of clergy, officials, and well-to-do Canadians continued to flourish — for French Canada was increasing in population and prosperity during the period. The difference came when portraits began to be painted of members of the English military and merchant classes, who participated in the opening up of the country after the Seven Years' War, and of the Loyalists and others who arrived from the United States after the Revolution. For in England and the Thirteen colonies the portrait was an accustomed means of recording a family's place in the community. As the period wore on, the painting of portraits eventually became available to the ordinary folk of the countryside.

Harper/Hubbard go on to indicate that

Three types of portrait painter catered to the rising demand. The first were the immigrants from abroad, who arrived in Canada most often in their youth and who had varying amounts of training. In most cases they formed their styles in Canada and consequently practised more or less naive manners. The second type were the visiting artists, trained abroad, who painted in Canada for a time and left for other parts. The third were the native-born. Among these latter two approaches are apparent, the one the naive artists and untrained amateurs (Légaré, Roy-Audy, Zacharie Vincent), the other the professional trained abroad who returned to work in the current European styles with a Canadian accent (François Beaucourt, François Baillairgé, Plamondon, Hamel).[14]

16

Possibly the earliest extant Canadian self-portrait canvas is that of François Beaucourt (1740-1794), in the National Gallery of Canada (Fig. 5). A tentative date is *circa* 1770—some forty years previous to one of the first self-portraits by an English-speaking artist to be painted on Canadian soil: the watercolour silhouette of the deputy postmaster of British North America from 1800 to 1816, George Heriot (1766-1844), a copy (?) of which in the J. C. Webster Collection of the New Brunswick Museum is inscribed 1810 (Fig. 6). This Woolwich-trained artist, like so many other officers on colonial tours of duty, brought with him to Canada his sketchbook and drawing implements. His employment of them in the "taking" of outdoor "views" was for his own enjoyment, rather than for the purpose of supplying information for military surveys, and this freedom from the contingencies of accurate topographical rendering translated itself into the addition of classical and romantic elements into his panoramas and intimate watercolour landscapes. But where, one wonders, is that indispensible scale-indicating figure-in-the-foreground, the artist himself, preoccupied with recording the scene schematically unfolding before him according to the compositional tenets of Claude Lorrain, John and Robert Cozens, and Heriot's teacher, Paul Sandby? This character is a constant of late-eighteenth and early-nineteenth-century landscape, appearing, for instance, in two watercolours in the National Gallery of Canada by Lieutenant-Colonel Thomas Davies (circa 1837-1812), *Quebec* and *The Falls of Chaudière near Quebec*, both painted in 1787. In the latter work

(Fig. 7) the artist is presented in greater-than-usual detail and prominence, as if to remind the viewer that so lovingly rendered a scene was the handiwork of someone who took pride in his craftsmanship and colour-sense and desired recognition of his abilities, amateur though he was.

A successor at Québec, Lieutenant-Colonel James Pattison Cockburn (1778/9-1847), another pupil of Sandby's, paid similar tribute to himself in the watercolour dated circa 1830, straightforwardly entitled *The Artist Sketching Quebec from Pointe Levis* (Fig. 8). In this highly finished work, Cockburn's own image is central but integrated with the foreground, providing a moment of human interest amid all the folial detail. In his *Artillery Barrack and Mess Room* (1829; Royal Ontario Museum Canadiana Collection), Cockburn introduced a sketcher into the lower middle of the watercolour, facing the viewer rather than Artillery Park and the harbour beyond — an indication that the figure may be a fellow officer or civilian rather than the artist himself. Neither Davies nor Cockburn was a figure-painter *per se*, both revealing the limitations of their training in their awkward and undifferentiated stick-people. They nonetheless looked upon figureless landscapes as incomplete, void of interest, too declarative of the uninhabited vastitudes surrounding the precarious St. Lawrence River settlements where the British maintained their garrisons and strove to retain the civilized customs (including cultural pursuits such as sketching and painting) of longed-for home. The convention of the artist-in-the-landscape lingered in Canada after the last troopships sailed

Fig. 5   Fig. 6

Fig. 7

Fig. 8

Fig. 9 Cornelius Krieghoff (1815–1872)
Death of the Moose, South of Quebec
(detail) 1859
Oil on canvas (45.7 x 61 cm.)
Glenbow Museum, Calgary

Fig. 10 William Kurelek (1827–1977)
The Painter 1974
Acrylic on canvas (121.9 x 94.1 cm.)
Isaacs Gallery, Toronto
Photo: T.E. Moore, Toronto

Fig. 11 Robert Shore Milnes Bouchette
(1805–1879)
*Imprisonment of R.S.M. Bouchette,
Montreal* 1837
Watercolour on paper (12.1 x 15.2 cm.)
Public Archives of Canada, Ottawa
(C-21554 [*recto*])

Fig. 12 Katherine Jane (Balfour) Ellice
(1814–1864)
*On board H.M.S. Hastings/Mrs. Ellice &
Miss Balfour reflected in the Looking Glass*
(1838)
Watercolour on paper (16.2 x 22 cm.)
Public Archives of Canada, Ottawa
(C-13377)

Fig. 13 B.C. Binning (1909–1976)
Self-Portrait in Ship's Cabin (1945)
Pen-and-ink (44.5 x 60 cm.)
Mrs. B.C. Binning, Vancouver

Fig. 9   Fig. 10

Fig. 11

Fig. 12

Fig. 13

back to Britain, with variants in mode of transport paralleling stylistic changes down the years. Cornelius Krieghoff, for example, depicting himself wearing snowshoes and carrying a portfolio in *Death of the Moose*, painted in 1859 (Fig. 9); over a century later, William Kurelek (1927-1977) represented himself working on a prairie landscape, using the driver's seat of his Volkswagen as a makeshift easel in *The Painter* (Fig. 10).

Another early treatment of the theme of artist-in-setting that has lingered is the "self-portrait-indoors", the sketcher-in-a-domestic-interior. Here the diaristic aspect of self-portraiture enters the picture. The desire to record one's participation in daily events, to commemorate an occasion, or simply to show oneself at work amid one's possessions and sketching-materials, is common to painters as well as to journal-keepers both professional and amateur. In certain circumstances the image serves as a reminder that enforced confinement sometimes inspires the captive to render for an audience of one the appearance of the prison and one's presence in it, whether for posterity or for entertainment. Incarceration can take many forms and inspire many responses, as is witnessed by painter and civil servant Robert Shore Milnes Bouchette's *Imprisonment of R. S. M. Bouchette*, a symbolic memorandum of the outcome of his participation in the Lower Canadian Rebellion of 1837 (Fig. 11): note the pet bird perched on Bouchette's right hand, the open cage hanging in the barred window. Such memorials were not the exclusive medium of male artists. Katherine Jane Ellice

(1814-1864), who accompanied her husband, Edward, on his voyage to Canada in 1838 to take up the position of private secretary to the Governor-General, Lord Durham, recorded the passage in her sketchbook, as was the custom of ladies of education and breeding (ability to handle a brush and watercolours being considered one of the polite endowments of both men and women of the day). *On Board H.M.S. Hastings/Mrs. Ellice & Miss Balfour reflected in the Looking Glass* (Fig.12) has its twentieth-century counterpart in an amusing pen-and-ink drawing by the British Columbian painter and architect B. C. Binning (1909-1976), *Self-Portrait in Ship's Cabin*, of 1949 (Fig. 13). The device of the small mirror included within the larger context of a room, allowing the artist to "frame" his or her reflected image in his or her surroundings, is a fairly rare but notable sub-species of self-portraiture; Frederick Varley employed it metaphorically in his *Mirror of Thought* (See Cat. Nos. 32-33, Fig. 1). In Fig. 13, Binning takes the image-within-image possibilities a step further by showing his hand drawing the bespectacled face he sees in the oval mirror hanging beside the porthole; in fact, the sketch-in-progress on Binning's lap will become the finished *Self-Portrait in Ship's Cabin*.

Such *jeux-d'esprit* remind us that the self-portrait need not always be deadly serious; the element of play is an integral element of art, especially art-about-art, which self-portraits by definition are. Nonetheless, the majority of eighteenth- and nineteenth-century examples that have come down to us evince a sobriety of mien in

Fig. 14 William Berczy (1744–1813)
Self-Portrait (c. 1762)
Gouache (12.4 x 10.2 cm.)
Royal Ontario Museum Canadiana
Collection, Toronto
Note: probably painted in Vienna.

Fig. 15 William Berczy (1744–1813)
Self-Portrait (c. 1790)
Watercolour and gouache (27 x 21.6 cm.)
Royal Ontario Museum Canadiana
Collection, Toronto
Note: unfinished and retouched around
hands, coat.

Fig. 17 William Bent Berczy (1791–1873)
Self-Portrait (c. 1815)
Watercolour
Private collection, Montréal
Note: left half of double (marriage)
portrait, right half representing artist's
wife, Amélie Panet.

Fig. 16 William Berczy (1744–1813)
Self-Portrait (c. 1805)
Graphite (30.5 x 24.1 cm.)
Private collection, Emsworth, England

18 keeping with the public rather than with the private function of portraiture. The self-portrait generally was treated as a vehicle for the conveying of a carefully considered image, rather than for psychological interpretation or character revelation. "This is how I wish to be seen, to be thought of, to be remembered," a self-portrait of this period seems to announce; the viewer is not invited to probe behind the mask. We can best witness the incidence of this tendency in "sequential" self-portraits — that is, self-portraits painted or drawn by the same artist over a number of years. One such series is that executed by the ambitious immigrant settler, William Berczy (1755-1813), a Vienna-trained itinerant limner who brought a group of German-speaking expatriates with him from New York State to Markham Township, Upper Canada, in 1799. The disappointed Berczy, one of the true founders of Toronto, was subsequently to earn a modest living as a portrait and landscape painter in Montréal. When he painted his first two self-portraits, in 1762 and 1790 respectively (Figs. 14, 15), his career was only at its formative stages: in 1762 he was enrolled as a student at the Academy of Arts, Vienna, and from 1785 to 1790 he travelled about Italy, probably studying art. In 1790 he was appointed drawing-master to the household of the Marquis of Bath, and associated in London with Andrew Tendi and the German artistic community. His best-known work, *The Woolsey Family* (1808-1809; National Gallery of Canada), considered to be the first Canadian conversation-piece, reflects a familiarity with the decorative group-portraits of Zoffany. By 1805, the date

of Berczy's last self-portrait (Fig. 16), his early confidence had been shaken by the unsuccessful litigation in which he had engaged to secure promised grants for his settlement from the government of Upper Canada, and by his visit of 1799-1801 to England, where he was jailed as a result of financial difficulties. The sanguine mask had slipped, if only slightly. It is firmly back in place in a marriage-portrait miniature (Fig. 17) by Berczy's son, William Bent (1791-1873), whose apprenticeship consisted of painting backgrounds for his father's compositions and copying old masters in Montréal; his wife, Louise Amélie Berczy (née Panet), was herself a painter and art-teacher who had taken lessons from William Berczy Senior. Undoubtedly intended as a gift for his fiancée, the double miniature at once proclaims their union and gives it a public face; the artist presents himself in the uniform of a soldier rather than in the garb of an artist.

The habit of returning to the contemplation and delineation of one's own countenance, as if to record the marks of the passage of time and the impress of experience as well as to reacquaint the likeness-maker with the essential identity lurking behind the gradually changing features, served a more mundane purpose for image-conscious artists who wished by means of periodic self-portraits to inform the world of the quality of the artist's appearance as an index of growing prosperity, respectability, and skill. In as conservative and reserved a colony as Canada, the Rembrandtesque practice of chronicling in oils one's ever-altering moods, of exploring the profundities of a troubled spirit by

Fig. 14

Fig. 15

Fig. 16

Fig. 17

Fig. 18 Zacharie Vincent (1812–1886)
Chef Huron Zacharie Vincent et son fils
Oil on canvas (48.4 x 41.1 cm.)
Musée du Québec, Québec

Fig. 19 Zacharie Vincent (1812–1886)
Zacharie Vincent dit Teliarolin, autoportrait
1850
Oil on paper (75 x 55.9 cm.)
Musée du Chateau Ramezay, Montréal

Fig. 18

Fig. 19

means of a paintbrush, of baring the secrets of personal character to an eternally guarded society that accepted artists only as artisans, — decorators, copyists, souvenir-sellers, — was unthinkable until the second half of the nineteenth century. Even then it was an act to be carried out in private, not for public consumption except very selectively (as in the instance of the most prolific of Canadian self-portraitists, Robert Harris [see Cat. Nos. 6 and 31]).

An exception to this rule of reticent non-assertiveness was the afore-mentioned exotic primitive, Zacharie Vincent, reputedly the last surviving pure-blooded Huron Indian: a belief to which Vincent attempted to give credence through his habit of regularly portraying himself in native costume. Perhaps the best-known of his numerous *autoportraits* is the handsome oil in le Musée des Beaux-Arts de Montréal, depicting the Chief armed with a tomahawk and his young son with bow-and-arrows (Fig. 18). The cradled calumet reappears in a magistral but worried-looking self-portrait of 1850 (Fig. 19); however, in two of Vincent's eight documented treatments of his own likeness the artist has traded his armaments for a paintbrush and palette — as if in acknowledgement of the fact that his prosperity now lies not with the continuation of his race but in his perpetuation of its memory through the passing on of visual reminders of his and other native Canadians' existence after all other traces had been erased. Vincent's initial instigation had been the experience of posing for Antoine Plamondon (1802-1895), who, had explored the theme in a portrait that won the art prize of the Concours de la

Société littéraire et artistique de Québec for 1838. In the words of Marie-Dominique Labelle and Sylvie Thivierge,

Selon Gérard Morisset [*i.e., La Peinture traditionnelle au Canada français,* Ottawa, 1960], le toile de Plamondon a joué un role prédominant dans le déclenchement d'une carrière artistique chez Zacharie Vincent . . . Comme nous le raconte Morisset, c'est en effet après avoir posé pour Plamondon que le Huron décida d'entreprendre son autoportrait en utilisant un miroir. Ceçi donna lieu ensuite à toute une série d'autoportraits. Toujours selon l'historiographie, il semble que Plamondon ne soit pas contente de fournir un exemple, mais qu'il n'ait pas hésite à prodiguer à son élève les conseils artistiques nécéssaires . . .[15]

And so, too, did Plamondon (Fig. 20) supply his student Théophile Hamel (1817-1870) not only with a precedent for engaging in self-portraiture, but with a model of how to proceed in the business. In a sense, such acts of exemplification merely sum up in little the process of instruction and imitation by which a new culture is informed by an old and then proceeds to develop, along lines determined by environmental factors and heritage, the national character these formative elements help to shape (Figs. 21, 22, 23).

Such chronologically scannable image-clusters are so rare in Canadian art for it to be assumed that portraiture flourished here only briefly, and most noteworthily in Québec, where a combination of state, church and private patronage kept at least a dozen

professionals busy at any given time until the modern era and the break-down of traditional lines of communications between these institutions and the art community. In the rest of Canada there was simply no market for most varieties of figure-painting (especially, of course, the nude), and an artist who wished to avoid starvation had to eschew introspection, probity and wit if he or she hoped to win commissions to immortalize premiers and lieutenant-governors, captains of industry and society hostesses. The restrictions to artistic liberty, observable everywhere on the globe where portraiture is practised, naturally were exaserbated in so sparsely populated, so pragmatic-minded, and so anti-individualistic a nation as this colony-turned-dominion. The advancement of portraiture can occur only under conditions approaching the ideal: open-spirited sitters, courageous artists, the presence of constant stimulation, a cultural atmosphere congenial to experimentation — and an easy-going, accepting attitude toward the human body and its most expressive appendage. There is no point in lamenting the absence of such circumstances for creativity except when there is yet some possibility of altering the situation for the better. For the human presence truly and enduringly to be accepted in Canadian art, it must first truly and enduringly become an identifying quality of our essential makeup. Unable yet to achieve a *rapprochement* between themselves and their country's geography, Canadians are unlikely to transcend self-loathing and mutual distrust to the extent that celebration can succeed mere ''survival'', and that exultation can replace revulsion with

20

Fig. 20

Fig. 21

Fig. 22

Fig. 23

the body and its acts, the mind and its works.

As the study of portraiture demonstrates, the proliferation of likenesses of fellow creatures, whether widely recognized or anonymous, can have a beneficial effect on the witnesses to such evidence of dignity, humour, and magnanimity as certain of our citizens have been able to exemplify through deeds and words. This may sound like an argument for renewed government involvement in the commissioning of commemorative public portraiture and statuary — artforms that rarely appeal to non-academic painters and sculptors, for obvious reasons. More commonly accessible art clearly is needed before popular attitudes toward it change for the better; abstraction works only in certain contexts, and too extreme a divorce from expressions that are recognizably human results in alienation and the wholesale dismissal of all attempts to present the idea of the creative and the aesthetic as alternatives to the violent and the nihilistic. Unfortunately, however, the portraiture with which the public is most familiar — besides, of course, the masterworks of the past, which retain their universal currency through colour reproductions — is of a stiff, formulaic, ''official'' character, which causes portraits and statuary to be reduced to the status of background details, components of architecture, interior décor, or streetscapes, rather than integral objects deserving individual consideration.

It is hardly surprising, then, that the one form of portraiture *not* generally condemned to this limbo of parliamentary, judicial and social images is that which is engaged in the penetration of disguises (uniforms, formal costumes, symbols of status and power) and in the examination of the mentality of the sitter. Concentration on the self as subject does not, of course, eliminate the possibility of ''improvement'', flattery, and outright deception; it does, however, inform us that the impulse behind the creation of the likeness was one of two things: voluntary and spontaneous, or else irresistable and coercive. The artist, in other words, was not working for money or preferment. Self-portraits rarely sell before their authors are dead. Even when guilty of twisting the facts, they possess an innate honesty to be found in no other replicatory genre. In a sense they are closer to landscapes or abstractions than to commissioned portraits, and, unlike the majority of the latter, are of interest to us not simply as depictions of people to whom we might have some familial connection, or for whose memory we retain a sentimental attachment, or about whose lives and careers we happen to be knowledgeable or curious: they transcend the plane of history (time) to seek admission to that of art (timeless). To this statement I must add the conditional proviso that the implicit split between ''official'' or ''public'' (by definition or inference ''bad'', according to modernist criteria) and ''personal'' or ''private'' (that is, ''good'') art is less prevalent in the portrait legacy of New France and post-Conquest Québec than it is, say, in late-nineteenth- and twentieth-century English-speaking Canada, where institutional support for any form of visual culture has always been sporadic, inconsistent, and unreliable. That this has been, and remains to be, the case is palpably evident in both the

Fig. 24 Charles-Édouard-Masson Huot
(1855–1930)
Autoportrait (c. 1880)
Oil on wood (22.2 x 15.9 cm.)
Mme. Gérard Huot, Québec

Fig. 25 Charles Huot (1855–1930)
Autoportrait
Oil on canvas (48.4 x 35.9 cm.)
Musée du Québec, Québec
Photo: Patrick Altman

Fig. 24

Fig. 25

quality and number of portrait paintings and sculptures to be seen in museums, galleries, public places and private homes. A united sense of the importance of community or collectivity and of individual human worth is an absolute requisite before artists can escape the solipsistic isolatedness (a species of domestic exile) that breeds romantic neuroses and misanthropic rage.

To rephrase my point: good portraiture is reliant upon the prior existence of a habit among artists of experimenting with *self*-portraiture. Historically, the considered, self-consciously conceived self-portrait required the precedent of the so-called ''psychological'' portrait, that indispensible contribution of the international humanistic movement (which also produced the scientific method, the modern novel, the confessional memoir, the sonnet-sequence, and the most flexible of dramatic forms, the tragi-comedy). This is true of Canada as elsewhere; but in short order the artistic (as opposed to merely functional) portrait was to go underground, to emerge with exceeding and almost accidental rarity. Indeed, it was only with the establishment, after Confederation, of art societies and their invitational and competitive exhibition-systems, that a forum for such portraiture became available. Through the exposure of self-portraits artists could achieve not only public recognition but also public *recognizability* over a period of time (Figs. 24, 25). As often as not appreciated only by their peers, their experiments in self-interpretation, produced when no other models are to be procured (no *double entendre* intended), and in response to the

irresistible beckoning of that merciless perscrutator, the studio mirror, survive and engage our sympathies long after their bread-and-butter work may have vanished into the oblivion of the not-quite-good-enough. The self-portrait is more than a confession or a gasconade, a self-grilling or a self-commendation: it is, or should be, an earnest of all that an artist hopes to achieve through, and for, art. I am not the first to contend that the greatest self-portraits are not really vehicles of ''self-expression'' — at least insofar as their latterday viewers are concerned. After all, some of the most hauntingly memorable likenesses with which posterity has rewarded us are unsigned, undated, and unattributed, their designation as self-portraits (or at least as portraits-of-artists) deriving solely from the presence of a brush or pencil in the subject's hand.

The establishment of art societies for the promotion of the profession and the holding of exhibitions in the Maritimes, Québec and Ontario was part of the Victorian-age self-improvement and educational movement, paralleled by the founding of mechanics' institutes, provincial agricultural fairs, public libraries, free universities, and cultural organizations designed to implant an appreciation of the polite graces and accomplishments in a rude colonial populace. The major such officially sanctioned bodies — the Art Association of Montreal (1860), the Society of Canadian Artists (1867), the Ontario Society of Artists (1872), and the Royal Canadian Academy (1880) — were modelled, of course, on British, European and American precedents, and all accepted the operative premise enunciated as the goals of the S.C.A.: ''the

advancement'' of ''the Fine Arts in the Dominion of Canada by elevating the standard of art, training artists throughout the Dominion, and inciting them in emulation in the production of works of art for public exhibition . . .''

To further this educative end, the R.C.A. began subsidizing life-classes in Montréal, Toronto and Ottawa, to be run by the academicians in co-operation with the local institutions. Most of these, such as Montréal's Conseil des Arts et des Manufactures and the Ontario School of Art, founded by the O.S.A. and taken over by the provincial government in 1884, offered training of a practical nature to suit industrial requirements (e.g., mechanical drawing), and artists unable to avail themselves of the Academy classes were compelled to set up their own informal organizations where life-study could be pursued according to the continental or British practice. Models were hired to pose clothed or nude, and outdoor sketching-trips were organized on weekends and holidays; instruction and discussion usually were reserved for evenings, as most members had to work days in the lithography and engraving shops where their skills in design and draughts-manship might be traded for art-supporting salaries. One such alternative group was the Toronto Art Students' League, founded in 1886 and disbanded in 1904 (but continuing its life as the Canadian Society of Graphic Art). The camaraderie and friendly mutual criticism that enlivened the League's after-hours sketching-sessions offered participants at least a simulacrum of the *Atelier* and *Académie* training that increasing numbers of Canadian artists

22 were then seeking in the capitals of Europe. Those who returned to Canada from Paris, London, Antwerp, or Berlin — a typical example is Joseph-Charles Franchère (1866-1921), who studied at the École des Beaux-Arts in Paris under Gérôme and then at private school under Joseph Blanc, and at the Académie Colarossi, before opening a studio in Montréal in 1890 (Fig. 26) — brought with them their experience in drawing and painting the human figure as an essential exercise. The principles of scientific anatomy as applied to art were also disseminated by Canadians who (like George A. Reid and Frederick S. Challener) were determined to ensure the successful transplantation at home of the standards expounded by such influential instructors as the Philadelphia Academy's Thomas Eakins and the Art Students' League of New York's George B. Bridgman (and, later, Kimon Nicolaides). An inevitable outcome of such steadfast (if academic) engagement with the human figure was a concomitant production of self-portraits and portraits-of-artists; where there was no model to draw or paint, there was always a handy mirror to be consulted, or a fellow student to sketch instead.

A sub-genre of sorts resulted from the proliferation of the public academies and private ateliers: the artists' conversation-piece or studio-portrait, a Canadian example of which is the now-lost painting by William Bengough (1863-1932), *At Work at the League* (1891); formerly in the possession of the Arts and Letters Club, Toronto, and supposed by William Colgate to be ''On loan to the Art Gallery of Toronto'' in 1954, the date of the publication of his Ryerson

Press monograph on the Toronto Art Students' League) (Fig. 27). Bengough's crowded canvas, dedicated to the League by the artist on the eve of his departure to New York to pursue a career as an illustrator and portraitist, depicts no fewer than twenty-four members — among them C. M. Manly, C. W. Jefferys, Robert Holmes, William Cruikshank, F. H. Brigden, J. D. Kelly, Gertrude Spurr, and W. J. Thomson — grouped around the sketch-subject, a bagpipe-playing Highlander whose bearded countenance and kilted form crop up in a number of extant drawings by participants in the session recorded by Bengough (who naturally included himself in the picture). This canvas belongs to a category of portraiture that was examined in a 1978 Cleveland Museum of Art exhibition entitled *The Artist and the Studio in the Eighteenth and Nineteenth Centuries*, which focused ''on the simple belief that the place where an artist worked contained profound significance, especially when 'the studio' became a prevalent visual theme over a one-hundred-year period.''[16] Bengough was probably aware of such iconographic antecedents as Zoffany's *The Academicians of the Royal Academy* (1771-1772; The Royal Collection, London), Leon Mathieu Cochereau's *Interior of David's Studio* (1814; Musée du Louvre), and perhaps even Jean Georges Vibert's *The Sketching Class* (Collection of Mr. and Mrs. Noah L. Butkin, Cleveland, Ohio).

While it is undeniable that a motivation for self-portraiture can be demonstrated as springing from the standard academic disciplines, few art-educational programmes have ever stressed self-portraiture to the same

degree that sketching and painting from the nude and draped model (until recently) were emphasized. Figure-work of this latter kind concentrates on the depiction of the human body: its structures, volumes, contours, lines. The model is an anonymity; little time is spent delineating the face, except where the study of planes and of gradations of shading is being pursued. So where does the student develop expertise in the depiction of self and others, specifically in the treatment of the head, not just as a geometrical form but as the receptacle of spirit, character, and emotion? Abhorrence of portraiture as an essentially com-promised artform, and of portrait-

Fig. 26

Fig. 27

painting as a mercenary trade, for too long has relegated likeness-taking to a clandestine extra-curricular activity practised in solitude or among a small circle of co-conspirators. Much of the arrogance endemic in youthful self-portraits may be ascribed to the alternative tendency underlying swagger and smirk: abject terror in the face of the soul-searching glass. The most trenchant and scarifyingly pitiless self-portraits are seldom the handiwork of the self-conscious but unintrospective young. With Titian, Rembrandt and Hödler no less than with Yeats, it is the masks of age that hypnotize through the power of their emblematic declarations of truth-to-life, however difficult to countenance:

Old Rocky Face, look forth;
Things thought too long can be no
  longer thought,
For beauty dies of beauty, worth of
  worth,
And ancient lineaments are blotted
  out.
We that look on but laugh in tragic
  joy.

As Yeats sagely observed, '''A young man in the dark am I,/but a wild old man in the light . . .''' For artists, perhaps, the ''young man in the dark'' never dies, nor loses his fear of the shadows. Playing the wild old man at night, they contemplate within the unlit corners of their deepest, darkest selves the colours they perceive in the recollected daylight of the past. Out of such self-delving is occasionally extracted an image of the struggle that takes the form of a self-portrait; without it, the replica of reflected features is that and nothing more: a superficial duplicate of what the mirror neutrally shows. The history of

Canadian self-portraiture, it might be contended, is by and large one of avoidance rather than of confrontation, of evasion rather than of coming-to-terms. The social and cultural reasons for this overall failure are too complex for analysis here; suffice to accede, in general terms, to the premise that, as with other modes of expression, one is dealing with a genre whose potential has hardly been explored, much less exhausted. The problem is not simply one of the artists being incapable of or unwilling to deal with the human presence in their art. There is plenty of evidence to the contrary; unfortunately, too rigid categorization and specialization by art historians and curators have ghettoized portraiture and figure-painting as minor genres that do not fit into any convenient niche. When Canadian art is discussed as a broad canvas, the combinative composite image consists of (as Paraskeva Clark impatiently put it) ''landscapes, landscapes, land-scapes''. Welcome signs that this ritual of ignoration is finally being phased out by the proselytes of non-reductive cultural awareness are beginning to manifest themselves on our bookshelves and in our galleries. I distrust all movements that feel compelled to prefix their stylistic ''isms'' with ''neo-'' or ''post-''; only insecure or slavishly imitative artists participate in cults, whether revolutionary or reactionary: either one leads or one labours alone. The honestly talented adherents to ''new-imagism'' will go on painting people after the fad has passed, thereby joining (no doubt incognizant of the fact) generations of strugglers for the same cause.

Originally, or course, it was that seventeenth-century *parvenu*, the

''pure'' landscape, emerging out of the theatrical tableau by way of the *paysage moralisée*, that had to fight for acceptance as a major mode. By mid-century the apparent disappearance of the former primary subject of all artistic media from serious consideration by its practitioners could present so baffling an aspect as to lead one critic—the soon-to-be-expatriate Hugh Kenner—to label the mystery, ''The Case of the Missing Face'', which title I have borrowed for a chapter-heading in my forthcoming expanded study of Canadian self-portraiture.

III A Case and a Place for (Self-)Portraiture?

"The Portrait, that type of painting which appears to be modest, calls for an immense intelligence. No doubt the artist's submissiveness must be great, but his power of divination must be equally so."
    –Charles Baudelaire, "Portraiture", "The Salon of 1859: Portraiture", *Art in Paris 1845–1862: Salons and Other Exhibitions* . . . Translated by Jonathan Mayne (London: Phaidon Press, 1965), p. 189.

"The painting of a portrait may be either a quixotic adventure or a spiritual exercise . . . What is the difference between a likeness and a portrait? Many people are unaware of the distinction."
    –J. W. L. Forster, "The Painting of a Portrait", *Sight and Insight* (Toronto: Oxford University Press, 1941), p. 30.

By and large, the portrait has not fared well in the twentieth century. Needless to say, too few artists specializing in portraiture in modern times have managed to make profound statements in their medium. Reasons for this failure seem endemic in the sitter-painter relationship itself. Writing of one of Canada's most successful professional portraitists, Sir Edmund Wyly Grier, C. W. Jefferys noted in 1935 that

> It has always seemed to me that the occupation of a portrait painter must present difficulties more acute and more constant than those which attend any other department of artistic practice. It is a succession of problems peculiar to itself. First of all, if the painter is to get portraits to paint, he must please his sitters, and — a still more difficult task — their friends and relatives.
>
> If he pleases them, will he please himself? If he pleases them *and* himself, will he please his fellow-painters and the critics? His portrait must be biography, character analysis, and decoration; the painter must be at once artist and psychologist. And, in addition to these qualities, he must possess also a certain social tact that will evoke a suitable response in sitters.[17]

Small wonder that so many contemporary artists consider the disadvantageous demands of portraiture to outweigh by far the rewards. Prejudice against portrait-painting has always been rife among those whose temperaments and convictions prohibit their acceding to the conventions of realistic rendering of the features of others (or, for that matter, of the self). Max J. Friedlander contended that the reluctance exhibited by Pieter Breughel, Hieronymus Bosch and Michaelangelo to commit themselves to portrait-painting was based on the objection that "The job of painting a portrait entails something akin to obsequiousness, against which creative power puts up a fight." Furthermore,

> Apart from the fact that the object, the appearance as given, demands to be observed accurately and objectively, thus limiting the artist's freedom, his imagination, his spirit, the portraitist is quite specifically in a subservient position to the patron — who, even if he does not consider himself knowledgeable in matters of art, still thinks he knows himself better than the artist and therefore feels entitled to pronounce judgment on the portraitist's performance. From the degrading pressure exerted by the pretensions, wishes, vanity of the patron no

successful portraitist — apart from the greatest, like Holbein, Velasquez or Frans Hals — could escape.

More or less fruitfully we may distinguish as follows: portraitists who make use of the medium of painting, and painters who make portraits.[18]

(As Augustus John snorted, "*A portrait is a picture that has something wrong about the nose.*") From the perspective of 1967, John Berger could dismissively announce:

> It seems to me unlikely that any important portraits will ever be painted again. Portraits, that is to say, in the sense of portraiture as we now understand it. I can imagine multi-medium memento-sets devoted to the character of particular individuals. But these will have nothing to do with the works now in the National Portrait Gallery.
>
> I see no reason to lament the passing of the portrait — the talent once involved in portrait painting can be used in some other way to serve a more urgent, modern function . . . .
>
> The beginning of the decline of the painted portrait coincided roughly speaking with the rise of photography . . . Photography was more accurate, quicker and far

cheaper; it offered the opportunity of portraiture to the whole of society; previously such an opportunity had been the privilege of a very small elite.

To counter the clear logic of this argument, painters and their patrons invented a number of mysterious, metaphysical qualities with which to prove that what the painted portrait offered was incomparable. Only a man, not a machine (the camera), could interpret the soul of a sitter . . .

All this was doubly untrue. First, it denies the interpretative role of the photographer, which is considerable. Secondly, it claims for painted portraits a psychological insight which ninety-nine per cent of them lack. If one is considering portraiture as a genre it is no good thinking of a few extraordinary pictures but rather of the endless portraits of the local nobility and dignitaries in countless provincial museums and town halls . . . The comparatively few portraits that reveal true psychological penetration . . . suggest personal, obsessional interests on the part of the artist which simply cannot be accommodated within the *professional* role of the portrait painter. Such pictures have the same kind of intensity as self-portraits. They are in fact works of self-discovery.[19]

Berger concludes on a McLuhanesque note:

It seems that the demands of a modern vision are incompatible with the singularity of viewpoint which is the prerequisite for a static-painted likeness. The incompatibility is connected with a more general crisis concerning the meaning of individuality. Individuality can no longer be contained within the terms of manifest personality traits. In a world of transition and revolution individuality has become a problem of historical and social relations, such as cannot be revealed by the mere characterizations of an already established social stereotype. Every mode of individuality now relates to the whole world.[20]

At the same time, however, that our individual identities are being stripped from us by the ceaseless bombardment by the mass media of our conscious and subconscious beings, there has resulted a reaction in favour of "self-realization," self-assertion, self-integration. The incidence of a "return to the figure" in art during the so-called "Me Decade" may not be coincidental. Despite Berger's claim that the painted portrait is obsolete and irrelevant, there is mounting evidence that not only artists themselves but the public upon which they depend (and whose hunger both for novelty and for continuity artists try to assuage) are interested in the restoration of portraiture as a convenable mode of expressing, honouring, and commemorating human truths and values. The painters and sculptors of the past who made their livings executing "portraits of record" and catering to the vanity of private patrons rarely, as Berger observes, indulged in psychological interpretation, leaving this dangerous and exacting act of daring up to the artists who, whatever their major media and favourite genres, essayed *self*-portraiture out of aesthetic rather than economic necessity.

Even a passing familiarity with Canadian art history confirms that few professional portraitists are taken into account in the critical analyses of the country's visual records. Of the sixty-odd artists represented in this exhibition, only a handful made their livings through portraiture, though a fair number may, at some time in the course of their careers, have turned the odd dollar by doing a likeness. But for most the impulse to paint or draw others or themselves is instinct in their very identification with their calling.

Manuel Gasser expressed the appeal in simple and specific terms:

Looking at artists' self-portraits is like consorting with eminent people — and it enables us to enjoy the sort of intimacy an artist allows only to his closest friends. For when an artist is painting his own portrait, he does not wear the blank, public mask that keeps the idle and curious at a distance. What he puts on the canvas may not be the whole truth about his face, but at all events it is the face he wishes to present to his fellow-men and to posterity.

The self-portrait, furthermore, admits us to the painter's studio; it lets us breathe the air that he breathed, and take part in his act of creation, for it gives us a privilege that is rare and unique in kind — that of watching the artist at work.[21]

The continuing validity of self-portraiture owes much to the freedom to explore and experiment that the medium affords, while at the same time helping the artist to hone technical skills that can grow rusty from disuse. The self-portrait has always been a means of "keeping the hand in", as well as showing it at work. This liberty arises in part from the element of volition on the artist's part; compulsive or not, the self-portraitist *chooses* to portray him or herself, *chooses* his or her style, *chooses* the quality of emotion the portrait is intended to communicate, *chooses* the references and allusions embedded in the pigment or clay.

Just because self-portraiture does not tend to pay or to lead to lucrative commissions or to the approbation of reviewers is no reason for its champions not to press its case as one of the most flexible and non-cramping of contemporary approaches to the figure. Public, religious, or corporate portraiture probably cannot sustain genuine revivals in Canada: there is neither the audience nor the will to commit funds. Present-day activity in the more personal aspects of this genre, however, is neither a fluke nor a flash-in-the-pan. In fact, the word "renewal" is probably inappropriate: as I trust *"The Hand Holding the Brush"* amply demonstrates, concern with, if not always passionate commitment to, the human face and figure have been constants in our art. When critical interest looks elsewhere, this passion simply goes underground, waiting to be unearthed by sympathetic rescue-squads. What is happening today is a twofold phenomenon: artists are rediscovering — or, among the neophytes, discovering for the first time — our "lost" figurative tradition, while a revisionist art-historical preoccupation with looking beyond individuals and movements to their cultural contexts and antecedents is leading to the rethinking and rewriting of the entire record. As Canada increasingly recognizes its fundamentally regional

Fig. 28 Greg Curnoe (b. 1936)
April, May, London, Toronto, Montreal
1965
Oil and collage on plywood
(243.8 x 243.8 cm.)
Private collection, Toronto
Note: left to right: Jack Chambers, Greg
Curnoe, Shiela Curnoe, Robert Markle (on
motorcycle).

Fig. 29 Jack Chambers (1931–1978)
Self-Portrait No. 2 (1952)
Oil on canvas (68.6 x 48.3 cm.)
Olga Chambers, London, Ontario

26   character, it may learn to rise above xenophobic factionalism and accept the rich diversity of its peoples and places and the art created by and out of them.

That the London Regional Art Gallery—itself a ''local'' institution with a determinedly ''national'' programme—should be organizing a retrospective survey of the development of a specialized medium like self-portraiture, is felicitously apropos: for is not London the breeding-ground of *''Oregionalism''*, that portmanteau coinage of Greg Curnoe's (combining ''region'' and ''origin'') (Fig. 28)? London poet Christopher Dewdney defines this '''Pataphysical creed'' as ''a rigorous and disciplined philosophy'' predicated on the notion that ''the artist must have total integrity with his/her real self, and that this raw glow become a secularized hallmark, a tribalized identification such that poseurs would immediately become visible in the crossfire.'' According to Dewdney, Oregionalism's proponents also

> maintained that the chronological relationship of the work, its progression, would follow a personal and unadulterated development . . . The oregional work would in essence generate itself and would be jeopardized if the artist began, intellectually, to anticipate its development. Also that the interests of the artists be grounded in a field of knowledge ''outside'' the scope of art, and that the work be nothing more than what it is, without esoteric or symbolic meanings . . . There is no developmental trajectory to oregionalism in the above sense, it is totally lateral or it is nothing.[22]

Not all of these qualities and qualifications apply, of course, to all of the artists represented here, many of whom are obsessed with the development of their careers and with impacting their works with ''esoteric or symbolic meanings.'' But most, surely, would agree that ''development'' is inimical if not antithetical to self-portraiture, a genre that began in earnest with Brunelleschi and Ghiberti, Jehan Fouquet and Masaccio, Jan Van Eyck and Dirk Bouts, Benozzo Gozzoli and Domenico Ghirlandaio, Gentile Bellini and Botticelli, Fra Filippo Lippi and Filippino Lippi, Pietro Perugino and Raphael, Leonardo da Vinci and Albrecht Dürer, Giorgione and Parmegiano. All a contemporary self-portraitist can do is endeavour, however, unrealistically, not utterly to dishonour such a tradition. One does not ''improve'' on Holbein or Rembrandt, Münch or Van Gogh. The history of self-portraiture is lateral, and perhaps travels in a circular or spiral direction, constantly looping back on itself to re-establish contact with its roots. Self-portraiture is ''regional'' in that its locus is the person, and may display particular characteristics attributable to peculiar factors of time and place; the style employed is very much the man or woman who chooses it. Knowing exactly where one stands in the continuous pageant need not imply a humbling obeisance before the classics, nor produce slavish imitations of same. Modesty and self-portraiture may be mutually exclusive, but any other attitude than proud respect with regard to the genre's acknowledged masters smacks of emulative servility or ignorant hubris.

A number of recent exhibitions either mounted by, or on view as part

of national tours at, the London Regional Art Gallery have showcased self-imaging artists as diverse as the late ''perceptual realist'' Jack Chambers (Fig. 29), the modishly neo-expressionistic Oliver Girling (Fig. 30), and the aforementioned photo-constructionist, Sorel Cohen. A retrospective honouring the achievement of one of London's most effective teachers, Herb Ariss, curated by Paddy Gunn O'Brien, expressed Ariss's generosity of spirit through the vehicle of his many portraits and/or evocations of the work of fellow artists, past and present; his self-portraits likewise pay homage to the sources of his inspiration. Natalie Luckyj's *Visions and Victories*, which paid long-overdue tribute to such up-to-now neglected or underestimated figure-painters and sculptors as Prudence Heward, Jacobine Jones, Pegi Nicol MacLeod, and Elizabeth Wyn Wood, prominently featured Lilias Torrance Newton's *Self-Portrait* of 1920 (Fig. 31), as well as her memorable portraits of Louis Muhlstock (*circa* 1937; National Gallery of Canada) and Frances Loring (*circa* 1942; National Gallery of Canada). Also on view was Florence Wyle's impressive *Head of F. H. Varley* (*circa* 1922; Art Gallery of Ontario). An exhibition curated by Avis Lang Rosenberg and circulated by the Art Gallery of Mount Saint Vincent University during 1982-1983, *Mirrorings: Women Artists of the Atlantic Provinces*, included three works specifically titled *Self-Portrait* (by Susanne MacKay and Charlotte Wilson Hammond). The catalogue's introduction bears an epigraph lifted from an unsuccessful submission to the show by Jacqueline MacQueen:

Fig. 28

Fig. 29

Fig. 30 Oliver Girling (b. 1953)
Portrait of the Artist Disguised as Robert Mugabe 1979
Mixed media on paper (244 x 244 cm.)
Collection: the artist, Toronto

Fig. 31 Lilias Torrance Newton (1896–1980)
Self-Portrait (1920)
Oil on canvas (59.7 x 74.9 cm.)
National Gallery of Canada, Ottawa

Fig. 32 Joyce Wieland (b. 1931)
The Artist on Fire 1983
Oil on canvas (107 x 130 cm.)
Collection: the artist, Toronto/Isaacs Gallery, Toronto
Photo: T.E. Moore, Toronto

Fig. 33 Richard Cook (b. 1951)
Saint Richard (Self-Portrait) 1983
Mixed media (101.5 x 30.5 cm.)
Collection: the artist, Hamilton, Ontario
Photo: courtesy, the artist

Fig. 34 Joanne Tod (b. 1953)
Self-Portrait as Prostitute 1983
Acrylic on canvas (150 x 140 cm.)
Carmen Lamanna Gallery, Toronto
Photo: Peter MacCallum, Toronto

Fig. 30

Fig. 31

Fig. 32

Fig. 34

Fig. 33

28

Reflections always fascinate me, but particularly woman in relation to her own reflection—for instance, woman existing only as a reflection of society's view, her self-image received externally rather than created and centred internally. The distortion is a double one. Physically a mirror image is one-dimensional and reversed spiritually, one can't view anything beyond a shadow of flesh. It is not a good tool for self-exploration.[23]

But, as Rosenberg explains, the mirror is merely a metaphor for self-observation and meditative reflection. The theme of the exhibition (devoted, at conception, to "Body Image/Self Image") seemed, in her words, "to provide a suitable opportunity to reappropriate the mirror that has for so long been thrust into our hands and before our eyes as an emblem of our vanity, self-absorption, and carnal doom, and to reinvest it with one of its primary emblematic meanings: truth."[23] The literal mirror held up literally to individual human nature is the self-portrait's requisite go-between; it can distort no less misleadingly than can the camera, but the truth it tells is that male artists suffer equally from stereotyping and externally imposed self-images as do their female counterparts. The mirror is no more an oracle than it is a *tabula rasa*; it is an optical device to aid in the perceiving and replicating of the full, three-quarter, or profile face. Architect/artist Brian Boigon:

> The mirror reflects all and reveals nothing in itself. In this mirror I am enabled to see myself as an other would see myself. It is an object

which exists on the unreflective level of my consciousness. I am the author of the mirror, desperate to become an objective still life, a wall, part of a bathroom cabinet, absorbed by the interior.[25]

Three of the artists represented in "*The Hand Holding the Brush*" were included in the Art Gallery of Harbourfront (Toronto) exhibition, *New Perceptions: Portraits* (May-June 1983), curated by Anita Aarons: Graham Coughtry, Lynn Donoghue, and Joyce Wieland (Fig. 32), all of whom contributed self-portraits, as did Richard Cook (Fig. 33), Joan Krawczyk, Joanne Tod (Fig. 34) and Don Bonham (Fig. 35), a retrospective devoted to whose plastic man-machine mutants had previously been put together by the London Regional Art Gallery.

Further to denote this fevered early-'eighties irruption of the practice and scrutiny of self-portraiture, one only needs to consult recent issues of Canada's nationally distributed art periodicals. By way of but one random example: Vancouver's *Vanguard* featured Joanne Tod's 1982 *Self-Portrait* on the cover of the December/January 1982-1983 issue; a review in the February 1983 issue alluded to photo-artist Jeff Wall's *Double Self-Portrait* (Fig.36)—which turns out to be based on the same double-exposure trick employed by the eccentric British Columbia photographer Hannah Maynard in her experimental multiple self-portrait composites in the late 1880s. Paraskeva Clark's 1933 *Self-Portrait* was reproduced in the April *Vanguard*; the next issue illustrated Part 8 of Sorel Cohen's *An Extended and Continuous Metaphor.*

Fig. 35

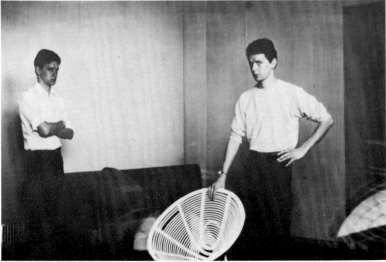

Fig. 36

Fig. 37 Richard Hambleton
"I only have eyes for you" 1980–81
Cut-out photo-poster (life-size)
Photo: John Kenny, 1981, courtesy, Flavio Belli, Toronto
Note: image reproduced from postcard announcing the artist's "urban installation, executed throughout 1980–81 in Los Angeles, San Francisco, Portland, Seattle, Vancouver, Toronto, Montreal, Washington D.C., Baltimore, Philadelphia and New York City."

Fig. 38 General Idea (a.k.a. Felix Partz, Jorge Zontal, A.A. Bronson, i.e., Ron Gabe, Jorge Saia, Michael Tims)
P is for Poodle 1983
Colour airbrushed black-and-white photograph (38.1 x 38.1 cm.)
Carmen Lamanna Gallery, Toronto

Fig. 37

Fig. 38

The summer 1983 number was full of extensions of the notion and norms of self-portraiture, from its cover — an image of the bleached-out, paint-obliterated photographic street-posters of ex-Vancouverite Richard Hambleton, who plastered walls and pillars as part of his "urban installation", *I only have eyes for you,* executed throughout 1980-1981 in seven American cities and in Vancouver, Toronto and Montréal (Fig. 37) — to its review section (a self-portrait photograph by Ian Wallace, a blackline tracing of which was reproduced on the installation's mailer and poster, whereby the artist's associates were invited to share in his working process between midnight and 1:00 a.m. in the Vancouver's Or Gallery for five days of the week during April 1983). In between these polarities, an article by Philip Monk, all-embracingly entitled "Colony Commodity and Copyright Reference and Self-Reference in Canadian Art", discusses self-referentiality in the work of photographer/sculptor/filmmaker Michael Snow, the performance-art, video-producing, scene-making Toronto collective General Idea (Fig. 38), multi-media sculptor Robin Collyer, linguistic poster-maker Andy Patton, and video-textualist Tom Sherman.

The artists of the moment who are championing new-imagism would argue that conceptualist intellectualizing, with its "fetishistic self-referentiality", its preoccupation with ideas at the expense of feelings, and with abstract processes rather than with tangible products, succeeded in alienating art from the consumers on whom its wellbeing ultimately depends, through the agency of taxpayer-supported arts councils, the private, public, and non-profit "parallel" gallery system, government patronage, and the Canada Council Art Bank. That there has been a wholesale abandonment of formalistic as well as philosophical foxholes is evidenced by the official recognition now being accorded to a genre which never really disappeared from the scene, but which merely lost favour among those who make aesthetic judgements on our complaisant behalf.

*

The Canadian writer Ralph Gustafson sought to epitomize what a classical sensibility perceives as the decadence of contemporary western art in a short poem called "Outburst for February":

The archaic Greeks carved smiling
        naked men.
Michaelangelo cut stone.
Beethoven, so the story goes,
Poured soup
Over the talker's head.
Now fools praise self-portraits.
To the solitary mountains, the pools,
Whatever fresh cold lake water there
        is to dive into . . .

Yet may not the fools who praise (or at least discuss) self-portraits, no less than those who paint or sculpt or photograph them, no less indeed of those who paint or sculpt the portraits of those who paint and sculpt, also be in thirsty search of the deep, clear pool of quiet reflection that is *not* the fateful habitat of Narcissus, but rather the unfathomable speculum of the universe itself: the glass held up to the hand and to the face (as to nature itself) for information, for affirmation, and for witness? "Painting", Leonardo contended, "can be shown to be philosophy", because "philosophy" deals with the increase and decrease through motion . . . ; or we may reverse the statement and say that the object seen by the eyes gains in size, importance and colour as the space interposed between it and the eye which sees is diminished." In no other artform than self-portraiture is the distance between artist and audience so critically diminished. Or put it this way: *La pittura essere filosofia* not only because it "deals with the motion of bodies in the promptitude of their actions, and philosophy too deals with motions,"[26] but because self-portraiture deals not just with motions but the emotions, and not just with bodies but with minds and spirits as well.

29

IV   Excuses and *Excursus*

"All of it, all of selecting, all of a pleasant thing is what has been a bigger thing than a piece of it taken away from it and not forgotten. A pleasant thing and some one selecting is selecting something, a pleasant thing and many of them can be found when everything is found that is pleasant and when everything that is selected is selected again."
> –Gertrude Stein, "G.P.M.", *Matisse Picasso and Gertrude Stein with two shorter stories* (New York: Something Else Press, 1972), p. 201.

"Curators are all masochistic dogs . . . They plunge their faces into mounds of image garbage, gorge themselves on cerebral mush and wallow in the chaos that culture truly is . . . Curators make temporary sense out of the chaos and still we make them roll over and beg for the footnotes. The task is simply impossible."
> – David Hlynsky, "New (?) Canadian (?) Photography (?) . . .!", *Image Nation* No. 26 (Fall 1982):7.

"*The Hand Holding the Brush*" does not—cannot—pretend to be anything more than a tentative setting-forth of available instances. The original idea had been to select a cross-section of past and present Canadian artists who, whether privately or for public consumption, not only delineated themselves so faithfully and so frequently as to deserve the title of inveterate rather than occasional or "Sunday" self-portraitists, but who also portrayed at least one other artistic contemporary—and in turn were portrayed at least once *by* them. Each "pairing" would thereby result in a nexus of, at minimum, four intimately related works. (A sample matchup: Goodridge Roberts and Allan Harrison, who, by virtue of friendship and associational propinquity, sketched one another as well as executing numerous self-portraits.) One benefit of such an arrangement would be the opportunity afforded to reveal how artists have responded over the years to *direct* influence—influence that can be measured and evaluated from documented relationships, member-ships, and collaborations. How does

the way in which artists see themselves differ from how others see them? What similarities of interpretation prevail? The interest in such revelations is, of course, as much biographical as it is aesthetic, but the curator can always hope that the viewer will be sufficiently excited by the conjunctions to transcend mere curiosity and become sensually and intellectually involved with the works of art on view, approaching them on art's own terms.

It eventually emerged, however, that the plan of choosing artists who regularly depicted themselves and their colleagues and who, conversely, were regularly depicted by self-imaging colleagues, would prove problematical, not to say impracticable. Such phenomena as the concatenations described above *do* exist, and in greater numbers than might be conceived. But to locate and secure for exhibition even a random culling from the hypothetical crop would take years of research, travel, and letter-writing, especially since so many of the requisite works are in private collections (or have disappeared from view altogether). This factor, along

with other equally discouraging practical considerations, rendered it imperative that the scope of the show be narrowed; hence my decision to focus on self-portraiture alone. All too familiar am I with the perils attendant upon attempting to organize an exhibition from the vantage-point of previously arrived-at conclusions arising out of the study of a whole range of material that might *potentially* be available for loan. As it transpired, many crucial paintings and sculptures remained untraceable despite intensive investigation, or else were found to have been consigned to permanent institutional installations and could not be borrowed for any purpose or any length of time. Even the decision to try to concentrate on such artists as had produced a sizeable self-portrait *oeuvre* was effectively sidetracked by the coincidence of a number of recent, ongoing or forth-coming retrospectives, such as those of Paraskeva Clark, Ghitta Caiserman-Roth, Frederick Varley, Zacharie Vincent, Pegi Nicol MacLeod, Alex Colville, and Robert Young, to name but a few. Not only do many private

Fig. 39 Paul-Emile Borduas (1905–1960)
Autoportrait (c. 1928)
Oil on canvas mounted on board
(21.6 x 15.9 cm.)
National Gallery of Canada, Ottawa

Fig. 39

collectors not care to lend out their treasures for extended periods; public institutions are becoming increasingly wary of long and arduous tours that will subject paintings and works on paper in their care to undue strain, and are now insisting on a minimum of a year's "rest and restoration" for a piece after it has been returned from a travelling exhibition. Among the artists not represented in "*The Hand Holding the Brush*" (where obviously they belong, if anything like comprehensibility is to be claimed for it) are several who helped to spark my interest in the subject of self-portraiture in the first place, such as Théophile Hamel and his master, Antoine Plamondon, Zacharie Vincent, and Paul-Émile Borduas (Fig. 39). Despite attempts to make amends for these involuntary omissions, their absence leaves an unfillable gap.

So, too, does the unhappy lack of more contemporary representation from Québec. This failure to offset so obvious an imbalance might be excused by the protestation that the continuing influence of *Automatisme* on québécois painting has militated against that much-vaunted "return to the figure" which has been heralded in the art-centres of English-speaking Canada on numerous occasions over the past two (or even three) decades. Limitations of curatorial time, travel funding, paucity of contacts, and scarcity of up-to-date, accurate, *accessible* documentation in French as well as in English all contributed to this apparent neglect of post-modern québécois self-portraiture.

Another touchy point. Where, some will feel compelled to demand, are the obligatory specimens of the Neo-Expressionist/New Image figure-

painting that has invaded Canada's major art-centres from Berlin and Rome, Milan and New York? Where is evidence of the influence of *Zeitgeist*, or at least of the Toronto *Monumenta* exhibition, the 'eighties' equivalents of the 1913 Armoury Show? My only response can be that, at this stage, I find most contributions to this "movement" imitative, hysterical, gratuitous, and unconvincing from the standpoints both of art and of politics. Too much of it strikes this viewer, at least, as the whipped-up products of a desire to paint according to the internationally dictated mode of the moment, rather than as sincere expressions of the urgent compulsion implied by the illiterate rhetoric and tortured Baconianisms so predictably deployed in canvas after clumsy, scrawly, sprawly canvas by the *wunderkinder* of the week. Regardless of what we are being told by those who should know better (or, worse, by those who do *not* know better), there is nothing to say in favour of bad painting, even and especially "deliberately" bad painting. When the angry young No-Futurists of today agree to learn something about and from the first-generation Expressionists bred in Canada by the Depression, and by the threat and then the actuality of World War II, then perhaps their prematurely apocalyptic visions will be exanded beyond the tunnel of personal panic and disaffection to admit of historical perspectives. The self-portrait is by nature a type of propaganda: propaganda for the working artist who paints or sculpts, performs or conceptualizes, photographs or videotapes his or her own image. The self-portraits cherished by posterity are those which transcend self

and serve the purpose of honouring art. Careless workmanship is a blatant confession of contempt for a vocation to which true artists are called and which true artists are powerless to deny. It should be noted here that I am equally unenamoured of that most unmagical of mechanistic styles, Magic Realism — a nominal contradiction in terms – with its penchant for highschool metaphysics and its craven dependence on the Kodachrome transparency. Realistic illustration is an honourable craft; would that more of our limn-every-grassblade literalists would leave painting to serious artists — painters, that it, who know by heart the protocols of technique (with which few copycat Magic- or Photo-Realists have more than a passing familiarity), but who dedicate their skill and science to the service of Vision, the aims and attributes of which are insight, inscape, inspiration.

Similarly, because of personal ignorance as well as an antipathy that I trust is not entirely hidebound and inflexible, I have neglected several other media or genres that might arguably be deemed either extensions of self-portraiture or forms of para- or anti-self-portraiture which a self-respecting semiotician or structuralist would regard as falling within the scope of this discussion: namely, video, performance art, "body art", and that application of installation art in which the artist's presence is either implied or integral. A colleague whose opinion I respect (if not always concur with) informs me that much of the most valuable Canadian video, especially that of the early 1970s, was concerned with "self-investigation but not with self-display", being preoccupied with "content" rather

Fig. 40 Iain Baxter (b. 1936)
President of a Company Blowing Bubbles
1969
Kodak type C prints (151.5 x 107 cm.)
Canada Council Art Bank, Ottawa
Photo: courtesy, Art Gallery of Ontario,
Toronto

Fig. 41 Richard Buff (b. 1947)
Split Image 1983
Mixed media (life size)
Collection: the artist, Kingston, Ontario
Photo: courtesy, the artist

32

than with navel-gazing, camera-noodling, gross exhibitionism, or the mimetic lampooning of commercial television — a medium that more than adequately parodies itself. I infer that the same may be said of the serious and witty performance art of today that refuses to wallow in vapid mannerism and *angst*-for-the-memories public tantrum-throwing.

Nevertheless, my inexpert outsider's impression is that, despite certain structural, thematic, or iconographic allegiances to self-portraiture (an Italian Renaissance invention, with Northern European antecedents), video and performance art, with their roots in commercial television, *avant garde* film, and the alternately optimistic or nihilistic antics of the Futurists and Dadaists, are only coincidentally or tangentially "about" the art-making *artist*: their employment or deployment of the person or persona of the visualizer-become-the-visualized is as often accidental or unavoidable as it is deliberate and calculated. Where and when I am able to make it out (TV-dyslectic that I am), the "issue" of a self-referential tape is rarely the character and appearance of the *animateur/auteur* in front of or behind the Portapak or out there on the gallery floor enacting the scripted or spontaneous "contemporary rituals" (Jack Burnham's term) of performance art or body art.[27] There are exceptions, of course, and numerous instances might be cited of works that are entirely predicated upon attempts to deal with the quandaries, paradoxes and contradictions of selfhood and self-image through the media of autobiographical psychodrama, the enactments of artistic functions on several planes of reference and within

several historical frames, and the paradigmatic maskings and unmaskings of ego and id. But to denominate these mysteries as *self-portraits* according to the classical Vasarian formula is to misunderstand the function as well as the perimeters of self-definition through self-depiction in two-and-three-dimensional formats which, through plastic, are static, fixed in time, concrete, and of the nature of surfaces (however much imbued they may be with illusory depth).

It is interesting to observe that many multi-media artists who have created performances, films and videotapes of a pronounced "self-portrait" or autobiographical nature have tended to back them up with more conventional and less ephemeral interpretations, or at least with records of themselves making art about themselves making art (query: when can we stop adding "making art" and agree that the real and final subject is "themselves"?). Thus the photo-sequences and constructions of Iain Baxter (Fig. 40) and Michael Snow (whose experimental films are all, of course, about Snow-the-artist); or the photographic storyboard that accompanied Suzy Lake's 1975 tape, *A Natural Way to Draw* (which itself was an essay in "translating" a graphic arts handbook into the meta-language of contemporary performance); or, more recently, Richard Buff's *Split-Image*, of 1983 (Fig. 41). This infinitely self-referential construction consists of a painted rubber statue of the artist (life-size, and designed to look like a dummy); videocam aimed at same, and a TV monitor showing what the lens (and the spectator) sees when contemplating the tableau; and (here comes infinity again), two holographic

images of the vulcanized sculptor in his chair inset in the seated mannikin's eyeglass-frames.

All of these "photo-extended" works (to borrow another curator's generic term) can legitimately be classified as generic sub-species, or at least as genetic deformations, of self-portraiture. Hence the inclusion in "*The Hand Holding the Brush*" of a small (and admittedly unrepresentative) selection of pieces that bear witness to the widespread trading-in of brushes and drawing-tools in the late 1960s and '70s for video-cameras, photocopy-machines, Polaroid SX-70s and laser-beam generators. (One latecoming would-be contributor even proposed having himself radially replicated by axial tomographic scan.) "Technique" does not always keep pace with "technic", but technology, by the same token, can never comprehend all the arcane, intuitive necromancy of inspired artistic execution. And so we return to the phenomenologically intriguing fact that the most chronologically up-to-date experiments in self-portraiture in this exhibition are exercises by artists determined to teach themselves the representational and psyche-probing secrets of the Northern and Italian Renaissance masters who almost single-handedly originated the inwardly speaking likeness of the outward self.

The news is not exactly new that the hour of mediumistic purism along Greenbergian lines is long past — though not, let us hope, the concern for appropriateness of form to medium and medium to form that Modernism's theoreticians articulated, but which the most serious artists had been practising since before the invention of the colour-wheel. Performance art, body

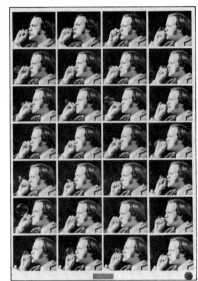

Fig. 40

Fig. 41

Fig. 42 Rae Johnson (b. 1953)
Self-Portrait 1980
Acrylic on canvas (243.8 x 182.9 cm.)
Collection: the artist, Toronto
Photo: courtesy, the artist

Fig. 42

art, installation art, video, *et al*, are at once too independent, vigorous, and endowed with powerful proselytes in Canada to need co-opting into so old-fashioned a camp as that of the painted, drawn, carved, cast, or photographically generated self-portrait. What has remained central to the study of this latter genre is the perception, through the medium of largely hidden omnipresence in our art history, of a quickening on the part of our artists to the notion of *continuity*, of a shared devotion to the cause of the human form as the primal and final tenet of pictorial faith. My point is not that there is anything "new" in the phenomenon of self-portraiture's recent return to favour as one of the major sources of imagery, hence one of the central *foci*, of a rising generation of bold (if not always articulate or coherent) statement-makers in paint (Fig. 42). To separate the genuine from the fraudulent, the truly *nouveau* from the merely trendy, requires not only a firm grasp on the overall picture of the passing moment, but an informed consideration of what has gone before, without which latter knowledge it is impossible to predict where individual artists, much less mass movements, may be headed. All this is obvious enough and hardly needs reiteration, yet the repeated follies of our arbiters of quality and "importance" provide ample evidence of an embarrassing failure on the part of the taste-makers (and -breakers) to provide the guidance and leadership their audience not only craves but deserves. Again and again a revolution is declared that turns out to be yet another belated and wrongheaded reaction. If we are to remain resolute in our intention to go on learning nothing from history, then at least we should be keeping such records and leaving such traces as will allow history to learn from us.

It is not Toronto's faddishistic gallery ghettos alone that are periodically "hit", in John Bentley Mays' cautionary words, "with tides of this or that fashion, from colour field painting to new image painting, from abstract weldings to photo-narratives. Criticism invariably responds with some new, sexy language to describe the new art — a kind of parallel to changing fads in ad copy. Potential unwary buyers are treated exactly the same." Unfortunately, artists are included among these contemporary consumers, eager to be the first in their loft-warren to adopt the latest "ism". If only they would stop reading the semiotextual gobbledegook of the 'eighties' heirs of Dryden's MacFlecknoe and Pope's Bayes and get back to the conscientious contemplation of their materials, their subject-matter, their common visual heritage, and the obligations as well as the privileges of a late-twentieth-century painter, sculptor, photographer, filmmaker, or whatever.

The proper study of mankind, for artists religiously inclined toward the resurrection of the human form and its fate in art, is *artmaking mankind*: before endeavouring to depict his or her species, the neophyte begins with the mastering of the face returning the limner's earnest gaze in the glass, the awkward, worried-looking, or falsely swaggering brushholder before the daunting void of the mirror-substituting canvas. There is a double paradox here: for while self-portraiture has been associated with the two-edged sword of romantic individualism, the Enlightenment's discovery and subsequent exultation of the Self by, among others, Rousseau, with the *Confessions* (written between 1764 and 1770, but published posthumously, and finding its visual correlative in Jacques-Louis David's 1794 *Autoportrait* in the Louvre), became implicated with the excesses of the egotistical sublime. The absurd overestimation of inventiveness and novelty, and, ultimately, the moral bankruptcy of Romanticism's "deliberate regression", have been anatomized by Robert Harbison. "The furthest excess of Romantic individualism", Harbison wrote in 1980, "is to recreate a god in the self out of just those parts beyond one's conscious control, so the unconscious and ungovernable is elevated as the true beyond, the highest part of the individual no longer individual."[29] "Make it new", Ezra Pound's Confucian battle-cry and challenge to the enemy, declined through rote repetition into a general order to the mechanically obeisant rank-and-file, which never asks "why?", or what "new" means, or what "it" might be.

The corruption of unrestrained Romanticism came to be "illustrated" by the proliferation of self-portraiture as a symptom of the self-absorption of a materially progressive but spiritually depressed and regressive age, hence the genre's bad reputation among prophets and profiteers of Modernism. (If an artist is patently incapable of objectivity, better he should paint non-objectively.) The Abstract Expressionists mistakenly conceived their revolt as a violent foreswearing, carried out through the agency of automatic *tachisme* (action or intuition *vs.* meditation or volition), of the very personalism and subjectivity they identified as the backward factor in

33

their romantic progenitors—who all too easily had been seduced, in middle-age, into accepting the blandishments of academe and exhibiting at the *Salon.* An expressed desire to draw or paint well was deemed a sign of a repressed or immature nature. There must be no retreats or regroupings, only advances, even if the reconnoiterers had no maps to plot their assault on the citadel of established, representational values. From the fortified tower of sceptical revisionism it is possible to observe patterns of recurrence not visible from ground-level.

Too much freedom induces giddiness, a feeling of imbalance and insubstantiality; too much discipline, conformity and humility have equal and opposite side-effects as well. Herbert Read was perhaps wrong to predict, in 1962, that modern artists would *not*, in future, seek a mutually beneficial compromise between tradition and individualism.[30] There will always be singular cases who believe in the marriage of craft and inspiration in whatever artform they practise, but sooner or later the moral-istic young *sans-culottes* reacting against the apolitical self-indulgence of their neurotic, alcoholic, style-obsessed elders are going to have to come to terms with the fact that, to participate in the great self-portrait tradition to which so many now make so many art-school allusions, they must acquaint themselves with the technical skills and iconographic literacy of the masters. For too long, evidence in paintings or drawings of hard artistic labour was dismissible as indicative of a latent puritanism, of an attachment to the discredited and irrelevant protestant work-ethic, or of a desire to please a

materialistic bourgeois market that favours pictures or sculpture which manifestly betoken the effort that had been put into them, and so possessed a proved moral as well as monetary value. The youngest contributor to "*The Hand Holding the Brush*" has spent a total of ten years struggling to teach himself the "renaissance techniques" of the painters with whose compositions he hangs his mental gallery; in his *Self-Portrait* of 1983 (Cat. No. 21) he perhaps sacrificed spontaneity and expressiveness (as he confesses in his artists' statement), but in persevering in his pursuit of the elusive secrets of his long-deceased mentors, the stubborn autodidact has learned even more deeply than before to appreciate the true arduosity as well as the ardour of good painting. It was through the medium of self-portraiture that this quest was undertaken; now the artist wishes to continue the search through the united but not parallel pursuits of landscape, portraiture, and still-life. His ambition is not to become rich and famous (though that, of course, would be nice, allowing him to move out of his parents' basement and into a studio of his own, rendering affordable the high-quality materials he needs to advance beyond his present level, permitting him to give up the unrewarding freelance illustration-work by which he pays for the "privilege" of making art), but to seek means of developing into an enduringly good painter. He is not alone in the crux in which he finds himself, but, a resolute avoider of "scenes", he experiences all the more keenly the isolation and sense of frustration romantic individualists with classical inclinations have to endure in

this and in other countries, at this and in other times. The instant (and no doubt temporary) repute enjoyed by immature cult-followers who publicly exhibit—to loud and influential approbation—student work which artists imbued with the conscientious-ness of craft would be ashamed to line their wastebaskets with, is a mark of the inconsistent development of taste in our culture. While it is praiseworthy that undergraduate painters who wish to learn to draw from life but who are not being taught to do so in art-college should be hiring models and forming sketching-groups as of old, there is nothing commendable about the haste with which they rush to show the results of their sessions round the dais, and something at once condescending and derisory in the laudation by post-modernist critics of this premature display of good intentions insufficiently realized.

*

In an attempt to convey not only the variety and numerosity of Canadian self-portraiture, but also the internal consistency and integrity of develop-ment within the self-portrait *oeuvre* of such dedicated practitioners as W. G. R. Hind, Robert Harris, Joseph Saint-Charles, L. L. FitzGerald, Jean Dallaire, Miller Brittain, Jack Humphrey, Maxwell Bates, Goodridge Roberts, Paraskeva Clark, Greg Curnoe, Dennis Burton, Tony Urquhart, Robert Young, Joyce Wieland, Michael Snow, and Suzy Lake, I originally had intended to include interpretive commentaries on their work—chronicling, for instance, the development of the auto-biographical and symbolic imagery of Ivan Eyre from the 1960s to his

culminatory allegory in acrylics, *Birdmen*, painted in 1981 (Cat. No. 67), or the stylistic evolution of FitzGerald's extraordinary self-portrait-in-watercolour series of 1942-1943 (Cat. No. 51). (It was these latter disturbingly inquisitional images that prompted Ferdinand Eckhardt in 1963 to make the startling statement that self-portraiture was "a field which is rare if not non-existent in Canadian art.") Unfortunately, time and space restrictions meant that these descriptive and critical analyses had to be cut (perhaps to be restored in my projected dictionary of Canadian self-portraits and portraits of artists). Nor did the exhibition's truncated gestation and production period allow for the researching and annotating of exhibition and publication histories of individual works in the show; much of this information, at any rate, is available in other catalogues and books. Readers here will have to make do with biographical outlines of each contributor and with a selection of comments by the artists, where such were available, either on self-portraiture *per se* (with emphasis on their own examples), or on more general themes relating to painting or sculpture which have pertinence to the subject under review. Appending the catalogue entries is a series of bibliographies on portraiture in Canada and elsewhere, and on the individual artists in the exhibition, listed alphabetically.

*

A final quandary: organization. There are any number of ways in which so much stylistically diverse but thematically related material could be presented. To hang the works

Fig. 43 Ernest Lindner (b. 1897)
Self-Portrait 1927
Charcoal, yellow chalk, heightened with
white, on beige construction paper
(46.2 x 32.7 cm.)
National Gallery of Canada, Ottawa
Photo: Hans Blohm, Ottawa

Fig. 44 Ernest Lindner (b. 1897)
Self-Portrait 1941
Charcoal (36.1 x 28.7 cm.)
National Gallery of Canada, Ottawa
Photo: Michael Neill, Ottawa

Fig. 45 Ernest Lindner (b. 1897)
Self-Portrait 1976
Watercolour on paper (75.6 x 53.9 cm.)
Saskatchewan Arts Board, Regina

Fig. 43

Fig. 45

Fig. 44

loners in Canadian art who resolutely turned down invitations to join societies, to exhibit with this or that movement or group, to be conscripted into the Academy of the École? A separate gallery of eccentrics and solitaries is conceivable, of course, but the forcible roping together of unclubbable mavericks and hermits would be as frivolous as the yoking of neo-expressionist to photo-realist merely because the surname of one follows that of the other. Biographical linkages are themselves distractive, drawing attention away from the work and fixing it on the life of its creator, the "facts" of which, when obtainable, tend to be inaccurate and open to misconstruction.

The simplest and most acceptable approach, from an art-historical standpoint, would probably be the predictable but convenient chronological tactic: stick them up according to when they were done, or when their artists were born or flourished or died. At least by this unimaginative strategy a horizontal line of development (or regression) could be observed from past to present. Arrangement by date also permits, in microcosm, the surveying of the maturation of individual artists — assuming (and it is a very large assumption) that the crucial works with which to document this transition over the course of a career may be borrowed or at least reproduced in the catalogue. For instance, through his self-portraits Ernest Lindner (not in this exhibition) might be shown in episodic fashion on the way to his close-focused vegetational style, retaining his allegiance to naturalism but interpreting it, in his figure-and-ground fantasies, allegorically rather than literalistically. This face is

recognizably that of the young man who drew his frowning self-image in 1927 and 1941, but a transformation occurred in the thirty-five years between the rather stiff draughtsman of the middle self-portrait and the confident, Düreresque master of the 1976 watercolour-on-paper *Self-Portrait* (Figs. 43, 44, 45). In that neglected interval Lindner discovered his subject-matter and *métier*. The number of Canadian artists in whom we can witness this innocence-to-experience-to-experienced innocence progression is small and all-too-rarely exhibited or reproduced.

Then again, there is classification by medium or style, by political orientation or "contents" of works chosen for display. Too vague, not enough focus; curatorial motivations and conflicts of interest also too much in evidence. Employed with sensitivity to historical as well as aesthetic concerns, the formalistic philosophy is as bereft of justification as the biographical or psychological. These works are not "just" paintings or sculptures or photo-constructions, granted; likewise and equally, they are not "just" self-portraits. How to emphasize the importance of *both* factors, medium and message, signifier and sign?

The curators of two fairly recent exhibitions of self-portraits took two quite different organizational tacks, both of which have their advantages and disadvantages. Ann Van Devanter and Alfred V. Frankenstein ordered their National Portrait Gallery (Washington) show according to the above-mentioned chronological scheme, numbering works according to the birthdates of the artists represented in *American Self-Portraits, 1670-1973.*

alphabetically-by-artist might occasion some serendipitously eye-opening juxtapositions of old and new, of *avant garde* and traditional, but the risk of allowing the diminishment of particular paintings, drawings or sculptures by uncongenial placements committed through the observance of too rigid a consistency to this arbitrary system of arrangement was too great. It was suggested to me that a sense of order and consequence might be imposed on randomness by the grouping of pieces according to the associational principle — showing together, say, the *autoportraits* of French-Canadian painters who had studied in Paris in the 1880s and '90s, and perhaps contrastingly collocating the self-portraits of their English-Canadian counterparts. But where then does one place the congenital

Fig. 46 Albert Dumouchel (1916–1971)
[*Autoportrait*]
Note: reproduced from Guy Robert, *Albert Dumouchel ou la Poétique de la Main* (Montréal: Les Presses de l'Université du Québec, Collection Studio, 1970), p. 96.

36 On the other hand, Siegmar Holsten's aforementioned *Das Bild Des Künstlers* breaks his material down into a number of helpful and provocative categories, under five major headings, as follows: "*Emanzipation und Selbstbehauptung*" (Emancipation and Self-assertion), "*Aug in Auge mit sich selbst*" (Eye-to-eye with Oneself), "*Im Konflikt mit der Gesellschaft*" (In Conflict with Society), "*Im Bund mit anderer*" (In League with Others), and "*Neu Aspekte der Selbstdarstellung*" (New Aspects of Self-Portraiture). Holsten's sub-classes within these general topics of discussion range from the treatment of artists by themselves as subservient to ecclesiastical or princely authority, to their self-discovery as confident individuals. One chapter deals with confronting the countenance of death, and another with the game of grimacing or "pulling faces". The theme of the mirrored image and the imaging mirror is dealt with in a section entitled "*Im Zweigesprach mit dem Spiegelbild*" (literally, "in dialogue with one's reflected visage"). Among other issues: melancholy and despair; the artist in the role of martyr; "aura" as self-protection; woman and artist; artist and family; artist united with friends and the like-minded; self-direction and self-estrangement; and, finally, "*Selbstaufspurung*" — the "tracking down of the self". To have set out to locate Canadian self-portraits answering to these categorical descriptions would have been foolhardy, not to say arrogant. That such qualities may be read into or extracted from the visual record is obvious, especially to a taxonomically inclined Teuton. However, a less deterministic *modus operandi* would

be to collect as much historically representative (and at the same time aesthetically stimulating) material together, and then try to allow *the works themselves* to "crystallize" into similar, though not necessarily identical, clusters. The harder and longer one thinks about a collection of images, the more those images begin to sort themselves into position: and while there are areas of overlap, and perhaps some contentious or question-able consociations, the five sections into which the contents of "*The Hand Holding the Brush*" are unscientifically "classified" do have the advantage of isolating some of self-portraiture's prevailing concerns, and of illustrating the manner in which Canadian artists have conformed to expectations or divagated from the well-blazed trail. More than one work could be placed in *any* of the groupings without violence being done to itself or to its neighbours. By emphasizing (if only inadvertently) the conventions observed, rather than the originality with which these have been subverted or avoided, "*The Hand Holding the Brush*" may convey a curatorial bias against experimentation. Rather, the basis of these choices was a conviction that the new needs the old not only for something to rebel against but for energizing sustenance, and a belief that much art that appears, at the time of its conception, to be without precedent and unique, in fact fits into the line of generic succession which contributes to any medium its hidden order and logical unity. "All art is about other art" may be a trite truism, but like all indefensible generalizations it bears itself out through the witness of those who *act* upon such precepts. Certainly, many artists have been

influenced in their self-portraits by other self-portraits, and have chosen to announce their gratitude through parodistic or homilitic lines — some even to the extent of presenting themselves in the garb, headgear and familiar poses of the past patterns to which they wish to pay homage, or from whose overwhelming presence they long to be delivered: hence Albert Dumouchel's and Mashel Teitelbaum's self-portraits-as Rembrandt (Figs. 46, 47), Lilian Freiman's Cranach-quoting *Early Self-Portrait* (Fig. 48), and Robin Page's summation of the modern-day dilemma of lost contact with omnipresent masters, *Call Michael-angelo* (Fig. 49). The answer, as J. W. Morrice indicates in his undated self-caricature (Fig. 50), is to return with humour as well as with humility to one's own experience and *métier*.

The sequence of the five historical, thematic, or formalistic categories into which this exhibition has been organized follows, roughly speaking, that the self-portraiture in Canada itself, from self-conscious self-advertisements (complete with career-identifying props), to the photographically generated serial imagery employed by contemporary artists interested in exploring the phenomena of their presences (or absences) in time as well as in space. And with photography we come full circle, ending this survey of ways and means, why and why-nots, with a quotation from Barbara Rose that coincidentally echoes the passage from W. G. Constable's technical manual from which this exhibition derives its title:

In self-portraits, the relationship of objective perception to subjective interpretation is particularly complex.

Fig. 46

For in a self-portrait, the artist is both observer and observed. One cannot remember one's own features; therefore, to portray himself or herself, the artist must observe the reflection in a mirror. Beginning in the 19th century, photographs could also be used. When relying on a reflected image, the artist was forced to pose in a position that enabled him to refer constantly to the mirror. As a result, the use of mirrors determined the formula for the self-portrait until the invention of photography: typically, the artist is seen in three-quarter view, both eyes focused to one side — a position that permits the head to remain fixed while the eyes move from mirror to canvas. Normally, one hand — the painting hand — is hidden, since it is virtually impossible to depict the hand in motion. In rare instances, an artist might use a print or painting of himself to vary this

Fig. 47 Mashel Teitelbaum (b. 1921)
Self-Portrait as Rembrandt 1979
Graphite and acrylic on paper
(35.5 x 42.5 cm.)
Private collection, Toronto

Fig. 48 Lillian Freiman (b. 1908)
Early Self-Portrait
Pastel and acrylic on blue paper
(26.5 x 26 cm.)
National Gallery of Canada, Ottawa

Fig. 49 Robin Page (b. 1933)
Call Michaelangelo 1973
Acrylic on canvas; marble
(200 x 120 x 55 cm.)
Galerie Müller, Köln, West Germany

Fig. 50 James Wilson Morrice (1865–1924)
Autoportrait (peignant au chevalet)
Graphite on paper (16.5 x 21.6 cm.)
(paper size)
National Gallery of Canada, Ottawa

Fig. 47

Fig. 48

Fig. 49

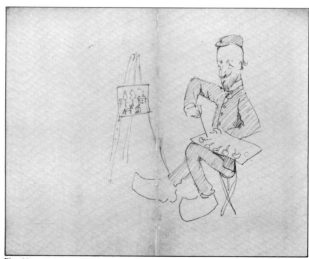

Fig. 50

rather strictly adhered-to format, but basically, full-frontal and full-profile self-portraits are inventions of the 19th century, made possible by photography.[32]

Rose broke her examination of the common theme of self-portraiture — "self-consciousness" — into three major subsections: "Thinkers and Workers", "Witnesses and Voyeurs", and "Martyrs and Madmen". Into such dualistic divisions or subdivisions — an interesting synonym for "class" is "predicament" — Canadian art history, and certainly its artists, art historians, and critics, could also be distributed. To close with Rose:

Because looking in the mirror is a primal act of self-consciousness, the theme of the self-portrait is a natural origin of the artists' initial consciousness of himself as a creator, with all the joy and misery that role implies, and of his art as deliberate illusion. Because the self-portrait is the first subject in art history to deal with self-consciousness as a theme, to disengage subject from object and recast them as observer and observed, the self-portrait is among the first crucial manifestations of the modern mind.[33]

That such crucial manifestations also took place, are taking place, will take place in Canada, as the mind — always unto itself "modern" — continues to contemplate its workings, is reason enough to pay special attention to this "primal act". Universal in motivation, local in feeling, agelessly contemporary because renewed by every sensitive contact between observer and observed, self-portraiture and self-portraits serve as indispensible mediators between face and mirror, eye and canvas, hand and brush.

Introduction: Endnotes

38

1) W. G. Constable, ''Preliminaries to Making a Painting'', *The Painter's Workshop* (London: Oxford University Press, 1954), p. 119.

2) Roland Barthes, ''The World as Object'', *A Barthes Reader*. Edited . . . by Susan Sontag. (New York: Hill and Wang, 1983), p. 73.

3) Marie-Dominique Labelle et Sylvie Thivierge, ''Un peintre huron de XIXe siècle: Zacharie Vincent'', *Recherches Amérindiennes au Québec* 11 (1981): 326.

4) See Robert Graham, ''Sorel Cohen . . .'', *Vanguard* 12 (May 1983): 41. See also Monica M. Heim's review of the Optica Gallery (Montréal) showing of *An Extended and Continuous Metaphor* in February-March 1983, and subsequently at PS 1, New York, published in *Parachute* 31 (June, July, August 1983): 49-50.

5) Ludwig Goldscheider, *Five Hundred Self-Portraits: From Antique Times to the Present Day in Sculpture, Painting, Drawing and Engraving*. Translated by J. Byam Shaw (London: George Allen and Unwin, 1937), p. 12.

6) Ludwig Goldscheider, *Five Hundred Self-Portraits* . . . . , pp. 19-20.

7) John Pope-Hennessy, *The Portrait in the Renaissance*. Bollingen Series XXV. 12. (New York: Pantheon Books, 1966), pp. 3-4.

8) John Pope-Hennessy, *The Portrait in the Renaissance*, p. 8.

9) John Pope-Hennessy, *The Portrait in the Renaissance*, pp. 60, 62.

10) John Pope-Hennessy, *The Portrait in the Renaissance*, pp. 112-113.

11) John Pope-Hennessy, *The Portrait in the Renaissance*, pp. 124, 126.

12) John Pope-Hennessy, *The Portrait in the Renaissance*, p. 135.

13) The Public Archives of Canada is working toward building up such an image-bank within its Picture Division, concentrating on painted, engraved, lithographed, and photographed portraits within its own holdings and in other public institutions and in private hands. The $10,000 left by J. W. L. Forster (1850-1938) in his will to help finance his dream of a Canadian National Portrait Gallery is still under the custodianship of the Ontario Government, and the portraits he left as a proposed nucleus for that projected collection remain in the care of the Royal Ontario Museum, Toronto.

14) J. Russell Harper and Dr. Robert Hubbard, ''English Colonial Period: Portrait Painting / Période coloniale anglaise: Le Portrait'', *Treasures from Quebec / Trésors de Québec* (Ottawa: National Gallery of Canada / Galérie nationale du Canada, 1965), p. 35.

15) Marie-Dominique Labelle et Sylvie Thivierge, ''Un peintre huron du XIXe siècle: Zacharie Vincent'', *Recherches Amérindiennes au Québec* 11 (1981): 326.

16) Gabriel P. Weisberg, Foreword, *The Artist and the Studio in the Eighteenth and Nineteenth Centuries*. By Ronnie L. Zakon (Cleveland: The Cleveland Museum of Art, 1978), p. 5.

17) C. W. Jefferys, ''Portrait Painting'', *Canadian Comment* (January 1935): 22.

18) Max J. Friedlander, ''Principles and History of Portraiture'', *Landscape, Portrait, and Still Life: Their Origin and Development*. Translated by R. F. C. Hull (Oxford: Bruno Cassirer, 1949), pp. 232-233.

19) John Berger, ''The Changing View of Man in the Portrait'', *The Moment of Cubism* (New York: Pantheon Books, 1969), pp. 41-42.

20) John Berger, ''The Changing View of Man in the Portrait'', p. 47.

21) Manuel Gasser, *Self-Portraits*. Translated by Angus Malcolm (London: Weidenfeld and Nicolson, 1963), p. 7.

22) Christopher Dewdney, ''The Paradigm of Invention: Murray Favro'', *Artmagazine* 12 (September 1983): 12.

23) Jacqueline MacQueen, quoted by Avis Lang Rosenberg in *Mirrorings: Women Artists* of the Atlantic Provinces (Halifax: Art Gallery, Mount Saint Vincent University, 1982), p. 6.

24) Avis Lang Rosenberg, Introduction, *Mirrorings* . . . . , pp. 6-7.

25) Brian Boigon, ''A Mirror in the Window: A search for an Ontological Double in the City'', *Impulse* 9 (Spring 1981): 45.

26) Leonardo Da Vinci, *Paragone: A Comparison of the Arts*. With an introduction and English translation by Irma A. Richter (London: Godfrey Cumberlege, Oxford University Press, 1949), p. 30.

27) Regarding the categorical ''split'' between these two ''genres'', see Bruce Barber, ''Indexing: Conditionalism and Its Heretical Equivalents'' in *Performance by Artists*, edited by A. A. Bronson and Peggy Gale (Toronto: Art Metropole, 1979), especially the section of this essay subtitled ''Indexing: Problems for the Contemporary Art Researcher'', pp. 184-191.

28) John Bentley Mays, ''[David] Buchan sells revolution in the best satirical style'', *The Globe and Mail*, 24 February 1981.

29) Robert Harbison, Preface, *Deliberate Regression* (New York: Alfred A. Knopf, 1980), p. xv.

30) See Herbert Read, ''At the Turn of a Civilization'', *A Letter to a Young Painter* (New York: Horizon Press, 1962), p. 276.

32) Barbara Rose, ''Self-Portraiture: Theme with a Thousand Faces'', *Art in America* 63 (January-February 1975): 66.

33) Barbara Rose, ''Self-Portraiture: Theme with a Thousand Faces'': 73.

PART I: "ARTISTS AT WORK"

The self-portraits in this opening section represent the artist in the most familiar guise and stance associated with the genre: with brush, charcoal-stub, or pencil in hand, often armed with palette and maulstick and wearing a profession-identifying smock. Usually he or she positions him/herself before the easel or drawing-board, or else is shown contemplating his/her reflection in a mirror, or else gazing out toward the spectator (who assumes a position relative to the painter exactly parallel with that of the looking-glass in which the artist was staring at the time of producing his/her likeness).

Richard Ormond noted, in his introduction to a National Portrait Gallery (London) exhibition devoted to depictions of "the artist in his working environment", that

> The conventions of the artist's portrait are sometimes predictable. There is the artist with palette and brushes, the tools of his trade; the view of his studio is carefully selected; the picture is set up on the easel; the other props are consciously arranged about him. Interpretation is possible on a number of levels. The portrait is a record of the appearance and personality of the artist himself. It is an illustration of what an artist does and how he conducts himself. At a deeper level, however, interpretation becomes more subjective and complicated. How should one assess the symbolic importance of accessories? What do they tell us about the artist? How does he see himself? How does society view him? What were the aesthetic and stylistic preconceptions of a particular period? Some works are more deliberately weighted with meaning than others, more consciously seeking to express the inner creative spirit, without which no art can exist. It is the idea of creative genius that endows the portraits of artists with particular significance. They offer us a clue to the inner world of the spirit, however conventional their external appearance may be. And they are very personal statements as well, whether painted by the artist himself or by someone else. It is the individuality and intimacy of the images that remains striking.[1]

It is curious, incidentally, that so few professional portraitists, at least in recent times, have painted noteworthy self-portraits; very often the best examples of the genre are by artists who specialize in other fields, and who resort to portraiture only out of choice or creative compulsion, rather than out of economic necessity. Why, too, have so few Canadian women painters and sculptors, past and present, elected to record themselves in this conventional attitude, hard at work in the studio?

This is the earliest type of self-portrait to come down to us, dating from the late middle ages and the early years of the Northern Renaissance. Artists today who resort to the identifying formula of depicting themselves in the process of depicting themselves are, for the most part, self-consciously alluding to the rich iconographic tradition of the painter's "portrait d'apparat".

It is frequently remarked that the self-portrait is often, if not always, occasioned by the unavailability to artists of live models or sitters — hence their reversion to their own reflected or conceptual images as subject-matter. On the other hand, self-advertisement and self-commemoration are also potent motives, no less in 1983, the date of the latest self-portrait in this section, than in 1838, that of the earliest.

---

[1] Richard Ormond, Introduction, *Artists at Work* (London: National Portrait Gallery, 1981), pp. 2-3.

FRANCIS MATTE
(1809-1839)

Painter.

1 Francis Matte
Autoportrait 1838
Oil on canvas (79 x 64.8 cm)
Detroit Institute of Arts, Detroit, Michigan,
Founders' Society
Purchase, Director's Discretionary Fund

EZEKIEL SEXTON, JR.
(active 1842-c.1850)

Itinerant portrait painter.

2 Ezekiel Sexton, Jr.
Self-Portrait with Wife and Daughter
(c. early 1850s)
Oil on canvas (98.1 cm: diameter)
London Regional Art Gallery, London,
Ontario, gift of Edward McKone,
1964

40

Born: Les Ecureuils, Québec, 1809.
Studied under Antoine Plamondon,
1834-38, and James Bowman, c. 1835.
Opened own studio, concentrating on
portraits in Plamondon's manner.
Portraits of bishops in Ursuline
Convent, Quebec City. Died: Les
Ecureuils, 1839.

Probably from upper New York State.
Visited London, Ancaster, Nelson, and
Toronto, 1842, seeking portrait
commissions. Married Rhoda Shenich,
London, Ontario, 1849, and bought
two acres of land from her father,
1853. Failing at farming, resumed
itinerant career, moving with family to
Ohio. Became involved in spiritualism,
alienating wife, who returned with
daughter to London. Sexton later
followed, then left to seek fortune in
gold fields of California, where he
presumably died, c. 1850.

WILLIAM G.R. HIND
(1833-1889)

Painter, topographic draughtsman,
teacher.

3 W.G.R. Hind
Self-Portrait (c. 1862-63)
Watercolour (30.2 x 22.5 cm)
Inscribed (*verso*, in ink): *WILLIAM G.R.
HIND*
McCord Museum, McGill University,
Montréal

Born: Nottingham, England, 12 June
1883. Arrived in Toronto (following
brother, Henry Youle Hind), 1851.
Conducted drawing classes in Toronto
for two years, appointed "Drawing
Master" of Toronto Normal School,
1851-56. Exhibited at Upper Canada
Exhibition, Toronto, 1852. To
England, 1861. Joined H.Y. Hind as
official artist of Canadian Government
Expedition to Labrador, 1861.
Watercolours and drawings of local
scenery, Indians, etc., reproduced in
H.Y. Hind's *Explorations in the
Interior of the Labrador Peninsula* (2
vols., 1863). Left with Toronto party of
"Overlanders of '62" to go to Cariboo
gold fields of British Columbia, spring
1862. Painted incidents connected
with expedition from Ft. Garry
through Rockies to Lillooet, B.C., then
along Fraser River to Victoria. To San
Francisco and California gold fields,
fall 1862. In Victoria, 1863-65,
working as professional artist.

Collaborated with a Mr. Tomlinson in
landscape paintings, 1865. Resident of
Red River Colony, 1870, then to
eastern Canada, making headquarters
at brother's house at Windsor, Nova
Scotia. Worked for railways in N.S.
and New Brunswick, possibly as
draughtsman. Continued painting
Maritimes landscapes. Settled in
Sussex, N.B. 1879. Died: Sussex,
N.B., 1889. Collection of Cariboo
sketches discovered in Nova Scotia
attic, 1927. Retrospective exhibition
mounted by Willistead Art Gallery,
Windsor, 1967.

Fig. 1 W.G.R. Hind
Self-Portrait (c. 1865)
Oil on board (15.9 x 15.9 cm)
Provincial Archives of British Columbia, Victoria

Fig. 2 W.G.R. Hind
Self-Portrait (c. 1870s)
Oil or encaustic on board (35.7 x 25.4 cm)
Public Archives of Canada (C-13964)

Fig. 3 W.G.R. Hind
Self-Portrait (c. 1870?)
Oil on paper (16.7 x 9.7 cm)
John Ross Robertson Collection, Baldwin Room,
Metropolitan Toronto Library (JRR 3250)

Fig. 4 W.G.R. Hind
Self-Portrait (c. 1876)
Watercolour and graphite (17.6 x 12.5 cm)
National Gallery of Canada, Ottawa

Fig. 1

Fig. 2

Fig. 3

Fig. 4

WILLIAM SAWYER
(1820-1889)

Portrait painter and photographer.

Born: Montréal, Québec, 9 November 1820. Learned art by copying engravings, drawing from casts and from life. Working as portrait-painter, Montréal, 1840s. Began to work in communities along St. Lawrence River and north shore of Lake Ontario. In Kingston, Ontario, 1848; to Toronto, 1850; visited New York, spring 1852; returned to Kingston and set up studio. Moved back to Montréal, 1855, then returned to Kingston, working as itinerant portrait painter, travelling to Port Hope, Cobourg, Belleville, Toronto, Brockville, Peterborough, Ottawa, and Montréal. Began to use photography as an aid. Worked in Kingston and Montréal in late 1860s and early '70s. Advertised as photographer, Montréal, 1858. Travelled to Scotland, England, France and Belgium, 1862, copying old masters and visiting museums and galleries. Set up photographic and art studio, Montréal, 1871. Resumed intinerant career, 1870s. Worked as portraitist, teacher, ornamental painter, photographer, picture restorer, Kingston, 1880s. Exhibited with Montreal Society of Artists, 1847 and in Toronto Mechanics' Institute's province-wide exhibition, 1850, of works to be sent to Great Exhibition, London, 1851, receiving diploma from the Governor General, Lord Elgin. Exhibited photographs at 1859 Provincial Exhibition, awarded first and second prizes for portraits in oils in professional category, and award for best photographic portraits in oil, Provincial Exhibition, Kingston, 1863. Exhibited at Art Association of Montreal, 1864-70; Quebec Provincial Exhibition, Québec, 1865; Society of Canadian Artists, Québec, 1870-72; Upper Canada Provincial Exhibition, 1855-63; first exhibition of the Agricultural and Industrial Exhibition Association of Toronto, 1879; Royal Canadian Academy, 1883. Societies: Montreal Society of Artists (1847); Society of Canadian Artists (founder-member, 1867); Ontario Society of Artists (founder-member, 1872). Painted portraits of Sir John A. Macdonald, Sir Charles Tupper, Sir William Logan, Mackenzie Bowell, etc.; former mayors of Kingston for Corporation of City of Kingston; and series of official portraits for Parliament Buildings, Ottawa. Died: 9 December 1889. Retrospective exhibition mounted by Agnes Etherington Art Centre, Kingston, 1978.

COMMENTS BY THE ARTIST

Invention in painting must not be confounded with that of *Creation*, but a subject found and gathered from Poetry and History, or personal observation of the visible universe that envelops our senses, ready to be called up in the visions of fancy, giving to them a "local habitation, and a name".

…

Along with Invention, may be placed that subtle quality emanating from the soul, and, like a soul, pervading the whole representation — call it character, sentiment, feeling; — for one word seems to render that of which we perceive at once the presence or the absence, though it escapes definition. For not only will it be sublime, grand, graceful, truthful, pathetic or tender in accordance with the subject represented, but it will be essentially modified by the temperament of him who represents it. Where it is, it atones for many deficiencies; where it is *not*, no merits supply its place.

…

Expression is the vivid image of the sentiment or passion that affects the mind, its language and the portrait of its situation; the index without that registers the mind within, indicating joy or grief, love or hatred, charity or envy, hope and fear, intelligence or dullness, firmness or indecision, common to all in its elements of passion yet differing in its energy according to the character of sanguine, phlegmatic or melancholic, and must thus be true in the first place as to situation and emotion as in the second proper to the personage represented. It animates the features, attitudes and gestures which invention selected and composition arranged and requires the most refined discrimination and labour to portray its various modifications with correctness.

– William Sawyer, "Lecture on Art Delivered to the Kingston Young Men's Church of England Association, 9 July 1861 and the Churchmen's Association, Montreal, 3 February 1865", *William Sawyer, Portrait Painter*, by Michael Bell (Kingston: Agnes Etherington Art Centre, Queen's University, 1978), p.81.

4 William Sawyer
Self-Portrait 1861
Oil on canvas (76.2 x 52.1 cm)
Signed and dated (l.r.): *W. Sawyer 1861*
Private collection, Kingston, Ontario
Photo: Sparks and Associates, Kingston,
courtesy, Agnes Etherington
Art Centre, Kingston

5 William Sawyer
Artist Inspired 1884
Oil on canvas (73.6 x 62.2 cm)
Signed and dated (l.l.): *W. Sawyer 1884*
Private collection, Kingston
Photo: Sparks and Associates, Kingston,
courtesy, Agnes Etherington
Art Centre, Kingston

Fig. 1 William Sawyer
Self-Portrait 1883
Oil on canvas (61.5 x 51.1 cm)
Signed and dated (l.l.): *W. Sawyer, 1883*
Musée des Beaux-Arts de Montréal, presented by
the artist' family, in memory of their father

ROBERT HARRIS
(1849-1919)

Painter, sculptor, illustrator, writer.

44   Born: North Wales, 17 September 1849. Emigrated with family to Charlottetown, Prince Edward Island, 1856. Worked as land surveyor after graduating from Prince of Wales College, 1863. Visited England, 1867-68; decided to become a painter. Commissioned to paint portraits of Speakers of P.E.I. House of Assembly, 1871. To Boston, 1872-73, studying anatomy and painting, then opened studio. Did book and newspaper illustration. Returned to Charlottetown, 1874. To England, 1876. Enrolled at Slade School for one term under Alphonse Legros, 1877. To Paris, entered studio of Léon Bonnat, 1877 (re-enrolled , 1881). Moved to Toronto and exhibited with Ontario Society of Artists, 1879. Did illustrations for *Picturesque Canada*, 1881. To Paris, 1881. Exhibited at Paris Salon, 1882. Took studio in London, 1883, and exhibited at Royal Academy. Returned to Canada to work on *Fathers of Confederation*, 1883 (completed, 1885, destroyed by fire, 1916).

Directed Art School of Art Association of Montreal, 1883-87. Frequent trips to Europe and Great Britain, to 1911. Societies: Ontario Society of Artists (elected 1879, vice-president, 1881, resigned, 1881); Royal Canadian Academy (charter member, 1880, president, 1893-1906); Pen and Pencil Club, Montréal (elected president, 1892). Won gold medals at Pan-American Exposition, Buffalo, 1901, and Louisiana Purchase Exposition, St. Louis, 1904. Created C.M.G., 1904. Died: 27 February 1919.

Fig. 1 Robert Harris
On St. Helen's Island 1884
Watercolour on paper (19.5 x 43 cm) (sight)
Signed (l.r.): *R. Harris*
Inscribed and dated (l.l.): *St. Helen's Island, Montreal — June 7th, 1884*
Confederation Centre Art Gallery and Museum, Charlottetown, Harris Trust

Fig. 2 Robert Harris
Mahogany Sketch Box with Self-Portrait 1892
Oil on mahogany (portrait on sketch-box lid)
Confederation Centre Art Gallery and Museum, Charlottetown, Harris Trust
Photo: Wayne Barrett, St. Catherine's, P.E.I.

Note: see also Catalogue No. 31

LOUIS-PHILIPPE HÉBERT
(1850-1917)

Sculptor.

7 Louis-Philippe Hébert
Autoportrait (c. 1901)
Bronze (50 x 23 x 16 cm)
Signed (on edge of base, at back): *P. Hébert*
Art Gallery of Hamilton, Hamilton,
Ontario
Gift of Canadian Westinghouse Co., 1966

8 Louis-Philippe Hébert
L'Inspiration 1904
Bronze (height: 57.2 cm)
Inscribed (on base): *L'Inspiration*
National Gallery of Canada, Ottawa, Royal
Canadian Academy Diploma Collection
(deposited 1906)

Born: Ste. Sophie d'Halifax, Lower Canada, 27 January 1850. Began carving figures in wood at age seven. Joined the Papal Zouaves and served in Rome, 1869. Returned to Canada, 1871. Began career as sculptor. Apprenticed to Alfred Rho. Taken into studio of Napoléon Bourassa, worked in church decoration, 1879-80. On return from Paris, 1880, began to do historical statuary (e.g. Sir Georges-Etienne Cartier, Alexander MacKenzie, Sir John A. Macdonald, etc., for Parliament Hill, Ottawa; Monument Maisonneuve, Montréal; Parlement du Québec, etc.) Also sculpted portrait busts, statuettes and ornamental works for churches. To Paris, 1879-80, 1887, 1888-94, 1897-1902, 1906, 1907, 1911-14. Father of painter Adrien Hébert and sculptor Henri Hébert. Societies: Royal Canadian Academy (elected Associate, 1880, full academician, 1886). Awards: Canadian Government Centennial Medal, 1894; Chevalier de la Légion d'honneur, 1901; C.G.M., 1903; Knight of the Order of St. Gregory the Great, 1903. Died: Westmount, Québec, 13 June 1917.

SIR EDMUND WYLY GRIER
(1862-1957)

Portrait and genre painter.

9 Sir Edmund Wyly Grier
Self-Portrait or *Portrait of the Artist* 1914
Oil on canvas (100.3 x 74.9 cm)
Signed and dated (1.1.): *E. WYLY
GRIER/1914*
National Gallery of Canada, Ottawa

46   Born: Melborne, Australia, 26 November 1862. To Toronto with family, 1876. To England with family after graduating from Upper Canada College. Studied at Slade School under Alphonse Legros, 1879; evenings at British Academy, London (sculpture in wax and clay); Scuola Libera, Rome, 1881; for three years at Académie Julian, Paris, under Bougeureau and Tony Robert-Fleury. Exhibited at Royal Society of British Artists, 1886, and at the Royal Academy, 1889, '90, '92, '95. Won gold medal, 3rd class, at Paris Salon, 1890, for *Bereft*; silver medal at Pan American Exposition, Buffalo, 1901. Returned to Toronto, 1891, opened studio, specializing in portraits. Served with Royal Canadian Artillery, 1897-1903, rising to rank of Major; exhibited at National Academy of Design, New York, 1906 and '07, and at Munich, Berlin, and Düsseldorf. Societies: Royal Canadian Academy (elected associate, 1893, full academician, 1895, president, 1930-39); Ontario Society of Artists (elected 1896, president, 1908-13); Arts and Letters Club, Toronto (founding member, 1908, president, 1910-12). Honours: Hon. Doctor of Civil Law, University of Bishop's College, 1934; knighted, 1935. Commissioned by Nova Scotia government to restore and clean portraits in Province House, Halifax, 1936. Died: Toronto, 7 December 1957.

ARTHUR LISMER
(1885-1969)

Painter, teacher, writer.

Born: Sheffield, England, 22 June 1885. Won seven-year scholarship to Sheffield School of Art, 1898. Apprenticed to photo-engraving company, Sheffield, 1899-1905. Studied at Académie Royale des Beaux-Arts, Antwerp, Belgium, 1906. Worked at commercial art studio, Sheffield, 1908-10. Sailed for Canada, January 1911, settling in Toronto. Joined Grip Engraving Company as commercial artist under A.H. Robson. Co-workers included Tom Thomson, J.E.H. MacDonald, Frank Johnston, Franklin Carmichael, F.H. Varley (*q.v.*), Tom McLean, and W.S. Broadhead. To England and Belgium, 1912. Returned to Canada, August 1912. Became freelance illustrator. First sale: *The Clearing* purchased by Ontario government, 1913. First trip to Dr. James M. MacCallum's island, Go Home Bay, Georgian Bay, Lake Huron, September 1913; returned March 1915, worked with Thomson and MacDonald on decorative wall panels for cottage. First painting expedition to Algonquin Park, May 1914, with Thomson; returned with wife, daughter, Thomson, A.Y. Jackson and Varley in fall. Moved to Thornhill, Ontario, spring, 1915. Recorded Halifax harbour, shipping, military activities for Canadian War Records, 1918-19. To Algoma with Jackson, Lawren Harris, Dr. MacCallum, spring 1920; returned spring and fall, 1921, and spring 1924 and '25. To England to see Wembley Exhibition, London, 1924. During summers of 1927-30, sketched in Gaspé Peninsula, Rocky Mountains, McGregor Bay (Georgian Bay), New Brunswick, and Nova Scotia; summered in Wickaninnish Bay, Long Beach, Vancouver Island, 1951-67. Teaching: Ontario College of Art Teacher Training courses, 1915-16; instructor, Teachers' Summer Course in Art, Ontario Department of Education, 1915-16; principal, Victoria School of Art and Design, Halifax, 1916-19; principal of Teacher Training in Art, Ontario Goverment Summer Courses, 1919-32, vice-principal, 1919-27; appointed to direct art education, Art Gallery of Toronto, 1927 (became supervisor, 1929); started Children's Art Centre, A.G.T., October 1932; Visiting Professor of Fine Arts, Teachers' College, Columbia University, New York, September 1938; director of educational programmes, National Gallery of Canada, Ottawa, 1939-40; supervisor of art education, Art Association of Montreal, 1941; sessional lecturer, School of Architecture, McGill University, September 1941; principal of School of Art, Art Association of Montreal, 1942-67; opened Children's Art Centre, Art Association of Montreal, 1946; assistant professor, Department of Fine Arts, McGill University, 1948-55. To Europe as participant in Sixth World Conference of the New Education Fellowship, 1932; then led art-appreciation tour of Italy and France. Lectured in western Canada for National Gallery of Canada, 1932, '35, '40, and in Maritimes, 1940. To South Africa (Cape Town and Johannesburg), 1934; to South Africa, teaching and lecturing, May 1936-May 1937; to Australia and New Zealand, 1937; to Honolulu, July 1938; to Cranbrook and Ann Arbor, Michigan, July 1941. Societies: Arts and Letters Club, Toronto; Ontario Society of Artists (1913-16); Royal Canadian Academy (elected associate, 1919, full academician, 1947); Group of Seven (1920-32); Canadian Group of Painters (founder-member, 1933, president, 1954-55 and 1956-57); Fellow, Royal Society of Art, London, 1950. Exhibited sixteen works in first Group of Seven exhibition, Art Gallery of Toronto, May 1920. Lismer retrospective (108 works) shown at National Gallery of Canada and Art Gallery of Toronto, 1950. Awards: Honorary Diploma, Nova Scotia College of Art, Halifax, 1940; Honorary LL.D., Dalhousie University, Halifax, 1942; University of Alberta National Award for Painting and Related Arts, 1953; Greer Memorial Award, presented by Ontario Association of Teachers of Art, 1956; Canada Council Medal, 1963; Honorary LL.D., McGill University, 1963; Centennial Medal, 1967; Companion of Order of Canada, 1967; Royal Canadian Academy of Arts Medal, 1969 (posthumous). Film, *Lismer*, premiered at Montreal Museum of Fine Art, 1952. Died: Montréal, 23 March 1969. Ashes buried at McMichael Canadian Collection, Kleinburg, Ontario, April 1969. Retrospective exhibition mounted by National Gallery of Canada, 1969.

10 Arthur Lismer*
In My Studio 1924
Oil on canvas (91 x 76.3 cm)
Dated (*verso*): *1924*
The McMichael Canadian Collection,
Kleinburg, Ontario
Gift of Mr. J.A. Latner

COMMENTS BY THE ARTIST

...a nation's artists are true nation builders. They re-create in terms of line and tone and colour the aspects of nature, and excite the consciousness of the participator or spectator into kinship and response.

> – Arthur Lismer, quoted by J.B. McLeish in *September Gale: A Study of Arthur Lismer of the Group of Seven* (Toronto: J.M. Dent & Sons, 1955, reprinted 1973), p. 74.

Moderns may need a touch of sanity but not so much, comparitively, as academicians and official painters need a touch of madness. Let there be differences and claims—foolish and otherwise—it's the stuff of life—and especially of the artist's life. Out of the madness of others there have come rays of life giving elements...When a sound painter gets it [i.e., "the spark"] keeping his mind open and his mind selective, then he helps to change the convention that we know as painting into an interpretive art.

Mediocrity we can never move and there is more of that than any other thing in painting and it is only dead minds that try to prevent people from experiencing all kinds of expression.

Your real modern painter has not a scrap of antiquarian interest or historical bias and why should a sober technician, excellent in every way and contributing his soundness to others resent the brilliances of others. It is like beating pans in the dark to scare away an eclipse.

> – Arthur Lismer, undated letter to Frederick B. Housser (typed transcript in artist's file, Fine Art Department, Metropolitan Toronto Library).

Art is a way of life. It is experience lived, shared, and enjoyed. It is in the painting and the poem. It is in the rhythm and order of nature. It is in the child's drawing as well as in the great periods of art. But it seeks expression. It cannnot be a dead spot in the nature of the individual to be revived by historical or civilization memories — or by the erudition of the aesthete. It cannot thrive on words and precepts — only by active expression and self-criticism, by the activities of wise guides and teachers...

> – Arthur Lismer, quoted by Marjorie Lismer Bridges in *A Border of Beauty: Arthur Lismer's Pen and Pencil* (Toronto: Red Rock, 1977), p. 3

Everything is expanding, including the horizons of vision and art.

> – Arthur Lismer, quoted by Marjorie Lismer Bridges in *A Border of Beauty...*, p. 152

Fig. 1 Arthur Lismer
Self-Portrait from the Artist's Sketchbook (detail) (1916/17)
Charcoal on paper (12 x 16.5 cm) (overall)
Private collection, Toronto

Fig. 2 Arthur Lismer
Never Look Back, B.C. (1960s)
Ink on paper (14.5 x 9.5 cm)
Private collection, Ashton, Maryland, U.S.A.

Exhibited at the London Regional Art Gallery only.

ERNST NEUMANN
(1902-1955)

Painter, printmaker, teacher.

11 Ernst Neumann
Self-Portrait 1930
Oil on canvas (76.2 x 63.5 cm)
Signed and dated (l.l.): *E. NEUMANN '30*
National Gallery of Canada, Ottawa

Born: Budapest, Hungary, of Austrian parentage, 1907. Emigrated with parents to Canada, 1912. Studied: Ecole des Beaux-Arts, Montréal, and Royal Canadian Academy life-classes at Art Association of Montreal. Entered lithography shop as apprentice; developed interest in lithography, woodcuts, other graphic arts media. Did illustrations for *New Frontiers*, 1930s. Shared studio with Goodridge Roberts, Montréal, fall of 1936; co-founded Roberts-Neumann School of Art, 1936. Exhibited at Royal Canadian Academy annual shows, 1927-43; at Art Association of Montreal, 1939, '50, '52; Arts Club of Montreal, 1941, '45; etc. Delegated by Canada Arts Council to attend UNESCO-sponsored General Assembly of the International Association of Plastic Arts, Cini Palace, Isle of S. Giorgio, near Venice, 1954. Awarded government overseas fellowship by Royal Society of Canada, 1955, to study in France. Retrospective exhibitions sponsored by National Gallery of Canada, 1945, and by Art Gallery of Hamilton (posthumous), 1958. Died: Vence, France, 1955.

COMMENTS BY THE ARTIST

...painting is good in so far as it resembles sculpture.

...

[Rembrandt was the] supreme master [of portraiture, because he] developed his artistic abilities continually through his life.

The great works of art blend qualities apparently irreconcilable. Rembrandt combined the monumental with the intimate...

...

Van Dyck is considered the first painter to betray art — because he taught other painters to flatter the subject...Following the tradition, Gainsborough's work was vague — he was the sort of man who appeared to expect someone to object every time he expressed a definite opinion — so he never did...

After Gainsborough, art entered the realm of cold cream, tea parties and the Ladies Home Journal...Artists thought more of their customers and less of their art.

And with the age of Romney, portait painting received a blow from which it has not yet recovered.

– Ernst Neumann, quoted in ''Nobility In Art Declared Thing of Past: Ernst Neumann Gives Illustrated Lecture at Museum'', *The Montreal Star*, 14 April 1953.

Fig. 1 Ernst Neumann
Self-Portrait
Oil on board (42.6 x 35.6 cm)
University of Guelph Art Collection, Macdonald Stewart Art Gallery, Guelph, Ontario

Fig. 2 Ernst Neumann
Self-Portrait 1947
Oil on masonite (60.5 x 45.8 cm)
Signed and dated (l.r.): *E. Neumann '47*
Public Archives of Canada, Ottawa (C-18781)

JEAN DALLAIRE
(1916-1965)

Painter, teacher, tapestry artist.

12 Jean Dallaire
Autoportrait 1938
Oil on canvas (71.1 x 55.8 cm)
Signed and dated (l.l.): *DALLAIRE 1938*
Familie Jean Dallaire

50 Born: Hull, Québec, 9 June 1916. Studied: technical school in Hull, 1931-32; Central Technical School, Toronto, and Grange Art School, Toronto, 1933-34, under Charles Goldhamer, Peter Haworth, and Elizabeth Wynn Wood (sculpture); Boston Museum of Fine Arts (free student), 1937; Ecole des Beaux-Arts de Montréal, 1938 (won Quebec Government scholarship to study in France); Atelier d'Art Sacré, under Maurice Denis and Georges Desvallières, and at the atelier of André Lhote, Paris; studied tapestry, 1944, and 1949 with Jean Lurçat at Aubusson, France. Worked with Henri Fabien and Henri Masson, Hull, 1936. In internment camp, Saint-Denis, near Paris, 1940-44. Teaching: professor of painting, drawing and tapestry, Ecole des Beaux-Arts de Québec, 1946-52. Worked for National Film Board, Ottawa and Montréal, 1952-57, illustrating educational filmstrips on historical and folkloric subject. Studio in Montréal, 1957-59. Canada Council grant, 1960. To Paris and Vence, France, 1959; summers at Vence and Péone, to 1965. Commissions: murals for chapel, Monastère des Dominicains, Ottawa, and Dominican Monastery, Fall River, Massachusetts, 1936-38; mural for la Compagnie d'assurance l'Industrielle de Québec, 1952. First group show, Ottawa Art Association, 1937; participated in group exhibitions of Concours artistiques de la province de Québec, 1949-50; Salon de Printemps, Musée des Beaux-Arts de Montréal, 1952-54. Included in *Canadian Painting*, National Gallery of Art, Washington, D.C. (travelling), 1950; Biennale de São Paolo, Brazil, 1953. One-man exhibitions at Galerie de la Maison des Beaux-Arts de Paris, 1945; Cercle universitaire de Montréal, 1947; l'Atelier, Québec, 1949; Dominion Gallery, Montréal, 1954; Robertson Galleries, Ottawa, 1955; Musée des Beaux-Arts, Montréal, 1958; Galerie des Mages, Vence, 1959; Galerie Dresdnère, Montréal, 1960. Died: Vence, 27 November 1965. Posthumous retrospective exhibitions mounted by Dominion Gallery, Montréal, 1966; Musée du Québec, 1968; Musée d'art contemporain, Montréal, 1979 (touring).

COMMENTS BY THE ARTIST

De méthode, je n'en ai pas. Comme dans le surréalisme, c'est le subconscient qui s'exprime et se concrétise à travers la forme et la couleur dans mes tableaux.

– Jean Dallaire, quoted by Guy Robert in *Dallaire ou l'oeil panique* (Montréal: Editions France-Amrique, 1980)

Pellan [*q.v.*], c'est autre chose, c'est un peintre complet. Le côté plastique est chéz lui trés développé...J'ai trop veçu dans son sillon à Paris pour en avir véritablement subi l'influence. Et puis, un ami devient difficilement un mâitre. Je ne pourrais guère parler, en ce domaine que de Maurice Denis, d'André Lhote et de l'art mural. Du premier, j'ai retenu la superposition des tons, du second la forme.

– Jean Dallaire, quoted by Roger Mondoloni in ''Une heure avec Jean Dallaire'', *Le Droit* (Ottawa), 11 June 1952.

Fig. 1 Jean Dallaire
Autoportrait en corsaire 1936
Charcoal on paper (49.5 x 38 cm)
Signed and dated (l.r.): *Dallaire 1936*
Private collection, Rouyn-Noranda, Québec

13 Jean Dallaire
Autoportrait 1938
Charcoal on paper (43 x 54 cm)
Signed and dated and inscribed (l.r.):
Dallaire/1938/CANADA
François Dallaire, L'Acadie, Québec

EDMOND DYONNET
(1859-1954)

Painter and teacher.

14 Edmond Dyonnet
Portrait de l'Artiste 1940
Oil on canvas (73.6 x 61 cm)
Signed and dated: (l.l.): *E. Dyonnet/1940*
Musée des Beaux-Arts de Montréal

Born: Crest, France, 25 June 1859. Moved with family to Turin, Italy, 1873. Attended school there until 1875. To Montréal, 1875. Studied at Ecole des Arts et Matières, Montréal, copying lithographs and drawing from the antique cast. To Italy for four years' study (Turin, Naples, Rome), 1886-90. A portrait and two landscapes accepted for exhibition in Rome. Returned to Montréal, 1890, opened studio (moved into new studio, 1916). Appointed drawing master of Conseil des Arts et Métiers, 1891-1922. Taught at Ecole Polytechnique, 1907-22, reforming course of art education; also taught at McGill Unversity, 1920-36, and for five years at Art Association de Montréal. Assumed post of Professor of Drawing, Ecole des Beaux-Arts, Montréal, 1922-24 (founded by Dyonnet, Suzor-Côté and Alfred Laliberté [*q.v.*]). Silver medals at Pan-American Exposition, Buffalo, 1901, and Louisiana Purchase Exposition, St. Louis, 1904. Societies: Pen and Pencil Club, Montréal; Royal Canadian Academy (elected associate, 1893, full academician, 1903, secretary, 1910-1947). Collaborated with Hugh G. Jones on history of R.C.A., 1934. Wrote *Mémoires d'un artiste canadien* at age 92 (manuscript circulated in typescript, 1949, published, 1968).

Appointed Officier d'Académie by French Government, 1910, for services rendered in the cause of education. Died: Montréal, 8 July 1954.

COMMENTS BY THE ARTIST

N'importe la langue que l'on parle si l'oeuvre elle-même parle le langage que tout le monde comprend, celle qui s'adresse au coeur, celle qui émeut? L'émotion, voilà la pierre de touche du véritable artiste, voilà ce qu'il doit ressentir et communiquer.

– Edmond Dyonnet, ''L'Art chez les canadiens-francais'', reprinted from *The Yearbook of Canadian Art* (Toronto: J.M.Dent and Son, 1913) in *Mémoires d'un artiste canadien*, ed. by Jean Ménard (Ottawa: Editions de l'Université d'Ottawa, 1968), pp.105-106.

Ce n'est pas en dessinant quelques heures par semaine que l'on peut acquérir la maîtrise de l'art.

– Edmond Dyonnet, *Mémoires d'un artiste canadien...*, pp.30- 31.

Fig.1 Edmond Dyonnet
Portrait de l'Artiste
Oil on canvas (61 x 45.7 cm)
Musée des Beaux-Arts de Montréal

Note: reproduced in catalogue of 1938 R.C.A. annual exhibition (Cat.No.66).

FREDERICK B. TAYLOR
(1906-   )

Painter and teacher.

52

Born: Ottawa, Ontario, 27 July, 1906. Studied: McGill University, Montréal (B.Arch. degree, 1930); University of London, Goldsmith's College of Art; London Central School of Arts and Crafts; Byam Shaw School of Painting, London, England. Teaching: McGill University, School of Architecture, drawing and modelling, 1940-43. Fourteen solo exhibitions in Montréal, Toronto and Ottawa, 1932-63. Executed commissions for Government of Canada and major industrial corporations in Canada and U.S.A. Societies: Society of Canadian Painter-Etchers and Engravers (elected 1934; life member, 1959); Canadian Society of Graphic Art (1943); Royal Canadian Academy (elected associate, 1948; full academician, 1967). Exhibited with R.C.A., 1932-67. Sketched in Canadian Pacific Railway's Angus Shops, Montréal, as part of private war records project; produced 114 drawings and 85 paintings of war-production subjects from 1942 to '45. Survey of war-production art shown in meeting rooms of Lodge 712 of the International Association of Machinists, Montréal, 1944. Paints landscapes, portraits, urban scenes.

Lives and works in San Miguel de Allende, Mexico. Widely represented in Canadian public and corporate collections.

COMMENTS BY THE ARTIST

My experience in painting war industry completely explodes the widely held idea that art only concerns the privileged and the initiated. This idea, or myth, is that art is not good for the people. It is false. Workers are quick to discern gold in the muck, quick to recognize that art and life are one, they are quick to learn and anxious and quick to broaden their intelligent appreciation of the said-to-be intangible which they find tangible and very good.

– Frederick B. Taylor, quoted by Barry Lord in *The History of Painting in Canada: Towards a People's Art* (Toronto: NC Press, 1974), p. 197.

LOUIS MUHLSTOCK
(1904-   )

Painter and draughtsman.

16 Louis Muhlstock
Portrait of the Artist as a Younger Man 1946
Oil on canvas (55.9 x 48.3 cm)
Signed (l.l.): *Muhlstock*
Collection: the artist, Montréal
Photo: Brian Merrett, Montréal

Born: Narajow, Poland, 1904. Emigrated with family to Canada, fall 1911. Studied: evening classes at Monument National, Montréal, under Edmond Dyonnet (*q.v.*); Council of Arts and Manufactures, Montréal; Royal Canadian Academy evening classes at Art Association of Montreal, 1920-27, under William Brymner, G. Horne Russell, Charles S. Simpson, A.H. Robinson, Maurice Cullen, and Edmond Dyonnet; night classes at Ecole des Beaux-Arts, Montréal, under Charpentier, 1926-28; life classes, Grand Chaumière, Paris, then studio of Louis François Biloul, 1928-31. Exhibited two portraits at Art Association of Montreal annual spring exhibition, 1925. Worked as bookkeeper. To Paris, 1928-31; summered in Brittany, 1929, the Alps, 1930. Taught figure drawing at his Rue Ste.-Famille studio, 1935. Began painting in oils, 1936. Exhibited sixty-six drawings at Art Association of Montreal, 1935. Solo exhibition at Eaton's Department Store, Montréal, 1936, and at Picture Loan Society, Toronto, 1937, '38, '39, '45. Societies: Canadian Society of Graphic Art (joined 1937), Canadian Group of Painters (1939-69), Contemporary Arts Society (founder-member, 1939);

Federation of Canadian Artists (1941). Muhlstock's and Fritz Brandtner's drawings and paintings of workers in United Ship Yards and Canadian Vickers plant, Montréal, exhibited, at instigation of F.C.A., in Ottawa and Toronto, 1943. Cross-Canada exhibitions 1949 and '50. Painted series of twenty-eight small oil "Non-objectives", 1951. Then concentrated on heads, nudes, landscapes, studies of animals, still- lifes. Contributed to 400th Anniversary Exhibition, São Paulo, Brazil, 1954, and Pittsburgh International, 1955. Retrospective exhibition mounted by Art Gallery of Windsor, 1976. Lives and works in Montréal.

COMMENTS BY THE ARTIST

...something that has been neglected very, very much because so few people in all of Canada draw for drawing's own sake and so few people here acquire a drawing for its own sake. There seems to be very little understanding or feeling or need for drawing — it has to and must be a painting or it isn't enough.
...

...there is always something new to find in nature and rather than repeat or draw from within me I prefer to continually learn from nature and to draw out of nature.
...
You have to be moved by your subject in order to paint.

– Louis Muhlstock, quoted by Lawrence Sabbath in "Louis Muhlstock", "Artist in Action Series: I", *Canadian Art*, 18 (July 1960), pp. 218, 220, 222.

I had but one or two portrait commissions where I had to flatter, otherwise they would not have been accepted. From then on I refused commissions and preferred to pick up some unemployed or homeless people and *pay them* to sit for me. Here I was free to express myself and draw and paint for the pleasure of it.

– Louis Muhlstock, letter to Robert Stacey, 1 May 1983.

A true artist doing a self-portrait will not lie. One has but to see the many Kaethe Kollwitz or Rembrandt self-portraits. Each one was as they saw and felt about themselves — that particular day or time of their life. And when Rembrandt felt like an old drunk, he painted himself that way.

Last week I saw some very fine Fantin-Latour self-portraits. There was no attempt in any of the drawings or paintings to flatter himself. There was just a concern about good painting. I know that he admired Delacroix, but one also felt that he knew and loved Rembrandt's self-portraits.
"Self-flattery and self-deception" also spells bad painting. Slick! slick!

– Louis Muhlstock, letter to Robert Stacey, 30 May 1983.

Fig. 1 Louis Muhlstock
Self-Portrait 1940
Charcoal on paper (50.8 x 38 cm)
Signed and dated (l.r.): *Muhlstock 1940*
Collection: the artist, Montréal
Photo: Brian Merrett, Montréal

EDWARD B. PULFORD
(1914-)

Painter and teacher.

17 Edward B. Pulford
Self-Portrait (Diploma Piece) 1948
Oil on canvas (101.5 x 75.5 cm)
Signed and dated (l.r.): *E. Pulford '48*
Owens Art Gallery, Mount Allison
University, Sackville, New Brunswick
Photo: John Tamblyn, London
Note: Mount Allison University Fine Arts
Department student diploma piece,
submitted 1949

54 Born: Saskatoon, Saskatchewan, 1914. Began drawing and painting at an early age. Studied: University of Saskatchewan night classes, under Augustus Kenderdine; Saskatoon Technical Collegiate night classes, under Ernest Lindner, 1930s. Joined R.C.A.F., June 1940, served in Europe, Africa, Asia, to 1945. Returned to Canada, 1945. Studied: Fine Arts Department, Mount Allison University, Sackville, N.B., 1945-49, under Lawren P. Harris and Alex Colville. Teaching: basic courses in drawing, painting and design, Department of Fine Arts, Mount Allison University, 1949-1980. Students included Christopher Pratt (*q.v.*), Mary Pratt, Tom Forrestall, D.P.Brown, Ken Tolmie. Turned exclusively to direct painting from nature in watercolours of Maritimes scenery, 1960s. Awards: first prize, Maritime Art Exhibition, 1950; first prize, first Atlantic Provinces Competition, Beaverbrook Art Gallery, Fredericton, 1959. Painted large mural for Royal York Hotel, Toronto. Sketching trip to Baffin Island; painted from sketches a large oil of a D.E.W. line site for the Foundation Company of Canada. Received first sabbatical, 1964, travelled in Canada and abroad; second sabbatical, 1975. Exhibition of recent work travelled to Maritime art centres, 1965. Exhibition of watercolours officially opened by Alex Colville at Owens Art Gallery, Sackville, 1980, and circulated through Atlantic provinces Art Circuit. Retrospective exhibitions mounted by Owens Art Gallery, Sackville, 1983. Received honourary doctorate from Mount Allison University, May 1983. Subject of a 1983 C.B.C. television documentary.

COMMENTS BY THE ARTIST

...as my own painting developed, it was done only to satisfy an inner urge and desire and to gratify my own satisfaction and pleasure. The fact that my paintings are what I term, works of love, does not mean that they are done in an easy and facile way. To work in this non-professional way is a privilege that I have deeply appreciated.

– E.B.Pulford, artist's statement, *Watercolours by Edward B. Pulford, C.D., B.F.A.* (Sackville, N.B.: Owens Art Gallery, 1980).

GOODRIDGE ROBERTS
(1904-1974)

Painter and teacher.

18 Goodridge Roberts
Self-Portrait in my Studio (c.1955)
Oil on masonite (114.5 x 81 cm)
Signed (l.r.): *G. Roberts*
Musée des Beaux-Arts de Montréal, gift of
Dr. Max Stern

Born: Barbados, British West Indies, 24 September 1904. Family returned to Fredericton, N.B., 1905, then moved to London, England, 1908, and to France, 1910. Began to paint during this period. In England, 1914-19; returned to Canada, 1919, settling in Ottawa, 1919- 20, then Fredericton, 1920. Studied: Ecole des Beaux-Arts, Montréal, 1923-25; Art Students' League of New York, 1926-28, under John Sloan, Max Weber, Boardman Robinson. Moved to Ottawa, 1930. Teaching: art instructor, Ottawa Art Association, 1930; opened summer school for painting, Wakefield, P.Q., 1931; gave weekly painting lessons, Ottawa, 1931; first resident artist, Queen's University, Kingston, and taught at Kingston Art Association, 1933-36; summer school, Queen's University, 1934, 1935; partner in Neumann-Roberts School, Montréal, 1936; School of Art and Design, Art Association of Montreal, 1939-43, 1945-49, 1952-53; first resident artist, University of New Brunswick, Fredericton, 1959-60. Met John Lyman (*q.v.*), 1932. Painted for first time at Georgian Bay, Ontario, and in Gatineau Hills, 1934. Began to paint landscapes in oils, 1935. To Montréal, 1936; shared studio with Ernst Neumann (*q.v.*). Enlisted in R.C.A.F., August 1943; appointed official war artist, September 1943; overseas in November 1943 to December 1945. Returned to Montréal, December 1945. Painted in Laurentians, Eastern Townships, at Georgian Bay, Gaspé Peninsula, etc. Began series of self-portraits after father's death, February 1953. In France, England, and Italy, 1953-54. Societies: Eastern Group, Montréal (charter-member, 1938); Contemporary Arts Society, Montréal (charter-member, 1939); Canadian Society of Painters in Water Colour (elected 1939); Canadian Society of Graphic Art (elected 1939); Royal Canadian Academy (elected associate, 1952; full academician, 1956). Awards and honours: Canadian Government overseas fellowship for one year of work and study in France, 1953-54; Hon. LL.D., University of New Brunswick, 1960. First solo exhibition, Montréal, fall 1932; first major exhibition, Montréal, January 1938, with A.Y.Jackson; represented in 1939 World's Fair, New York; chosen for Canada's participation in Venice *Biennale* with Emily Carr, David Milne and Alfred Pellan (*q.v.*), 1952, and in several other international exhibitions. One-man exhibition, Paris, 1954. Retrospective exhibition mounted by National Gallery of Canada, 1969. Died: Montréal, 28 January 1974.

COMMENTS BY THE ARTIST

I have so often tried, with no hope of success, to find the key to the meaning of things. At that moment when, in the presence of the subject, my relationship to the subject induces in me a sensation that is not altogether free from what I can only describe as fear or awe — the moment when I realize that I have grasped and am setting down some inexplicable meaning that has hitherto lain sleeping among the trees and fields or within the fruit and dishes of a still life or in the body of a model — I ask myself, as I have a thousand times, what it is. This feeling of fear in the face of a mystery. What mystery? "Do you work in fear and trembling", Blake once asked his pupil Samuel Palmer. "Indeed I do, sir", replied Palmer. "Then you'll do", was the rejoinder.

– Goodridge Roberts, "From this Point I Looked Out", in *Goodridge Roberts: A Retrospective Exhibition* (Ottawa: National Gallery of Canada, 1969), p.190. (Originally published in *Queen's Quarterly*, Autumn 1953.)

Fig. 1 Goodridge Roberts
Self-Portrait (c.1950)
Oil on board (50.8 x 40.6 cm)
Signed (l.r.): *G. Roberts*
National Gallery of Canada, Ottawa
Photo: Merrett and Harper, Montreal

Fig.2 Goodridge Roberts
Portrait of the Artist (c.1951)
Oil on masonite (50.5 x 40.4 cm)
Signed (l.r.): *G. Roberts*
Edmonton Art Gallery, gift of Dr. Max Stern
Photo: E. Lazare, Edmonton

FREDERICK HAGAN

(1918-)

Painter, printmaker, teacher, carpenter.

19 Frederick Hagan
Trying to Paint in '72 1972-74
Polymer on plywood (107.2 x 68 cm)
Signed and dated (*verso*): *Frederick Hagan 1972-73*
Woodstock Art Gallery, Woodstock, Ontario

56

Born: Toronto, Ontario, 21 May 1918. Studied: Ontario College of Art, Toronto (evening classes), 1937-41, under John Alfsen and Frank Carmichael; Art Students' League of New York, spring-summer 1941, studying engraving and woodcut-making with Martin Lewis, and lithography in shop of George Miller. Teaching: resident artist, Pickering College, Newmarket, Ontario, 1942-45; evening art classes at Northern Vocational School, Toronto, 1945-46; Ontario College of Art (painting, drawing, composition and print-making), 1946 - 1983. Member: Ontario Society of Artists (elected 1968), Canadian Society of Graphic Art (1940-55). Has exhibited with Royal Canadian Academy, O.S.A., Canadian Society of Painters in Water Colour, and Canadian Society of Painter-Etchers and Engravers. Commission: mural, Oakville Library and Art Gallery, 1967. Subject of a film, *Fantasy of Print*, produced by Alan Jarvis and Paul Kimberley, 1962. Retrospective exhibition mounted by Grimsby Public Library and Art Gallery, Grimsby, Ontario, 1977. Lives and works in Newmarket, Ontario.

COMMENTS BY THE ARTIST

Stanley Spencer shows us that the heavenly forces are within us and that they do not possess us. I have sympathies in that direction.

– Fred Hagan, quoted by Gillian MacKay in ''Hagan, artist of monumental vision'', *The Kingston Whig Stardard*, 29 July 1977

Art is not entertainment nor does it necessarily reflect the artist's personality....Art has always associated itself with great experiences. It has to do with the great moving moments of time. Never does it concern itself with the trivial.

– Fred Hagan, quoted by Jane Grimshaw in ''Artist speaks of low periods of creativity and the meaning of art'', *Woodstock-Ingersol Sentinel Review*, 10 February 1977

Fig. 1 Fred Hagan
Trying to Paint in '72: original, unfinished version, in progress, 1974
Polymer on plywood (121.9 x 121.9 cm)
Right hand section: Woodstock Art Gallery; left hand section: the artist, Newmarket, Ontario

Fig. 2 Fred Hagan
Self at Pickering 1943
Oil on canvas (61 x 50.8 cm)
Collection: the artist, Newmarket

Fig. 3 Fred Hagan
Self with Daisies 1958
Lithograph (25.4 x 38.1 cm approx.)
Collection: the artist, Newmarket

Fig. 1

Fig. 3

Fig. 2

WALTER BACHINSKI
(1939-)

Sculptor, painter, draughtsman, printmaker, teacher.

20 Walter Bachinski
Self-Portrait 1983
Charcoal and black chalk on paper (96.5 x 59 cm)
Signed and dated (l.r.): *W. Bachinski '83*
Collection of the artist, Guelph, Ontario
Photo: courtesy, Walter Bachinski

Born: Ottawa, Ontario, 1939. Studied at Ontario College of Art, Toronto, in Drawing and Painting Department, 1961-65, working closely with Fred Hagan (*q.v.*) in printmaking. Won T. Eaton Travelling Scholarship, travelling to England, France, Spain, Belgium, Holland and Germany, 1965. Attended University of Iowa under Mauricio Lanasky, graduating with an M.A. in Printmaking, 1967. Associate Professor, Department of Fine Art, University of Guelph, Ontario, teaching drawing and printmaking, 1967 to present. Executed first relief sculptures in 1969, and first sculptures in the round in 1970; began work on "Fury" theme. Received Canada Council grant for production of portfolio of lithographs, *After Birth*, published by George C. Miller and Son, New York, 1969. Began *Revelations*, a cycle of large drawings, 1971. Travelled to Mexico City and Guadalajara, Mexico, to study murals of Orozco and Siquieros. First public commission: three relief sculptures on a humanitarian theme for the University of Waterloo, 1975. Began work on "Artist and Model" theme, 1975. Executed commission for Kitchener Court House, *Mother and Child* relief, 1977. Lived and worked in Flavingy-sur-Ozerain, France, 1978-79. Has won many awards; works in numerous public collections in Canada and abroad. Lives and works in Guelph, Ontario.

COMMENTS BY THE ARTIST

I consider the theme of "Artist and Model" to be firmly established within the visual tradition; I see it as a parallel to still life or landscape as an artistic motif. I have been working with the theme for close to ten years now. It grew out of a change in emphasis in my work, from portraying a reality concerned with historical events and a search for archetypal images to exemplify these subjects, to one where I wished to work out of my more immediate and personal surroundings. The studio has now become my world of activity, and within it I place the model(s), the nude or some sort of relationship between the artist and model. The studio has become a refuge from external forces; however, this refuge is not constant. My space is sometimes peaceful, at other times a battlefield, but the images worked on are a result of my personal expression. I try to show in a positive way my feelings toward life, based on an increasingly classical approach to art. The activities within the studio are autobiographical, but not primarily anecdotal; they combine my respect for life and the need to communicate that, with reference to the making of art, whether it be drawing or sculpture.

In terms of how I see myself in relation to the "Artist and Model" theme with reference to Picasso and Matisse, I would have to say "somewhere in between". Picasso is certainly the most autobiographical artist of the 20th century and he explored within the "Artist and Model" theme every nuance of his personal life, both real and imagined, and much of that material was connected to his dialogue with artists of the past, i.e.: Cranach, Delacroix, Toulouse-Lautrec. Matisse, on the other hand, when he does include the artist within a work, always uses a recognizable self-portrait. However, in most cases, the presence of the artist is played down, in relation to that of the model. Quite often the artist is sketchily drawn or left unfinished. It is interesting to note that of the two, Matisse used a model for almost all of his figurative work whereas Picasso relied primarily on his visual memory,

– Walter Bachinski, letter to Robert Stacey, 25 July, 1983.

Fig. 1 Walter Bachinski
Artist and Model I 1977
Sanguine on paper (155 x 138.4 cm)
Kitchener-Waterloo Art Gallery, Kitchener-Waterloo, Ontario

Fig. 2 Walter Bachinski
Sculptor Working on Standing Figure 1978
Pastel on paper (145.1 x 137.8 cm)
Private collection, Calgary

GLENN PRIESTLEY
(1955-)

Painter and illustrator.

21 Glenn Priestley
Self-Portrait 1983
Oil on masonite (60.5 x 50.5 cm)
Signed and dated (u.l.): G. *Priestley* 83
Collection: the artist, Scarborough, Ontario
Photo: T.E. Moore, Toronto

58

Born: Toronto, Ontario, 6 December 1955. Studied: Ontario College of Art summer course, 1972; Ontario College of Art (admitted into second year, Fine Arts Programme), 1973-76; Ontario College of Art off-campus studies programme, Florence 1975-76; graduated with honours diploma, 1976; University of Toronto Continuing Education course in Anatomy and Life-drawing, 1982-83. Travelled to Florence, Geneva, Zurich, Brussels, Amsterdam, Marseilles, and Arles, 1975-76. Sketching and printmaking, Amsterdam, New York, 1979 and 1981. Teaching: drawing and painting instructor, Burwash Correctional Institute, Burwash, Ontario, 1973; drawing instructor, Continuing Education Programme, Cedarbrae Collegiate, Scarborough, Ontario, 1978; painting instructor, Willowdale (Ontario) Art Guild and Don Valley Art Guild, 1979; painting instructor, Amsterdam Art Guild, Amsterdam, New York, 1981. Scholarship and awards: Reeves Vocational Art Scholarship, Cedarbrae Collegiate Inst., 1973; Josephine M. Harper Scholarship, O.C.A., 1973-74; Ontario Chapter of the I.O.D.E. Scholarship, O.C.A., 1974-75; Graphic Litho-Plate Award, Canadian Society of Painters in Watercolour, 1982. First group exhibition: *The Child in Ontario Art*, Macdonald Gallery, Queen's Park, Toronto, June 1979; first one-man show, Lemay Carell Gallery, Toronto, January 1981. Freelance illustrator, 1975 to present (*City Woman, Quest, Saturday Night*, etc.). Illustrated *Patrick and the Actors*, by Margaret Keith (Penumbra Press, 1981), and numerous textbooks. Did cover for 1983 Seal Book Award novel published by McClelland and Stewart. Founding member of notorious garage band, The Dead Bunnies, 1979-80. Lives and works in Scarborough, Ontario.

COMMENTS BY THE ARTIST

The self-portraits I have done in the past usually started out with no set purpose in mind. Generally they were begun in a spare moment, perhaps as relaxation from a larger, more demanding project, and only occasionally would I return to them once I had put them aside. Or else they get nibbled on in no particular sequence until they evolve into some kind of completed work. Since they don't start with any direct idea in mind, those I do complete don't get finished in any great hurry. I am interested in painting the human figure and I always seem to be around when I need a model (which is more

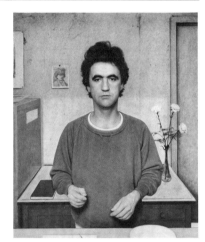

than I can say for my friends).

The *Self-Portrait* of 1983 (actually begun in 1982) was the result of a very different approach. It is the product of a rather long and involved, self-imposed post-O.C.A. study of painting styles and techniques in which I was concerned with traditional aspects of design, composition, perspective, etc. At the time, my preoccupation with Italian painters of the 15th century led me to a more formal structural organization than is usual with my work, and the painting makes no secret of this. While I consider it a success in that I achieved (to some degree) what I had set out to accomplish, I expect my work in the future to be a little less self-consciously "designed". In painting it I was dissatisfied with a looser approach and felt the need for a more formal grounding in the design elements (perspective, anatomy, composition— everything you *don't* get to study at art school anymore. It was back to school for me on this one.)

I have an unapologetic love of the painting of the past and I feel it is virtually impossible to ignore four centuries of artwork of staggering richness and scope. To be unaware of it is to experience a great loss. To choose to deny it would be foolish. To paint in the face of it is best left to the truly obsessed.

I hope that the essential elements of design and structure that I have learned from the Renaissance masters can be used less self-consciously when I turn my attention to a less formal, more expressive style. The reproduction of a postcard of a Rembrandt self-portrait on the wall behind me in the picture points in the direction [in which] I want to go.

– Glenn Priestley, artist's statement, September 1983.

Fig. 1 Glenn Priestley
Self-Portrait, Florence 1976
Graphite on paper (38 x 36 cm)
Signed (l.r.): G. *PRIESTLEY*
Collection: the artist, Scarborough, Ontario
Photo: T. E. Moore, Toronto

Fig. 2 Glenn Priestley
Double Self-Portrait Study 1983
Oil and graphite on paper (59 x 48.5 cm)
Collection: the artist, Scarborough, Ontario
Photo: T.E. Moore, Toronto

Fig. 3 Glenn Priestley
Study for Oil Self-Portrait 1983
Graphite on paper (84 x 59 cm)
Collection: the artist, Scarborough, Ontario
Photo: T. E. Moore, Toronto

Fig. 1

Fig. 2

Fig. 3

PART II: THE "RUMINATIVE" SELF PORTRAIT

With the Renaissance came a new evaluation of human individuality, which, in the portraits and self-portraits of Da Vinci, Raphael, and Dürer, resulted in the development of pyschological interpretation in art. John Pope-Hennessy, in *The Portrait in the Renaissance*, defines the "ruminative portrait" as "the painting of the man consumed by thought...[It] was taken up by Titian...and was handed on to Rembrandt..." — and so on to Van Gogh. In such works the subject appears to be involved in intense communion with the secret recesses of the psyche, rather than in visual dialogue with the outside world. Usually the composition concentrates on the head or, at most, the head and upper torso, seen at a three-quarter or full-frontal angle; profile self-portraits, which require two mirrors, or a reference image or photograph, are rare.

"To Ruminate", according to *The Shorter Oxford English Dictionary*, is "To revolve, turn over in the mind; to meditate deeply upon...To muse, meditate, ponder..." Whether or not all the self-portraits in this section do indeed convey a genuine sense of mental activity or emotional depth depends on the private responses of the viewer, as much as on the "expressive" qualities of the works which we instinctively "read" as codes to feeling and thought. Some (apparent) attempts at honest revelation may in fact be masks donned to disguise the truth... and *vice-versa.*

In all these Canadian resemblances, how much dissemblance is there; in all these disclosures and exposures, how much composing and disguising? Sir Richard Steele declared that "Simulation is a pretence of what is not, and Dissimulation a Concealment of what is"; in the words of Oscar Wilde, "It is only when you give the poet a mask that he can tell you the truth." Wilde also wrote that "A man's face is his autobiography." Our natural assumption is that ruminative self-portraits are visual exercises in autobiography, and so take the liberty of trying to draw conclusions about the personality traits of artists who may be composing subtle fictions in their work, just as they (and we) adopt various personae in their (and our) lives. It is always dangerous to use self-portraits as "evidence" for exercises in amateur psychologizing. The "facts" may be as misleading as those which make up most artists' biographies and autobiographies.

The self-portraits in this section are arranged in order by date — a coincidental result of which principle of organization is the grouping together of works by artists who happened to belong to several prominent societies, such as the Canadian Group of Painters (established in 1933 to replace the Group of Seven), the Contemporary Arts Society of Montreal (founded 1939), and its predecessor, the Eastern Group (1938-39). These "ruminative" painters and sculptors may have preferred to present themselves as brooding solitaries, but many were, or are, actively involved not just in professional associations but in society at large.

JOSEPH LÉGARÉ
(1795-1855)

Painter, art-restorer, civic politician.

22 Joseph Légaré
Autoportrait (c. 1825)
Oil on canvas (76.5 x 61.3 cm)
Louis Painchaud, Sherbrooke, Québec
Note: there is now some debate as to
whether this portrait is indeed a self portrait
by Légaré. The doubt stems from a
comparison with it of contemporaneous
portraits and figure-compositions by
Légaré, which are less competently handled.
There is a possibility that this work and its
companion-piece, a half-length portrait of
Légaré's wife, also dated c. 1825, are by an
itinerant portraitist, possibly an American.
According to John R. Porter, however, the
"self-portrait" and its pendant have always
remained in the artist's family, having been
passed down from Légaré's daughter Clina
to her own daughter, Marie-Thérèse, who in
turn left it to her eldest daughter, Mme
Edmire Painchaud, mother of the present
owner. Both canvases were restored by the
National Gallery of Canada in 1978.

60

Born: Quebec City, 10 March 1795.
Studied: Séminaire de Québec,
1809-11. Apprenticed as painter-
varnisher, 1812, painting carriages,
signs, home interiors, also did gilding,
picture-restoration. Purchased, then
began repairing and making replicas
of, works in art collection of Abbé
Philippe-Jean-Louis Desjardins,
Québec, 1817. Took on Antoine
Plamondon (1804-95) as assistant.
Awarded honourary medal by Quebec
City's Société pour l'encouragement
des arts et des sciences en Canada,
1828, for his *Le Massacre des Hurons
par les Iroquois* (c. 1828; Musée du
Québec, 1828). Copy of portrait of
George IV purchased by government,
1829. Member: Bureau de santé de
Québec, and relief committee during
cholera epidemic, 1832; founder-
member, la Société Saint-Jean-Baptiste,
1842. Involved in charity drives after
fires in Saint-Roch and Saint-Jean
quarters, Québec, 1845, and painted
depictions of these catastrophes.
Represented Palais quarter on le
Conseil de ville de Québec, 1833-36;
served as justice of the peace; three
times named to grand jury; elected
church-warden for parish of
Notre-Dame de Québec. Became
follower of nationalist politician
Louis-Philippe Papineau, 1827.

Involved in rebel activity in Quebec
City region, 1837; arrested and jailed
13 November 1837. Elected
vice-chairman of le Comité constitu-
tionnel de la réforme et du progrès,
1847. Defeated in Quebec City by-
elections, 1848 and '50. Named
member of Conseil législatif, 1855.
Exhibited art collection on premises of
La Société litéraire et historique de
Québec, then displayed paintings at
own gallery (built in 1833), 1838.
With lawyer Thomas Amiot opened La
Galérie de Peinture du Québec, 1838.
Proposed to municipal authorities the
creation of a "galérie nationale" in
Québec City, 1845 and '48. Opened
new gallery, allowing public free
access, and published catalogue of
personal art collection, 1852.
Collection acquired by l'Université
Laval (Séminaire de Québec), 1874.
On selection committee for provincial
representation at l'Exposition universelle
de Paris, 1854. Worked as portrait,
religious and landscape painter. Died:
Quebec City, 1855.

WILLIAM VALENTINE
(1798-1849)

Portrait painter and photographer.

23 William Valentine
Self-Portrait (c. 1835)
Oil on canvas (76.1 x 63.3 cm)
Public Archives of Nova Scotia, Halifax
Note: presented to the Nova Scotia
Museum by George M. Smith, Halifax, 1
June 1917 (acc. no. 4512). Transferred to
the Public Archives of Nova Scotia in the
1940s.

CORNELIUS KRIEGHOFF
(1815-1872)

Painter and teacher.

24 Cornelius Krieghoff
Self-Portrait 1855
Oil on canvas (29.2 x 25.4 cm)
Signed and dated (l.r.): *C. Krieghoff/1855*
National Gallery of Canada, Ottawa

Born: Whitehaven, Cumberland, England, 1798. Emigrated to Halifax, Nova Scotia, 1818. Studied: London, England, 1836; otherwise self-taught. Advertised as portrait and landscape painter, and as teacher of drawing and painting. Also worked as house-painter and decorator under trade name of Bell and Valentine, to May 1824, then under own name. Operated drawing school, 1821. Earliest dated portrait, 1828. Became chief successor of Robert Field (1769-1819). Influenced by Sir Thomas Lawrence and Gilbert Stuart. From 1830 worked chiefly as itinerant portraitist, travelling throughout Maritimes. Served on Halifax Mechanics' Institute Committee, 1832. In London, studying and making copies, 1836; returned to Halifax, 1837. Advertised rates for portraits in *The Nova Scotian*, 9 March 1837 (from £1.10 for a profile in oil to £30 for a half-length in oil). Introduced Daguerrotype-taking to Halifax, opening city's first photographic studio, 1844. Encouraged by Joseph Howe. Harry Piers estimated that he painted about 125 or 150 portraits in all; also did miniatures, copies, and historical and mythological canvases. Studio burned shortly before his death. Died: Halifax, 26 December, 1849.

Born: Amsterdam, Netherlands, 19 June 1815. Moved with family to Düsseldorf, then to Schloss Mainberg, near Schweinfurth, Bavaria, 1822. Father worked as supervisor at a wallpaper factory. Probably studied art at Düsseldorf Academy. Travelled throughout Europe as itinerant musician and painter. Emigrated to United States, 1837. Enlisted in American Army as artificer and served until 1840. Made drawings of Seminole War in Florida for American Army. Deserted, 1840. Married Emilie Gauthier *dit* Saint-Germain of Longueuil, Québec, 1840. Living in Montréal, 1841. Moved to Rochester after death of son, 13 June 1841; set up studio. To Paris, 1844. Returned to Canada, 1845. Visited Toronto, 1845. In Longueuil by 1845, then settled in Montréal, to 1853. To Québec, 1853. Toured Europe with wife, 1854-55, visiting London, Düsseldorf, Paris. Returned to Québec. Taught at Mrs. Brown's School. Held auctions in Québec, 8 April and 23 December 1862. To Europe, late 1863 or early 1864. Exhibited at Philadelphia Exhibition, 1876, and Colonial and Indian Exhibition, London, 1886.

Returned to Montréal, 1867. Joined married daughter in Chicago, c. 1870. Left Quebec City for last time late in 1871 for Chicago. Died: Chicago, 8 March 1872, buried at Graceland Cemetary.

Fig. 1 Anon
Mr. Valentine, Artist
Cut silhouette with ink and gilt (9 x 6.7 cm)
Nova Scotia Museum Historic House Collection
Note: formerly attributed to Valentine himself.

Fig. 1 Cornelius Krieghoff
The Death of the Moose 1859
Oil on canvas (45.7 x 61 cm)
Glenbow Museum, Calgary
Photo: courtesy, Dr. J. Russell Harper, Alexandria, Ontario
Note: see also introductory textual Figure 9.

FLORENCE CARLYLE
(1864-1923)

Painter and teacher.

25 Florence Carlyle
Self-Portrait
Oil on canvas (sight: 43.2 x 33 cm)
Signed (u.l.): *Florence Carlyle*
Florence Carlyle Johnston, Woodstock, Ontario

62 Born: Galt, Ontario, 24 September 1864, the daughter of William Carlyle, Oxford County school inspector and nephew of Thomas Carlyle. Moved with parents to Woodstock, Ontario, 1867. Educated at Woodstock. Recognizing her daughter's talent, her mother organized an art class, set up studio in Woodstock, and hired a teacher from New York. To Paris with Paul Peel (*q.v.*) and Mildred Peel, 1890. Studied for six years at several Parisian ateliers under Bouguereau, Delacleuse, L'Hermite, Rolshoven, Lefebvre, and Robert-Fleury. Painted in Barbizon and Normandy, summer 1890. Exhibited at Paris Salon, 1893, '94, '95; Chicago World's Fair, 1893 (silver medal); Pan-American Exposition, Buffalo, 1901 (honourable mention); Rochester Arts Club, 1902; Louisiana Purchase Exposition, St. Louis, 1904 (silver medal); Dominion Exhibition, Halifax, 1906; Walker Art Gallery, Liverpool, 1910; Winnipeg Industrial Bureau, 1912-14; Dominion and States Exhibition of the Royal British Colonial Society of Artists, 1913-18. Showed regularly with Ontario Society of Artists, Royal Canadian Academy, Art Association of Montreal, Canadian National Exhibition, Royal Academy, London. Returned to Canada, 1896. Taught at Havergal College, Toronto, and maintained studios in London, Ontario, Woodstock ("Englewoods", family home), and New York. Painted in British Columbia, 1897. Travelled extensively from 1896 (Netherlands, Belgium, Spain, Italy, France, England, New England). Settled permanently in England, 1912. Did work for War Memorials Committee and Canadian War Records in Britain during World War I. Societies: Ontario Society of Artists (1900-1906), Royal Canadian Academy (associate, 1897-1908, 1912), Canadian Alpine Club (elected 1897). Died at Crowborough, England, 7 May 1923. Memorial exhibition and sale of 86 of her works held at Jenkins Art Gallery, Toronto, 1925. Centennial exhibition of her work mounted by Woodstock Art Gallery/Oxford County Art Associaton, 1964. Represented in National Gallery of Canada, Woodstock Art Gallery, Art Gallery of Toronto, London Regional Art Gallery, Hamilton Art Gallery, Government of Ontario Art Collection, Toronto.

PAUL PEEL
(1860-1892)

Painter.

Born: London, Canada West (Ontario), 7 November 1860. Studied: under W.L.Judson, London, and at Western School of Art (founded by his father, John Peel), 1870s; Pennsylvania Academy of Art, Philadelphia, under Thomas Eakins, 1877-80; Royal Academy Schools, London, England, 1880; worked at British Museum, 1880; Ecole des Beaux-Arts, Paris, 1881, under Gérôme, Boulanger, Constant, and Lefebvre, 1881. Met George A. Reid and Mary Hiester Reid, Paris, 1888, and advised them to study under Constant. Spent summers sketching at Calais, Normandy; Concarneau, Brittany; and Pont Aven, 1882. Met Isaure Verdier, a Danish painter of miniatures, at Pont Aven; married her in Copenhagen, Denmark, 1882. Returned to Toronto and London, 1882-83. Societies: Ontario Society of Artists (elected 1880); Royal Canadian Academy (elected associate, 1882; full academician, 1891). Awards: honourable mention, Paris Salon, for *Que la Vie est Amère: (The Tired Model)* (Columbus Gallery of Fine Arts, Columbus, Ohio), 1889; third-class medal, Paris Salon, for *After the Bath*, 1890. Exhibited at Art Association of Montreal, 1883-89; O.S.A., 1880-89; R.C.A., 1881-1910; Toronto Industrial Exhibition, 1881-1902; World's Columbian Exposition, Chicago, 1893. *After the Bath* sold to Hungarian Government, hung in National Art Gallery, Budapest, until sold to art dealers H.Pocock and J.Colerick, of London, Ontario, 1922. *The Two Friends* (pastel) purchased by Princess Alexandra, 1890. Returned to Toronto for exhibition and auction of his pictures at Oliver, Coate and Co., October 1890; sixty-four works sold, but only c. $2,000 realized. Returned to Paris, 1890. Died: Paris, 12 October 1892. Memorial exhibition mounted by London Public Library and Art Museum, November 1974. *After the Bath* bequeathed by estate of Col. R. S. McLaughlin, Oshawa, Ontario, to Ontario Government, which turned painting over to Art Gallery of Ontario, 1972. Catalogue of 200 Peel works compiled by J.Edward Martin, 1970.

Fig. 1 Paul Peel
The Artist in his Studio (Self-Portrait) 1890
Oil on canvas (116.8 x 82.5 cm).
Signed and dated (l.r.): *PAUL PEEL*
London Regional Art Gallery, London, Ontario.
On permanent loan from Miss Margaret Peel, California, U.S.A.
Note: exhibited at London Regional Art Gallery only, as Cat. No. "0".

OZIAS LEDUC
(1864-1955)

Painter, muralist, teacher, writer.

27 Ozias Leduc
Mon Portrait 1899
Oil on paper laid down on board (33 x 27 cm)
Signed and dated (u.l.): *18/LEDUC/99* (monogram)
National Gallery of Canada, Ottawa

64 Born: Saint-Hilaire de Rouville (now Mont Saint-Hilaire), Québec, 8 October 1864. Worked as statue-master for a M. Beaulac of the atelier T. Carli, Montréal, 1883. Began frequenting studio of church-decorator Luigi Capello and did drawings for Louis-Philippe Hébert (*q.v.*), 1883. Worked for Capello on church-decoration, 1888. Became pupil of Adolphe Rho, 1888. Exhibited two paintings at *Exposition des beaux-arts*, Montréal, 1890. Exhibited fourteen times with Art Associaton of Montreal between 1891 and 1922; twelve times with Royal Canadian Academy between 1893 and 1920. Exhibition of *Quelques peintures et dessins de O. Leduc* held in Montréal, February 1916. Included in *Exposition d'art canadien*, Musée du Jeu de Paume, Paris, 1927. Exhibited twenty-six works at Musée de la Province, Québec, 1945. First church-decorating commission, 1892. Started large decorating project for Joliette cathedral, 1893 (twenty-eight paintings). Began construction of his studio, "Correlieu", Saint-Hilaire, c. 1894. To London, May 1897; then to Paris, May-June 1897, rejoining artists Joseph Saint-Charles (*q.v.*) and M.-A. de Foy Suzor-Côté. Worked at portraiture, church-decoration, allegorical paintings,

book illustrations until death in 1955. Began sketches for decoration of private chapel of Bishop of Sherbrooke, 1922 (completed 1932). Invited Paul-Emile Borduas (1905-1960) to work for him, 15 June 1922; collaborated with Borduas to 1932. Began decoration of church of Notre-Dame-de-la-Présentation, Almaville-en-bas, P.Q., 1942 (project completed by Gabrielle Messier after his death). Elected municipal counsellor, Saint-Hilaire, 1924, '26, '28, '30. Teaching: painting and drawing in convent of les Soeurs Jésus-Marie, Montréal, 1901; convent of les Réligieuses de la Présentation de Marie, Saint-Hyacinthe, 1913; elected school commissioner, 1917 and '21. Elected associate, Royal Canadian Academy, 1916, full academician, 1937. Received Doctorate *honoris causa*, Université de Montréal, 1938. Died: 16 June, 1955. National Film Board of Canada produced film on Leduc, *Correlieu*, 1958.

COMMENTS BY THE ARTIST

The substance of my creative work comes from the wide-open world of dreams. The substance of a living imagination, made almost tangible by the sign of a set of lines, shapes and colours. Therefore substances of the

universe. So it is a somewhat unreal world, but of precise appearance. The incarnation of the subtle, the magic, the infinite, the incarnation of meditation. Meditation before creation.

> – Ozias Leduc, quoted by Victoria Baker in "On Art, Beauty, and Imaginaton: Currents of Thought in the Writings of Ozias Leduc", *Ozias Leduc the Draughtsman*, Montréal: Sir George Williams Art Galleries, Concordia University, 1978), p. 129

I agree with you that…painting is a trade, so the painter must simply be a tradesman, plying a good trade, highly desirous to forcefully realize the plastic expression of his own vision. He will thus have recourse to a personal art to convey these thoughts that it is always our hope to see high and strong. By respectfully exalting the real (think for a moment that nature must be handled gently to extract poetry) this art will necessarily add beauty to the world (think here of the supreme goal of art.)

> – Ozias Leduc, letter to Olivier Maurault, quoted by Victoria Baker in "On Art, Beauty and Imagination…", p. 133

Fig. 1 Ozias Leduc
Autoportrait (c. 1900)
Charcoal on buff laid paper (36.5 x 26.5 cm)
Initialled (l.r.): *O.L.*
National Gallery of Canada, Ottawa
Photo: Michael Neill, Ottawa

ALFRED LALIBERTÉ
(1878-1943)

Sculptor, painter, teacher.

Born: Saint-Elizabeth de Warwick, Arthabaska, Québec, 1878. Family moved to Saint-Norbert, 1890. Began working as wood-sculptor, 1894. Executed a statue in wood of Sir Wilfrid Laurier, 1896. To Montréal, 1896. Studied at Conseil des Arts et Métiers de Montréal, 1896-99; Ecole des Beaux-Arts, Paris, under Gabriel Jules Thomas and Antoine Injalbert, 1902. Returned to Canada, 1907. Exhibited at Paris Salon, 1905, 1906, 1911; Annual Spring Exhibition, Art Association of Montreal, 1908-42 (192 works). Returned to Paris, 1910-11, 1917, 1923. Teaching: Conseil des Arts, Montréal, 1907-10; appointed professor, Ecole des Beaux-Arts de Montréal, 1922. Commissioned to sculpt statues of Père Marquette and Père Brébeuf, 1909. Purchased studio building, Rue Ste.-Famille, Montréal, 1917. Executed 215 statuettes in *Légendes* series, 1928-32 (Musée du Québec). Began

writing *Les Artistes de mon temps*, 1928; published album of *Légendes*, 1934. Elected associate, Royal Canadian Academy, 1912; full academician, 1919. Retrospective exhibition at Galerie des arts de Montréal, 1943. Received honourary degree, Université de Montréal, 1940. Died: Montréal, 13 January 1943.

COMMENTS BY THE ARTIST

A mon avis il n'y a pas seulement celui qui produit qui peut être artiste. Etre sensible, c'est déjà avoir une nature d'artiste. Si l'on ajoute l'imagination qui existe presque toujours chez un être sensible, c'est certes un artiste à qui il manque le métier. Celui-ci serait vite obtenu avec le travail et l'observation qui en est le complément.

Cet être sensible serait un artiste aussi qualifié que ceux qui font de la sculpture ou de la peinture avec compréhension.
…

Il y a des peintres et des sculpteurs qui, sans avoir vraiment la mentalité d'artiste, mais avec un métier tellement fort, ont réussi des oeuvres réellement belles. On se à demande la fin si tout homme sur terre avec du métier et du talent joints à un travail sérieux, ne pourrait pas devenir artiste, surtout s'il a un goût sûr. Nous pouvons placer au-dessus de cette catégorie le véritable artiste complet ayant produit les plus belles choses qui résistent aux jugements du temps et que les biographies placent au-dessus des hommes ordinaires pour leur supériorité. Nous en trouvons presque à toutes les époques de l'histoire de l'art.

– Albert Laliberté, "L'Artiste", in "Réflections", *Mes Souvenirs* (Montréal: Les Editions du Boréal Express, 1978), pp. 208-209.

28 Alfred Laliberté
Buste de l'artiste
Bronze (47 cm height)
Signed and inscribed (at back): *A. Laliberte/par lui même*
Royal Canadian Academy Diploma Collection (deposited 1923)
National Gallery of Canada, Ottawa

Fig. 1 Alfred Laliberté
Jeune Artiste
Bronze
Photo: Jean-Paul Laliberté (*La Patrie*)

Fig. 2 Alfred Laliberté
Autoportrait (c. 1920)
Oil on canvas (46 x 38 cm)
Michel Champagne, Québec
Note: reproduced from *Alfred Laliberté: 1878-1953* (Montréal: La Galerie l'art français, 1978), with permission.

JOSEPH SAINT-CHARLES
(1868-1956)

Painter and teacher.

29 Joseph Saint-Charles
Autoportrait (c.1910)
Oil on canvas (81.2 x 59.8 cm)
Signed (l.r.): *J. ST. CHARLES*
Musée du Québec, Québec
Photo: Patrick Altman

30 Joseph Saint-Charles
Autoportrait à la pipe 1913
Red chalk on paper (24.1 x 31.7 cm)
Signed and dated (l.l.): *Jos. St. Charles/1913*
Private collection, Outremont, Québec
Photo: Louis Prud'homme, Montréal, courtesy, Anna Saint-Charles

66 Born: Montréal, Québec, 10 June 1868. Studied: atelier of Edouard Meloche, *décorateur*, Montréal, 1884; Ecole des Beaux-Arts de Montréal, 1884-88, under abbé Joseph Chabert; Ecole des Beaux-Arts de Paris, 1888, under Jean-Léon Gérôme; Académie Julian, 1889, under Benjamin Constant, Jules Lefebvre, Joseph Blanc, 1889; Académie Colarossi, 1889; Ecole National des Beaux-Arts, 1890. Awarded third-class medal for figure drawing and gold medal for drawing, Ecole des Beaux-Arts, 1891. To Montréal, 1889, and 1891, returning to France with M.-A. Suzor-Côté. Returned to Canada with Suzor-Côté and Edmond de Nevers, 1894. To Rome, February 1896, then to Paris, April 1897, returning to Canada 1898. Settled in Montréal as portrait painter; also painted landscapes and still-lifes. Painted decorations for the chapel of Saint-Charles, Notre-Dame de Montréal, 1890, and chapel of Grand Séminaire de Montréal, 1905. Teaching: professor of elementary course in drawing, Conseil des Arts et Manufactures de Montréal, 1898; professor of drawing, Université de Montréal, 1910-25; professor of drawing, Ecole des Beaux-Arts de Montréal, 1925-42; drawing instructor,

Monument national, 1925. Pupils included Stanley Cosgrove, Francesco Iacurto, Robert LaPalme, and Dr. Paul Dumas. Exhibited at Annual Spring Exhibition, Art Association of Montreal, 1895-1933; Annual Exhibition, Royal Canadian Academy, 1895-1939; included in Louisiana Purchase Exposition, St. Louis, 1904. First large exhibition, Montréal, December 1945, with Edmond Dyonnet (*q.v.*), Ozias Leduc (*q.v.*), and Elzéar Soucy. Retrospective exhibitions mounted in Montréal, 1945 and 1966, and in Ottawa, 1971. Member: Royal Canadian Academy (elected associate, 1901; full academician, 1938). Died: 26 October 1956. Saint-Charles *catalogue raisonné* by François Laurin, Departement d'Arts visuels de l'Université d'Ottawa, 1974-77, turned over for completion to Centre de Recherche en Civilisation Canadienne-Française, Ottawa, 1977.

Fig. 1 Joseph Saint-Charles
L'Artiste par lui-même 1895
Oil on canvas (41.5 x 39.8 cm)
Signed (l.l.): *J. St. Charles*
Private collection
Photo: courtesy, Foundation Joseph Saint-Charles, Centre de Recherche en Civilisation Canadien-Français, L'Université d'Ottawa, Ontario.

Fig. 2 Joseph Saint-Charles
Autoportrait aux lunettes
Oil on canvas (22 x 27 cm)
Anna Saint-Charles, Outremont, Québec
Photo: Louis Prud'homme, Montréal, courtesy, Anna Saint-Charles

ROBERT HARRIS
(1859-1919)

See also Catalogue No. 6 for Biography.

31 Robert Harris
Self-Portrait 1908
Oil on pressed cardboard (26.7 x 23.5 cm)
Initialled (l.r.): *R.H.*
Dated (l.l.): *6 May/1908*
Agnes Etherington Art Centre, Kingston,
Ontario
Photo: Victor Sakuta, Kingston

FREDERICK H. VARLEY
(1881-1969)

Painter, illustrator, teacher.

Born: Sheffield, England, 2 January 1881. Studied: Sheffield School of Art, 1892-99; Académie Royale des Beaux-Arts, Antwerp, Belgium, 1900-02. Worked as commercial illustrator, London, 1903-08. To Canada, July 1912. Began working in Toronto for Grip Limited, under art director A.H. Robson, then at Rous and Mann Limited. To Algonquin Park, October 1914, with Tom Thomson, A.Y. Jackson and Arthur Lismer (*q.v.*). Began to do illustrations for *Canadian Courier*, 1917. Commissioned as honourary captain to paint for Canadian War Records, 7 February 1918; to Glasgow, 25 March, 1918, then to London; in France, August-October 1918. Worked in studio in London, October 1918-August 1919. *For What?* (1918; Canadian War Museum, Ottawa) displayed in *Canadian War Memorials Exhibition*, London, January-February 1919, and praised by Augustus John and William Rothenstein. Returned to Canada, August 1919. Took studio in Studio Building, Toronto. Spent summer painting with Arthur Lismer at Dr. James M. MacCallum's cottage, Georgian Bay, 1920. Assisted J.E.H. MacDonald in painting murals for St. Anne's Anglican Church, Toronto, 1923. Portrait commission, Winnipeg, 1924. To Vancouver, September 1926. Met Emily Carr, November 1927. Garibaldi period, c. 1930-35 (annual summer painting expeditions with J.W.G. MacDonald); Lynn Valley period, 1932-36. To Ottawa to paint portrait of H.S. Southam, April 1936. To Arctic on the *Nascopie*, with the Eastern Arctic Patrol, July-September 1938. Moved to Montréal, 1940. Painted portraits of Canadian soldiers, 1942. Living in Ottawa, 1943-44; wintered in Toronto, 1944; settled permanently in Toronto, 1946-69. To Soviet Union with a group of other Canadian artists, writers and musicians, 1954. Painting trip to Cape Breton, Nova Scotia, 1955. Summer painting trips to British Columbia, 1957-67. Continued to paint until 1967. Teaching: member, Board of Examiners, Ontario College of Art, 1916-17, 1919-20, 1921-22; summer course, O.C.A., Meadowvale, Ontario, 1922; appointed to full-time teaching post (instructor of drawing from the antique and drawing and painting from the draped figure), O.C.A., 1926-27; instructor of drawing and painting, Vancouver School of Decorative and Applied Arts, 1926-33; co-founded British Columbia School of Arts with J.W.G. MacDonald and Harry Tauber, 1933 (principal,

Fig. 1 Robert Harris
Self-Portrait (undated)
Oil on canvas (74.9 x 59.7 cm)
Signed (u.r.): *Robert Harris*
National Gallery of Canada, Ottawa (acquired 1913)

Note: see also Catalogue No. 6

32 Frederick H. Varley
Self-Portrait 1919
Oil on canvas (61 x 50.8 cm)
Signed (u.r.): *F H VARLEY*
National Gallery of Canada, Ottawa
Photo: B. Merritt

68 1933-35); Ottawa Art Association, 1936-39; Doon School of Fine Arts, Doon, Ontario, 1948-49. First group exhibition, Toronto, 1912; first one-man exhibition, Toronto, February 1916. First exhibited with Ontario Society of Artists, 1913; exhibited with Royal Canadian Academy, 1912-42. Participated in first exhibition of Group of Seven, Art Gallery of Toronto, May 1920. Solo exhibitions at Art Institute of Seattle, January 1930; and Vancouver Art Gallery, December 1932. First major solo show in eastern Canada at W. Scott and Sons, Montreal, May 1937. Numerous one-man exhibitions thereafter in Ottawa and Toronto. Portraits exhibition at Hart House, Toronto, October-November 1965. Travelling retrospective exhibition mounted by Art Gallery of Toronto, October-November 1954; retrospectives organized by Willistead Art Gallery, Windsor, April - May 1964, and Burnaby Art Gallery, May-June 1974. Centennial exhibition mounted and circulated by Edmonton Art Gallery, 1981-82. Societies: Arts and Letters Club, Toronto (elected November 1912); Ontario Society of Artists (1916-29); Group of Seven (1920-33); Royal Canadian Academy (associate, 1931-39); Canadian Group of Painters

(founder-member, 1933). Awards and honours: prizes and medals for drawing and painting, Académie Royale des Beaux-Arts, Antwerp, 1901, '02; first prize for painting, Willingdon Arts Competition, 1930; honourary LL.D., University of Manitoba, Winnipeg, 1961; Canada Council Medal, 1963; R.C.A. Medal, 1969. National Film Board documentary, *Varley*, by Allan Wargon, released 1953. Died: 8 September 1969.

COMMENTS BY THE ARTIST

''Feeling'' avails nothing without organization and restraint. Add ''intellect'' and ''will'' to emotion and you possess the three great qualities necessary for all aesthetic expression. *Emotion* senses the motif, *Intellect* the constructive, and *Will* the power to organize.

Art is not merely recording surface life — incidents, emotions. The Artist divines the causes beneath which create the outward result.

– F.H. Varley, ''Room 27 Speaking'', *The Paint Box*, Vancouver School of Decorative Arts, Vol. 2 (June 1927): 23.

...if there is composition of form, there must be composition of mind and orderliness of emotion. The machine of patterns is better ''scrapped'', for

mind surely only exists [when] woven through the fabric of all things.

– F.H. Varley, letter to L.L. FitzGerald, 25 September 1934. Archives of the FitzGerald Centre, University of Manitoba, Winnipeg.

I have nothing, no power to say — I will do this — or I will do that. My life has taught me that I have nothing to do about ''what will be''. *I believe!* I have been schooled in a way of life so that I am immune to praise or — condemnation. As long as I make contact with a great Unknown and recognize the privilege of living in a glorious world, it would be impertinence to say ''I will do this or that''.

– F.H. Varley, letter to his sister Ethel, quoted by Christopher Varley in *F.H. Varley: A Centennial Exhibition* (Edmonton: Edmonton Art Gallery, 1981), p. 168.

Fig. 1 Frederick H. Varley
Mirror of Thought
Oil on canvas (50.8 x 57.6 cm)
Signed (l.r.): *VARLEY*
Art Gallery of Greater Victoria, Victoria, B.C.

Fig. 2 Frederick H. Varley
Liberation. 1936
Oil on canvas (213.7 x 134.3 cm)
Signed (l.r.): VARLEY
Art Gallery of Ontario, Toronto
Gift of John B. Ridley. On loan to the
Art Gallery of Ontario from the Ontario Heritage Foundation.

INGLIS SHELDON-WILLIAMS
(1870-1940)

Painter, illustrator, teacher, writer.

Born: Elvetham, Hampshire, England, 1870. Studied: at Ghent, under Théophile Lybaert, 1885-86, winning Form Prize; Académie Colarossi, Paris, 1891-93; Ecole des Beaux-Arts, Paris; studied at British Museum, and at Slade School, London, under Sir Thomas Brock, 1893; Slade School, 1896, under Frederick Brown, Henry Tonks, Walter Russell. Emigrated to Canada, arriving in Brandon, Manitoba, March, 1887. Acquired full section for his widowed mother, began building a homestead at Cannington Manor. Returned to England, 1891-93. In Canada, 1894-96, then back to England. Assisted Henry Brewer in large mural decoration, London, 1897. House at Cannington Manor burned down, summer, 1897. Enlisted in British Army, 1899, serving as trooper in South Africa until June 1901. Worked unofficially for *The Sphere*, 1899; did illustrations for *Today*, 1902; for *The Sphere* in India, 1902-03, in Paris, Lisbon and the Azores, 1903, and covering Russo-Japanese War, 1904. Settled in Painswick, Gloucestershire, 1905. Returned to Regina, Saskatchewan, 1913, making trips to England, 1914 and 1915-16. Appointed official Canadian war artist, December 1917. Returned to England, c. January 1918. To France and Germany. Studio in London, 1919. Returned to Canada, 1919-20, 1922. To France and Italy on rest cure, 1925; working as landscape painter in Italy, 1927-34. Settled in England, 1934. Writing became main occupation. Teaching: Frank Calderon's School of Animal Painting, London, 1899; teacher of portraiture and landscape painting, Regina College, 1916-17. Exhibited at Royal Canadian Academy, 1914. Exhibited regularly at Fine Art Society, London; Royal Academy, London; Ridley Art Club, London; Royal Institute of Oil Painters, etc. Elected member of R.I.O., London, 1922. Died: Tunbridge Wells, Kent, 30 November 1940. Memorial exhibition (64 works) mounted by Kensington Art Gallery, London, 1950. Travelling retrospective mounted by Glenbow Museum, Calgary, 1982.

PARASKEVA CLARK
(1898-   )

Painter.

35 Paraskeva Clark
Self Portrait 1925
Oil on canvas (28.3 x 22.2 cm)
Signed and dated (l.l.): *Paraskeva Allegri/1925*
Collection Art Gallery of Ontario, Toronto, Purchase with assistance from Wintario, 1979.

70 Born Paraskeva Avdyevna Plisik, 28 October 1898, in St. Petersburg, Russia. Evening art classes with Savely Seidenberg, 1916-18. Attended "Free Studios" (formerly, Imperial Academy of Fine Arts) full-time under Vasily Shukhayev, 1918-20; transferred to Kuzma Petrov-Vodkin's class at the Free Studios, 1920. Married Oreste Allegri, Jr., 1922 (drowned 1923). Arrived in Paris with son, Ben, autumn 1923. Worked in interior design shop, 1929. Met visiting Torontonian, Philip Clark, whom she married in England, June 1931. Arrived in Canada 30 June 1931. First Canadian exhibition: Royal Canadian Academy, Art Gallery of Toronto, 1932. Exhibited with Canadian Group of Painters, 1933. Worked as window-designer for René Cera at Eatons College Street Department Store, Toronto, 1934. First solo show at Douglas Duncan's Picture Loan Society, February 1937. To New York to see Picasso retrospective, 1939. Attended Kingston Conference of Canadian Artists, 1941. Appointed by National Gallery of Canada to paint activities of Women's Division of Canadian Armed Services, 1944. First large exhibition (with son Ben) at Arts and Letters Club, Toronto, 1974. 1933 *Self-Portrait* reproduced on cover of *Canadian Painting in the 1930s*, organized by National Gallery of Canada, 1976; *Petroushka* purchased by N.G.C. Societies: Canadian Group of Painters (elected 1936); Canadian Society of Painters in Water Colour 1937, elected to executive, 1943, president, 1948); Candian Society of Graphic Art (1938, resigned 1940); Ontario Society of Artists (1954); Royal Canadian Academy (elected associate, 1956, full academician, 1966). Travelling retrospective exhibition organized by Dalhousie Art Gallery, Halifax, 1982-83. National Film Board of Canada documentary on her life and work, *Portrait of the Artist as an Old Lady*, released 1983.

COMMENTS BY THE ARTIST

Who is an artist? Is he not a human being like ourselves, with the added gifts of finer understanding and perception of the realities of life, and the ability to arouse emotions through the creation of forms and images? Surely. And this being so, those who give their lives, their knowledge and their time to social struggle have the right to expect great help from the artist. And I cannot imagine a more inspiring role than that which the artist is asked to play for the defence of civilization... Forget if you wish the troubles of Europe: there are plenty here. Paint the raw, sappy life that moves ceaselessly about you, paint portraits of your own Canadian leaders, depict happy dreams for your Canadian souls... Think of yourself as a human being, and you cannot help feeling the reality of life around you, and becoming impregnated with it.

> – Paraskeva Clark, "Come out from Behind the Pre-Cambrian Shield", *New Frontier*, I, (April 1937): 16.

Above all I am a realist. Reality of life around me fills me with everlasting admiration for its miraculous wonders —which I see spellbound — and full of desire to share my experiences with others. My powers of imagination are very limited perhaps because contemplation of the riches of reality made them unnecessary...

I want to make clear that these particular aspects of reality, presented in the painting, are not the product of my imagination or my deeply personal emotions aroused by them. *No*—they are "the emotions of that reality" the presence of which I want to put on canvas or paper...

> – Paraskeva Clark, "The Artist Speaks", *Canadian Review of Art and Music*, 3, (October-November 1944): 18.

Fig.1 Paraskeva Clark
Self Portrait 1933
Oil on canvas (101.6 x 76.2 cm)
Signed and dated (l.r.): PARASKEVA CLARK/33
National Gallery of Canada, Ottawa

Fig.2 Paraskeva Clark
Self Portrait 1937
Watercolour on paper (53.3 x 50.8 cm)
Signed and dated (l.l.): *paraskeva clark/37*
Dalhousie Art Gallery, Halifax

36 Paraskeva Clark
Self Portrait 1931-1932
Oil on cardboard (41 x 31 cm)
Inscribed (*verso*): *Painted in winter of
1931-32/Toronto — invited by Many* [i.e.,
sculptor Emanuel Hahn] *to Exhibit in*
[Royal Canadian] *Academy/was accepted by
jury and thus it became a 'foot/in the door'
into the Temple of Canadian Art"*
Harold Town, Toronto
Photo: courtesy, Harold Town

THOMAS REID MACDONALD
(1908-1978)

Painter, teacher, curator.

37 T.R. MacDonald
Self-Portrait 1934
Oil on canvas (61.4 x 51.2 cm)
Signed and dated (l.l.): *T.R. MacDonald
1934*
Private collection, Hamilton, Ontario
Note: see also Catalogue No. 60.

Born: Montréal, Québec, 28 June 1908. Studied under Adam Sheriff Scott, Montréal, 1928-30; under Edmond Dyonnet (*q.v.*) at Royal Canadian Academy Life Classes, Art Association of Montreal, 1930-33. Exhibited for first time at Annual Spring Exhibition, Art Association of Montreal, 1929, and Annual Exhibition, Royal Canadian Academy, 1931. To Europe, Holland and Belgium, 1934. Enlisted as trooper in 17th D.R.C. Hussars, 25 March 1941; overseas in August, receiving promotion to rank of sergeant. Commissioned as war artist with Army, with rank of lieutenant, 10 May 1944. Worked mainly in Italy, 1944-45. Appointed Director, Owens Art Gallery, Department of Fine Art, Mount Allison University, Sackville, N.B., 1945-46; Director and curator, Art Gallery of Hamilton, Hamilton, Ontario, 1947-73. Elected associate, Royal Canadian Academy, 1947, full academician, 1957. Married artist Rae Hendershot, Hamilton, 6 October 1950. Figure, portrait and city-scene painter. Retrospective exhibitions mounted by McMaster University Art Gallery, Hamilton, 1968; Laurentian University Museum and Art Gallery, Sudbury, Ontario, 1972; and Art Gallery of Hamilton, 1980. Received hononary LL.D., McMaster University, 1974. Died: Paris, France, 15 October 1978.

COMMENT BY THE ARTIST

Truly my outstanding quality is a mulish persistance.

– T.R. MacDonald, letter to Robert Pilot, 13 May 1964, quoted by Andrew Oko in his Introduction, *T.R. MacDonald: 1908-1978* (Hamilton: Art Gallery of Hamilton, 1980), p. 7.

JACK WELDON HUMPHREY
(1901-1967)

Painter.

72 Born: Saint John, New Brunswick, 12 January 1901. Studied: Mount Allison University, Sackville, N.B., 1917-18; Boston Museum School of Fine Arts, under Philip Hale, 1922-23; National Academy of Design, New York, 1924-29, under Charles Hawthorne, 1927-29; summers at Cape Cod School of Art, Provincetown, Mass., under Charles Hawthorne, 1925-27 and 1929; Hans Hofmann's School, Munich, Germany, March-May 1930. Travelled and studied in Europe for nine months, 1929-30. Painted in Mexico, 1938. In France, 1952-54, on overseas grant. Taught at Queen's University Summer School, 1945. Societies: Canadian Group of Painters (joined 1933); Eastern Group, Montréal (1938-39); Canadian Society of Painters in Water Colour (1939, elected director, 1944, vice-president, 1945); Contemporary Arts Society, Montréal (1939); Canadian Society of Graphic Art (Regional Representative, 1946, 1956, 1959, Eastern vice-president, 1951); Canadian Arts Council Committee of the International Association of Plastic Arts (1955). First one-man show, Toronto, 1938. Exhibited internationally. Awards and honours: LL.D. from University of New Brunswick, Fredericton, 1951; Canadian Government Royal Society Overseas Fellowship, 1952; Canada Council Senior Arts Fellowship, 1960; First Purchase Prize, First Atlantic Awards Exhibition, Dalhousie University, Halifax, 1961. Retrospective exhibition mounted by Beaverbrook Art Gallery, Fredericton, and circulated by the National Gallery of Canada, 1966-67.

COMMENTS BY THE ARTIST

My ambition for my painting is for it to grow in full equality with the painting that is done where conditions are at their finest. Am I merely making excuses? In my opinion, no. Painting is worthwhile when it is not a creature of habit. The great variety in visual art is due to the differences and shades of difference between organized perceptions and conceptual constructions. I feel it necessary to experience uniquely for myself the resources of mediums and concepts. To know without experience is not truly to know. To paint without curiosity and to live without seeking is to stop growing. I do a great deal of painting from nature following its forms. It is a way like those of Monet and Thoreau, by their ponds, savoring particularities. I also paint from my own inward nature following the various laws of contrast and the growth of free invention, truly a more radical exploration. I am glad to do both. As an artist, I like my experiments to surprise me. I also like to search out nature... I have painted psychological portraits. Then there is memory, and so the analytic quality of landscape and figure painting has its further use to authenticate invention. The most liberating surprise occurs when the hand is guided almost by trance. It is not enough that nearly all avenues have been already explored. One must arrive by personal experience.

– Jack Humphrey, quoted in *Bates-Humphrey* (Ottawa: National Gallery of Canada, 1958), reprinted in *Jack Weldon Humphrey (1901-1967): Early Portraits and Group Paintings* (Toronto: Galerie Dresdnere, 1980, unpag.

Fig. 1 Jack Humphrey
Self-Portrait undated
Oil on canvas (61 x 50.8 cm)
Private collection, New Brunswick

Fig. 2 Jack Humphrey
Self-Portrait c. 1934
Oil on canvas (76.2 x 61 cm)
Mrs. Jean Humphrey, Saint John, New Brunswick
Photo: Jim Chambers, Toronto

ALFRED PELLAN
(1906-)

Painter, sculptor, teacher, theatrical designer

Born: Quebec City, 16 May 1906. Began copying calendar and magazine pictures and sketching from nature. Studied: Ecole des Beaux-Arts, Québec, 1920-25 (in final year won all prizes given for drawing, painting, sculpture, pen drawing, and anatomy sketching); Ecole Supérieur des Beaux-Arts de Paris, 1926-30, under Lucien Simon. Remained in Paris to 1936, working in Grande Chaumière and Colarossi academies and then alone. To Québec, rejected for teaching position, returned to Paris, 1936. To Greece, 1937. Returned to Québec, 1940; set up studio in Montréal, 1941. Visited by Fernand Léger, 1945. In Paris, 1952-55. Teaching: painting instructor, Ecole des Beaux-Arts, Montréal, 1943-52; painting instructor, The Art Centre, Ste. Adéle, P.Q., summer 1957. Exhibited at Salon d'automne, Paris, 1934. First one-man exhibition, Académie Ranson, Paris, 1935; first Canadian solo show, Musée de la Province, Québec, 1940. Represented Canada at Art Institute of Chicago, 1945, and at World's Fair, Osaka, Japan, 1970. Retrospective exhibitions mounted by Musée de la Province de Québec, 1940; Musée national d'art moderne, Paris, 1955; National Gallery of Canada, Montreal Museum of Fine Arts, and Art Gallery of Toronto, 1960; Musée du Québec, Musée des Beaux-Arts de Montréal and National Gallery of Canada, 1972-73; National Gallery of Canada (drawings), 1980. Commissions: costumes and stage sets for *La Nuit des rois*, Les Compagnons, Montréal, 1946; Canadian Embassy, Rio de Janeiro, Brazil, two murals, 1942; Winnipeg Airport mural, 1963; Place des Arts, Montréal, stained glass window, 1963; National Library of Canada, Ottawa, two murals, 1968. National Gallery of Canada purchased *Coin du Vieux Québec*, 1922. Two Pellan paintings purchased by French State, 1937. Awards: first Quebec Government painting bursary, 1926; Ecole Supérieur first prize for painting, 1928; Prix de Peinture, Salon de Mural, Paris, 1935; first prize, Province of Quebec Competition, 1948; Royal Society of Canada bursary, 1952, to work in Paris; first prize, Canada mural competition, City Centre Building, Montréal, 1957; Senior Fellowship, Canada Council, 1958; National Award for Painting and Related Arts, University of Alberta, 1959; Canada Council Medal, 1965; Companion of Order of Canada, 1967; Centennial Medal, 1967; honourary doctorates from Canadian universities, 1969, 1971, 1974; Prix Philippe-Hébert, la Société Saint-Jean le Baptiste de Montréal, 1972; Molson Prize, Canada Council, 1972; Diplôme d'Honneur, Canadian Conference of the Arts, Vancouver, 1977. Societies: Contemporary Arts Society, Montréal (1940-48); Prisme d'Yeux, Montréal (co-founder, 1948); Royal Canadian Academy (elected associate, 1971, full academician, 1973). Member of visual arts panel, Kingston Conference, 1957; member of international jury, *Quatrième Biennale de Paris*, 1965; honourary chairman, Atelier International de Recherches Graphiques, Montréal, 1971-82; honourary committee, Rencontre des Arts et des Sciences de la Couleur, Centre Québéçois de la Couleur, Montréal, 1978. Has lived and worked at Ste.-Rose, north of Montréal, since 1956.

COMMENTS BY THE ARTIST

Je joue sur le hasard et j'élabore le problème que le hasard à posé.

– Alfred Pellan, quoted by Donald W. Buchanan in *Alfred Pellan* (Toronto: Society for Art Publications/ McClelland and Stewart, 1962), p.13.

—l'art n'est jamais statique, stationnaire; bien au contraire, il n'est que mouvement et dynamisme, comme la vie elle-même, et ainsi l'art ne saurait se dissocier de la vie;

—l'art est libre, indépendant, ouvert et dégagé de toute ingérence littéraire, idéologique, philosophique ou politique.

– Alfred Pellan, quoted or paraphrased by Guy Robert in *Borduas* (Montréal; Les Presses de l'Université du Québec, 1972), (*Cf*. Jacques de Tonnancour, Prisme d'Yeux manifesto, 1948, the sentence beginning "Nous cherchons une peinture liberée...".)

L'art, c'est la liberté…
…

L'abstraction pour l'abstraction nous fait tourner en rond. Si l'on travaille avec des taches abstraits, il faut les humaniser; c'est de cette façon seulement qu'on peut atteindre une dimension universelle.
…

Je suis si occupé à peindre que je n'ai pas le temps de fouiller tout ce qu'il peut y avoir derrière moi!

– Alfred Pellan, quoted in "La queue de la comète: Alfred Pellan: Témoin du surréalisme. Interview Vie des Arts", *Vie des Arts* 22 (automne 1975): 20.

39 Alfred Pellan
Autoportrait (c.1933-1935)
Charcoal on paper (27.6 x 17.6 cm)
Signed (l.r.): *Pellan*
Private collection, Auteuil, Québec (Pellan Inventory no.60d)
Note: "Although Pellan dates the work 1943..., both the signature and the similarity in style and composition to *Untitled...*, dated 1935, suggest that the work was executed earlier." — Reesa Greenberg, *The Drawings of Alfred Pellan* (Ottawa; National Gallery of Canada, 1980), p.109.

MILLER GORE BRITTAIN
(1912-1968)

74

Born: Saint John, New Brunswick, 1912. Began drawing under instruction of Miss E.R. Holt, 1923. Entered Saint John Vocational School as art student, 1926. Studied at Art Students' League, New York, under Harry Wickey (etching), George Wright, Mahonri Young, and William McNulty, 1930-32. Joined R.C.A.F., 1942, served overseas, 1944-45. Appointed Official War Artist, 1945. Returned to Saint John, 1945, discharged, 1946. Societies: Canadian Society of Graphic Art (elected 1936, elected Eastern section representative, 1957); Contemporary Arts Society, Montreal (elected 1942). One-man exhibitions in Daytona, Florida (1948); Saint John (1949); New York City (1950); St. Andrews, N.B. (1952); New York City (1953); Ottawa (1953); New York City (1955); Rome (1965); Palm Beach, Florida (1965); retrospectives in Halifax, N.S. (1965); Saint John (1966); Fredericton, N.B. (1975); Halifax (1978); Sackville, N.B. (1981). Died in Saint John, 21 January, 1968. Posthumously awarded the Canada Centennial Medal for his contribution to Canadian art and his distinguished war record, 1968. Subject of a National Film Board of Canada documentary, 1981.

COMMENTS BY THE ARTIST

I do not so much wish to record the rich and varied texture of human life as to let it work on me, the resulting visual image may take quite another form from the circumstances that prompted it.

– Miller Brittain, quoted by J. Russell Harper in *Miller Brittain - Painter* (Sackville, N.B.: Owens Art Gallery, 1981), unpag.

A picture ought to emerge from the midst of life and be in no sense divorced from it, and I call history to be my witness. And I think artists should be rooted in their native heath, not self-consciously but natually. And they will be so if their life and work are one and the same.

– Miller Brittain, quoted by Barry Lord, *The History of Painting in Canada: Towards a People's Art* (Toronto: NC Press, 1974), p. 184.

Fig. 1 Allfred Pellan
Autoportrait
Oil on masonite (40.6 x 23.2 cm)
Signed (l.r.): *PELLAN*
Musée du Québec, Québec
Photo: Neuville Bazin, Québec

40 Miller Brittain
Self-Portrait (c. 1934)
Oil on cardboard (53.3 x 41.9 cm)
Mr. and Mrs. Chen-Chi Ho, Moncton, New
Brunswick

41 Miller Brittain
Self-Portrait in a Blue Hat 1940
Oil and egg-tempera on masonite (55.9 x
45.7 cm)
Initialled (l.l.): *MGB*
Private collection, Toronto

Fig. 1 Miller Brittain
Self-Portrait (c. 1939-41)
Oil on masonite (dimensions unknown)
Miller Brittain Estate (in custody of Canada
Permanent Trust)
Note: reproduced from *Maritime Art* 1 (April
1951): facing p. 15.

Fig. 2 Miller Brittain
Self-Portrait
Pastel and white paint on paper (frame: 20.5 x
20.5 cm)
New Brunswick Museum, Saint John, N.B.
Photo: Micro Limited, Saint John

ALLAN HARRISON
(1911-)

Painter, illustrator, graphic designer, teacher.

42 Allan Harrison
Self-Portrait 1946
Charcoal on paper (27.6 x 20.3 cm)
Catherine Bates, Montréal

43 Allan Harrison
Self-Portrait 1978
Oil on canvas (35.7 x 46.1 cm)
Signed and dated (u.r.): *Allan Harrison '77*
Musée des Beaux-Arts de Montréal
Photo: Patrick Altman, Montréal

76 Born: Montréal, Québec, 27 December 1911. Studied: Ecole des Beaux-Arts de Montréal, 1930; Art Students' League of New York, under Kimon Nicolaides and George Bridgman, 1931; Atelier School, Montréal, under John Lyman and André Bieler, 1932-33; atelier of André Lhote, Paris, 1956. To London, then Paris, 1933-34, 1935, Paris again in 1938. Worked as advertising artist, Montréal, 1939-45. Professional positions: art director, J. Walter Thompson Company Limited, Montréal, 1940-46, and Rio de Janeiro, 1946-47. In Rio met refugee artists Vieira da Silva and Arpad Szènes. To Paris to work with Szènes, 1947-48. In Rome and Paris, 1948; returned to Montréal, 1949, then to New York for nine years, working as commercial designer (with Paul Rand and others). To France and Italy, 1956. Living and working in Montréal since 1959. Teaching: Montreal Museum of Fine Arts School (graphic design), 1941-46; Sir George Williams University, Montréal (graphic design), 1960-65; l'Université de Québec, Montréal (drawing and design), 1971-72. Lectures: School of Architecture, McGill University, Montréal; Mount Allison University, Sackville, N.B.; Alberta College of Art, Calgary. Societies: Contemporary Arts Society,

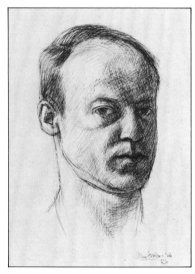

Montréal (founding member and secretary, 1939-48; exhibited with Society six times); Royal Canadian Academy (1979). One man exhibitions: Montreal Museum of Fine Arts, 1945; Instituto dos Arquitetos, Rio de Janeiro, 1947. Retrospective exhibition mounted by Musée des Beaux-Arts de Montréal, 1978.

COMMENTS BY THE ARTIST

I've long considered that only spatial relationships both in area and in colour

intensities…are worth slaving and suffering for… What materials are used is most secondary to me — even if it is part of the trade.

– Allan Harrison, letter to Robert Stacey, 5 July 1979.

Re art. I could say much more I suppose but it's a combination of intelligence, emotions and hard work. I started by falling in love with the three dimensional study of planes in whatever I tried to paint and under-

standing that the whole composition of a painting is a relationship of planes understood by colour changes. *Keen* visual capacity and sensitivity is the key once the intellectual understanding is there and a life long struggle. Content or no content, abstract or figurative — it's all the same problem…

– Allan Harrison, letter to Robert Stacey, 24 September 1979.

Fig. 1 Allan Harrison
Myself a bit complicated 1937
Graphite on paper (37.5 x 27 cm)
Collection: the artist, Montréal

JOHN LYMAN
(1886-1967)

Painter, sculptor, teacher, writer.

44 John Lyman
Autoportrait 1960
Oil on canvas (50.7 x 40.6 cm)
Signed (u.r.): *Lyman*
Musée du Québec, Québec (Succession John Lyman, 1970)

Born: Biddeford, Maine, U.S.A., 1886. Moved with family to Montréal. Studied: Hotchkiss School, Lakeville, Connecticut; McGill University, Montréal, 1905-07. To Paris, summer, 1907. Saw J.W. Morrice winter scene of St. Lawrence River at Salon. Enrolled in drawing classes of Marcel Béronneau, Paris. Made first landscape sketches in oils at St. Jean-du-Doigt, Brittany, 1907. Studied: Royal College of Art, South Kensington, London, 1907-08 (architectural design and life drawing); Académie Julian, Paris, under Jean-Paul Laurens, 1908-09. Opened studio, Paris, 1909. Met Morrice and visited his studio; saw Henri Matisse painting at Salon des Indépendentistes; met English painter Matthew Smith at Etaples, summer, 1909. Joined Académie Matisse with Smith. To Montréal, fall 1910. Honeymoon trip to Paris, Switzerland, Normandy, Munich, spring 1911. Spent winter of 1911-12 in Montréal, of 1913 in Bermuda. Exhibited four paintings at Art Association of Montreal spring show, 1913. First one-man exhibition, Montréal, May 1913; attacked in press. Returned to Paris with wife, 1913-14, then to Bermuda, to 1915. Joined Red Cross, served in France. Lived after war in

Paris, travelled in Europe, wintered in Bermuda and Tunisia. Bought villa near Nice. Solo show in Montréal, 1927; well-received. Returned to Montréal, fall 1931. Established The Atelier with Hazen Sise, George Holt, André Biéler; Lyman in charge of study classes. Established The Lyman Summer Art Class, St. Jovite, Québec, 1931. Began writing art reviews for *The Montrealer*, 1936. One-man show in New York, 1936. Met Paul-Emile Borduas, 1938. Co-founder and first president of Contemporary Arts Society, Montréal, 1939. Formed Eastern Group of Painters, 1939. Retrospective exhibitions at Dominion Gallery, Montréal, 1944; Montreal Museum of Fine Arts (sixty-two works), 1963; Musée du Québec (192 works), 1966. Published study of Morrice, 1944. Teaching: associate professor, Department of Fine Arts, McGill University, 1948-57 (appointed chairman, 1951). Died: Montréal, 1967. Large collection of his works donated by Mrs. Lyman to Musée du Québec; papers to Bibliothèque Nationale du Québec, Montréal, 1970.

COMMENTS BY THE ARTIST

The essential qualities of a work of art lie in the relationships of form to form, and of colour to colour. From these, the eye, and especially the trained eye, derives its pleasures and all artistic emotion. During, however, most of the 19th Century in the period known as the "Romantic Revival" the prevalence of a literary and sentimental point of view coupled with a representational technique resulted in a degradation of all "plastic" arts. The "modern" movement has been for the most part the return to a "classical" or formal point of view...

– John Lyman, "The Atelier, 1931" (brochure), quoted in *John Lyman* (Montréal: Montreal Museum of Fine Arts, 1963).

Feel truly, all the rest is eyewash.

– John Lyman, quoted by G. Campbell McInnes, "Contemporary Canadian Artists: No. 5 — John Lyman", *The Canadian Forum* (June 1937): 94.

I try to put the pervasive and permanent into a familiar mould.

– John Lyman, quoted by G.C. McInnes, "Contemporary Canadian Artists...": 94.

Fig. 1 John Lyman
Autoportrait 1918
Oil on canvas (73 x 60.3 cm)
Signed (u.l.): *Lyman*
Musée du Québec, Québec

GHITTA CAISERMAN-ROTH
(1923-   )

Painter, printmaker, teacher.

78   Born: Montréal, Québec, 2 March 1923. Began taking lessons from Alexander Bercovitch at age nine, 1931. Attended Montreal High School. Exhibited at Montreal Museum of Fine Arts at age twelve. First formal training at Parsons School of Design, New York, 1939-43; received Parsons Post-graduate Scholarship to study in Europe, 1942-43. Attended American Artists School for sketching classes and New York Art School under Moses Soyer, and later Art Students' League, New York, under Harry Sternberg, 1942-43. Then studied at Nova Scotia College of Art, Halifax. Returned to Montréal, 1944. Created Montreal Artists School with husband, Alfred Pinsky, Barbara Echkart and Harry Goodwin, 1946 (school closed 1952). Received O'Keefe Art Award, 1951, enabling her to travel to France and Italy. Won first Instituto Allende (Mexico) Scholarship, 1951. Began teaching at Sir George Williams University, 1952. Gave series of lectures on ''Turning Points in the History of Art'',

Montréal, 1952. Worked in graphics with Albert Dumouchel at Ecole des Beaux-Arts, Montréal, as part of Canada Council fellowship, 1961-62. Married Montréal architect Max Roth, 1962. Taught at Saidye Bronfman Centre, 1977, and at l'Université du Québec à Montréal and University of British Columbia, 1981; also at Mount Allison University Summer School and Queen's University Summer School. Societies: Federation of Canadian Artists (joined 1944); Canadian Group of Painters (1954); Royal Canadian Academy (associate, 1956); Print and Drawing Council of Canada. Awarded Canada Centennial Medal, 1967. Works in public and corporate collections across Canada. Travelling retrospective exhibition mounted by Sir George Williams University Art Galleries, 1981-82. Lives and works in Montréal.

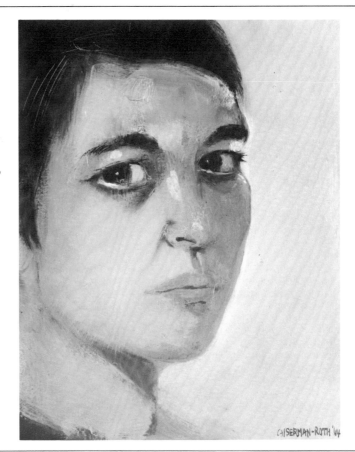

Fig. 1 Ghitta Caiserman-Roth
Self-Portrait in White (c. 1955)
Oil on masonite (60.9 x 30.5 cm)
Signed (l.r.): *CAISERMAN*
Private Collection, Montréal
Photo: courtesy, Sir George Williams Art Galleries, Concordia University, Montréal

CHRISTOPHER PRATT

(1935-   )

Painter and printmaker.

46 Christopher Pratt
The Graduate (Diploma Piece) or
Self-Portrait 1961
Oil on canvas (75 x 100.5 cm)
Signed and dated (l.r.): *Christopher Pratt '61*
Owens Art Gallery, Mount Allison
University, Sackville, New Brunswick
Photo: John Tamblyn, London

Note: Mount Allison University Fine Arts
Department student diploma piece,
submitted 1961

Born: St. John's, Newfoundland,
1935. Began painting with watercolours,
1952, while enrolled in Engineering,
Memorial University, St. John's.
Switched from pre-medicine, Mount
Allison University, Sackville, N.B., to
general arts course, Fine Arts
Department, 1953. Encouraged to
paint by Alex Colville and E. B.
Pulford (*q.v.*). Left before completing
course, 1955. Married fellow artist,
Mary West, 1957. Studied at Glasgow
School of Art, 1957-59 (drawing,
sculpture, design, lettering, crafts,
graphics), under Alex Dick. Returned
to Canada, 1959, and re-enrolled at
Mount Allison, graduating with B.F.A.
degree, 1961. Moved to St. John's,
became curator of Memorial University
Art Gallery and taught extension
classes at night, to 1963. Moved to St.
Mary's Bay, Newfoundland, 1964. First
group exhibition, London, Ontario,
1961; first solo exhibition, St. John's
Newfoundland. Participated in National
Gallery of Canada Biennial exhibitions,
1961-68. Travelling retrospective
mounted by Memorial University and
Gallerie Godard-Lefort, Montreal,
1970. Commissioned by Canada
Council Art Bank, 1978, to produce a
serigraphic print suitable for hanging
in government offices. Honours: Hon.
D. Litt., Mount Allison University,
1972; Hon. D. Litt., Memorial
University, 1972; Order of Canada,
1973. Elected associate, Royal
Canadian Academy, 1965. Works in
numerous public and corporate
collections.

COMMENTS BY THE ARTIST

When I was in art school,...we had a
very rigid form of instruction. We drew
from real plaster casts of Caesar — that
kind of thing. The teacher used to tell
us we had to remember that art was not
reality. And I've always remembered
that... I do try for precision... My
paintings are attempts to arrive at
precise visual definitions of things. It is
even possible to call them products of a
kind of personal research. My hope is
that the objects I paint have the kind
of intensity about them that incites the
viewer to introspection.

> – Christopher Pratt, quoted by Gary
> Michael Dault in ''Maritimes artist more
> than a realist'', *Toronto Star*, 25 October
> 1976.

It's a lonely, arrogant and selfish
business of researching your own
humanity, as if your own insights were
somehow worth recording or important
enough to be shared.

> – Christopher Pratt, quoted by Ann
> Johnston, ''A brooking vision'',
> *MacLean's* (21 September 1982): 37-38.

I never paint specifics. I avoid
identifying details. But I feel free to
return to my emotional and spiritual
sources. Everything I do is informed
and influenced by places I've been and
things I've seen. That's common to
anyone who makes something out of
''nothing'' — the nothing is really a
vast, complex range of experiences,
encounters and acquaintances.

> – Christopher Pratt, quoted in publicity
> package for *Christopher Pratt*, by David
> Silcox and Meriké Weiler (Toronto:
> Quintus Press, 1980).

Fig.1 Christopher Pratt
Self-Portrait 1968
Ink and gesso wash (20.3 x 10.2 cm)
Signed and dated (l.r.): *C. PRATT OCT.'68*
Inscribed (l.l.): *TO MARY*
Mary Pratt, St. John's, Newfoundland
Photo: T.E.Moore, Toronto

HUGH MACKENZIE
(1928-   )

Painter, printmaker, teacher.

47 Hugh Mackenzie
Self-Portrait 1965
Egg tempera on board (81.3 x 68.6 cm)
Signed and dated (l.r.): *HUGH MACKENZIE '65*
Musée des Beaux-Arts de Montréal, Horsley and Annie Townsend Bequest

80 Born: Toronto, 1928. Studied: Ontario College of Art, 1947-50, under Jock Macdonald, Carl Schaefer, Eric Friefeld; Mount Allison University, 1952-54, under Alex Colville. Lived and worked in Paris, 1950-51. Worked in Creative Department, Rolph, Clark, Stone Ltd., Toronto, 1954-55; illustrator, Avro Aircraft, Toronto, 1955-59. Teaching: instructor, H.B. Beal Technical School, London, Ontario, 1960-67; instructor, Art Gallery of Ontario, Toronto, 1967-69; instructor, Ontario College of Art, 1968-present; visiting lecturer, University of Waterloo, Waterloo, Ontario, 1973-75; visiting lecturer, University of Victoria, summer session, 1975. Societies: Ontario Society of Artists (elected 1961); Royal Canadian Academy (elected associate, 1972). Awards: J.W.L. Forster Award, Ontario Society of Artists, 1961; Special O.S.A. Award for *Self-Portrait*, 1966; Canada Council Grant, 1970. Commission: State portrait of the Hon. Lester B. Pearson for House of Commons, Ottawa, 1968. First solo exhibition, Hart House, University of Toronto, and London Art Gallery, London, Ontario, 1960. Paints in tempera and watercolours, does etching and lithography. Lives and works in Toronto.

COMMENTS BY THE ARTIST

I have always been my own painter. I paint what I want to paint. I am a realistic painter who is contemporary. I combine strong abstract with naturalism or realism.

···

The kind of painting I do is part of the culture around us.

···

My own training was too structured. I had to go out to work as an illustrator because all through my schooling and art training somebody told me what to do. I don't think I really started to pull it out of my own gut until I was almost thirty.

···

Their [i.e., art students'] drawing (or painting) is a way of finding information not only about the work but about themselves. This is difficult for them because they have been oriented to produce rather than experience. They will never do their good work until they have a sense of aloneness with their own work in their own studio...

···

You must know your own craft; you must be visually literate just as a writer is literate.

···

An artist is dealing with line, form, colour, space; all these things have to be orchestrated and it can't be done in a rational way. A lot of instinct is involved. Maybe it's all instinct.

···

I sure wouldn't like to live in a world without artists.

> – Hugh Mackenzie, quoted by Una O'Callaghan, in "'Real beauty must have strength,' painter says", *University of Waterloo Gazette*, 28 November, 1973.

Fig. 1 Hugh Mackenzie
Study for Self-Portrait 1965
Graphite on tracing paper (17.8 x 22.9 cm)
Collection: the artist, Toronto
Photo: T.E. Moore, Toronto

GREG CURNOE
(1936-   )

Painter, printmaker, filmmaker,
teacher, lecturer, musician

48 Greg Curnoe
Reggae Self-Portrait No. 4 1977
Pen-and-ink and watercolour
(61.4 x 45.8 cm)
Signed and dated (l.l.): *G. Curnoe/Jan. 20/1977*
Inscribed (u.c. to u.r.): *"I MAN WISH THAT I WOULD BRING BACK WHAT'S REAL AGAIN TO OUR LOVE"*
Collection: the artist, London, Ontario
Photo: London Regional Art Gallery

49 Greg Curnoe
Untitled Self-Portrait ("Canada") 1980
Watercolour on paper (30.3 x 30.5 cm)
Signed (l.r.): *Greg Curnoe*
Dated (u.r.): *June 26/80*
Inscribed (u.r.): *434 Pall Mall St.*
Danny and Paul Bercovitch, Montreal
Photo: Welt Studio of Photography
Limited, Montreal

Born: London, Ontario, 19 November 1936. Took art course at London Public Library and Art Museum, 1948. Attended H.B.Beal Technical and Commercial High School, London, studying in Special Art course under Herbert Ariss, John O'Henly, Mackie Cryderman, 1954-56. Art studies at Doon School of Art, Kitchener, Ontario, under Carl Schaefer and Alex Millar, 1956. Participated in first group exhibition at Garret Gallery, Toronto, 1957. Studied at Ontario College of Art, 1957-60 (failed May 1960, returned to London). Introduced to Dada in Toronto by Michel Sanouillet. Founded *Region* magazine, Spring 1961 (ninth and last issue, 1967). Organized first "happening" in Canada, London Public Library and Art Museum, 3 February 1963. Opened Region Gallery, London, November 1962 (in operation until end of 1963). First one-man exhibition at Gallery Moos, Toronto, September 1963. Nihilist Spasm Band formed, 1964 (Curnoe on kazoo). Founded co-operatively run 20/20 Gallery, London, 1966 (closed 1970). Received first Canada Council grant, 1966.

Painted controversial mural for Dorval Airport, Montréal, 1968. Began *View of Victoria Hospital, First Series*, 1968 (purchased by National Gallery of Canada, 1969). Among three Canadian artists represented at *X Biennial*, São Paulo, 1969. Wrote "Continental Refusal/Refus Continental" with John Boyle, 1970. Taught at University of Guelph, Ontario, 1979. First full-size bicycle cutout, *Zeus 10-Speed*, January 1972. Founded, with Pierre Théberge, the Association for the Documentation of Neglected Aspects of Culture in Canada, 1972. Taught at Emma Lake, Saskatchewan, July 1973. Artist in residence at University of Western Ontario, London, 1975-76. To England and Italy, 1976; represented Canada in XXVII Biennale di Venezia. Resident Artist at Ontario College of Art, 1976-77, Visiting Artist at Mount Allison University, Sackville, N.B., 1981. Travelling retrospective exhibition mounted by National Gallery of Canada, 1981-82. Lives and works in London.

COMMENTS BY THE ARTIST

My consciousness of regionalism is breaking down still further to my basic consciousness which is 75 Langarth Street East and most recently 38 Weston Street [London, Ontario]. And only after that: street, block, neighbourhood, city, township, county, province, dominion, world, solar system, cosmos, all of which become larger and more complicated. But because of mass media, I can sit in my house and an image of Egypt is on the T.V., Cuba is on the radio, and Edinburgh is on the 'phone. Are we always in balance between the macrocosm and the micrososm?

– Greg Curnoe, "Questions by Greg Curnoe", *Greg Curnoe: X Biennial Sao Paulo Brazil* (Ottawa: National Gallery of Canada, 1969), p. 67.

to be unselfconscious
to be anonymous
to be one with these legends…

– Greg Curnoe, "Statement", *Region* 2 (January 1962): 5

Fig. 1 Greg Curnoe seated beside his c. 1959 *Self-Portrait*, 21 June 1959
Photo: Don Vincent, London, Ontario

Fig. 2 *Self* 1960
Pen and India ink on paper (26.7 x 24.1 cm)
Walter Moos, Toronto
Photo: VIDA/Saltmarche, courtesy, National Gallery of Canada

Fig. 3 Greg Curnoe
1 Iron, First Hole, Thames Valley G.C., with Delaunay Sky 1971-78
Acrylic on plywood (243.9 x 243.9 cm)
Collection: the artist, London, Ontario
Photo: National Gallery of Canada, Ottawa

Fig. 1

Fig. 2

Fig. 3

PART III: FROM SELF-EXPRESSION TO SELF-IMPRESSION

For many artists, self-replication is not enough: their search for the essence of form and the communication of character extends itself beyond the devices of realistic portrayal into increasingly abstract, symbolic, or expressive realms. Ralph Mayer, in *A Dictionary of Art Terms and Techniques*, defines ''expressionism'' as

A concept of painting in which traditional adherence to canons of realism and proportion are over-ridden by the intensity of emotions, resulting in distortions of line, shape and color. Whereas the Impressionists were concerned with rendering nature in a new and more vivid way, such painters as the Fauves and Van Gogh, by considering their emotions as important as their subject matter, became the forerunners of expressionism. It was brought to the status of a full and vigorous movement by artists in Germany during the first quarter of the twentieth century...

Oskar Pfister, in *Expressionism in Art*, explains that The Expressionist wants to reproduce the intrinsic meaning of things, their soul-substance...From this point of view Impressionism appears as mere surface-art, and therefore a superficial art, a mechanical craft and not art at all. The Expressionist on the other hand creates out of the depth of things, the Absolute. The artist creates as God creates, out of his own inner Self, and in his own likeness.

The European Expressionist schools of the 1920s began to influence socially conscious Canadian painters in the Depression-ravaged 1930s, at the same time that the younger generation of artists began to rebel against the unpopulated northern wilderness subject-matter of the Group of Seven. This turn toward urban settings, the human presence, and overt political or psychological themes, however, was curtailed after World War II by the widespread adoption of Abstract Expressionism as the only acceptable style for the up-to-date artist. The modes that followed — Post-Painterly Abstraction, Minimalism, Concept-ualism, etc. — were not concerned with the representation of the body or of the face, although Pop Art did readmit the figure in an ironic context.

The Post-Modernist ''revolution'' of the 1970s has ushered in a so-called ''new spirit in painting'' in reaction to the formulistic proscription of human interest and content in art. The neo-expressionist movement of today happens to be largely a reaction to over-intellectualism on the part of artists who seek, in freeing themselves from formal rules of draughtsmanship, anatomy, and paint-application, an outlet for pent-up frustration, anger, *angst*, and longing. Also satisfied is the universal craving for recognizeable (even if not necessarily well-painted) images. This section of the exhibition traces the expressionistic impulse in Canadian art back to the late 1930s, and explores it forward into the late 1970s, the object being to demonstrate that the ''new-image'' boom follows upon a continuous, if not always well-known, orderly, or well-received, progression in our figurative art history. A constant throughout this process of synchronous development and return-to-basics is the confrontation of the eternal dualities of self and other, interior and exterior, negative and positive. Significantly, two of the artists selected for inclusion in this section represent themselves in the role of painter-at-work, as if in expression of the rigour behind the ritual of the creative act. The expressionistic mode has long served as a medium for the working out not only of emotional and sexual but of technical and aesthetic quandries. Reversion to self-portraiture (of an essentially symbolic nature) is an almost inevitable tactic for those engaged in the art-struggle who directly identify themselves with the subjects of their artistic endeavour and its problematic products. The age-old search for the essence of identity has forced self-portraitists of expressionistic bent to take again and again what Leslie Poole calls ''That one step...[of] looking in the mirror — to find the inside by painting the outside.'' But what of those artists who have attempted to go beyond the limits of self-obsession to address the hard facts of the physical world itself by pressing the substance of their beings up against the invisible but impenetrable barrier of the picture-plane (symbol of bounds as well as of horizons), or into the third dimension of solid matter itself? Those who deal creatively with the temporal, spacial, and spiritual dimensions are also participants in the ritual of self-expression-through-self-definition. In facing corporeal reality, all true artists, whatever their stylistic allegiances, concur with Kandinsky's fundamental dictum: *''Form is the outer expression of the inner content''*.

CAVEN ATKINS
(1907-)

Painter, printmaker, sculptor, designer, teacher.

84

Born: London, Ontario, 1907. Studied one year at Meyer Both Commercial Art School, Chicago, 1924, then at Winnipeg School of Art on scholarship under G.K. Gebhardt and L.L. Fitz-Gerald (*q.v.*), 1925-28. Worked as commercial artist at Bridgen's Ltd., Winnipeg, 1928. Toured art galleries in United States, 1929. Teaching experience: art instructor at Winnipeg School of Art, 1930-33; part-time classes at Central Technical School, Toronto, 1936; art instructor at University of Toronto, Hart House, Upper Canada College, Central Technical School and Queen's University Summer School, 1940; taught classes for the Windsor Art Association, 1945. Employed by Ford Motor Company, Detroit, Michigan, 1945-72. Societies: The Society of Manitoba Artists (elected 1929); Canadian Society of Painters in Water Colour (director, 1938-41, president, 1953-45); Canadian Group of Painters (1939); Canadian Society of Graphic Art (president, 1940-43); Federation of Canadian Artists (founding member, 1941); Ontario Association of Teachers of Art (2nd vice-president, 1944-45, 1st vice-president, 1945); Society of Engineering Illustrators, Detroit (organized first major exhibition, 1960). Donated the Atkins Memorial Collection to the Art Gallery of Windsor in trust for the people of Canada. Retrospective exhibition at the Art Gallery of Windsor, 1979. World War II paintings in National War Museum, Ottawa. Lives and works in Detroit.

COMMENTS BY THE ARTIST

I have never been really much into portraiture...other than the self portraits. The problems [are] particularly with the difficulties arising from the subject's and friends['] and relatives' differing views of what the subject should be like. Ugh!
...

An artist as a painter that knows what he is doing is formulating intellectually and isn't much of an artist in my view. He may be a good craftsman yes and worthy of respect but he is not what I call an artist. The true artist (painter) is a person who is looking and doing, he's reacting [—] "not this" [—] and changing or "accepting" and O.K.ing. To tell you true I still don't know how I painted the "Self Portrait After Shaving["]. It's always a fresh revelation to me.

— Caven Atkins, letter to Robert Stacey, 23 September 1983.

Fig. 1   Fig. 2   Fig. 3

LIONEL LEMOINE FITZGERALD
(1897-1956)

ch

at
s,

n
l
of
ba,

rt

gue

ly
n,
ng

.

Arts
ed

Appointed Principal of Winnipeg School of Art, 1929 (resigned, 1949). Travelled to U.S. and Canadian cities to look at art education facilities, 1930. Became member of Group of Seven, 1932, founding member of Canadian Group of Painters, 1933. Painted at Bowen Island, British Columbia, during summers of 1942-44. Met Lawren Harris in Vancouver, 1942. Entered ''abstract phase'' on retirement, early 1950s. To Mexico, 1951. Awarded honourary LL.D. from University of Manitoba, 1952. Died: Winnipeg, 5 August 1956. Memorial exhibition travelled to four Canadian galleries, 1958. *A New FitzGerald* (exhibition of 128 works) shown at Winnipeg Art Gallery, May 1963. Establishment of FitzGerald Study Centre, University of Manitoba, 1976.

COMMENTS BY THE ARTIST

It is necessary to get inside the object and push it out rather than merely build it up from the outer aspect... This requires endless search and contemplation; continuous effort and experiment; and appreciation for the endlessness of the living force which seems to pervade and flow through all natural forms, even though these seem on the surface to be so ephemeral.

– L.L.FitzGerald, ''FitzGerald on Art'', *L.L. FitzGerald 1890-1956: A Memorial Exhibition 1958* (Ottawa: National Gallery of Canada, 1958), unpag.

Consider technique as a means by which you say what you have to say and not as an end in itself. What you have to say is of the first importance; how you say it is always secondary.

– L.L.FitzGerald, quoted by Ferdinand Eckhardt, Introduction, *L.L. FitzGerald 1890-1956...*, unpag.

85

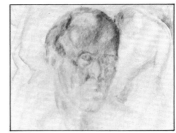

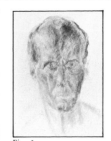

Fig. 1   Fig. 2   Fig. 3

MASHEL TEITELBAUM
(1921-)

Painter, teacher.

52 Mashel Teitelbaum
Dark Self 1957
Oil on canvas (101.6 x 76. 2 cm)
Signed (u.l.): *M. Teitelbaum*
Private collection
Photo: John Tamblyn, London

86

Born: Saskatoon, Saskatchewan, 1921. Studied: University of Saskatchewan, 1939-41; Mills College, Oakland, California, 1950, under Max Beckmann; California School of Fine Arts, 1950, under Clyfford Still, 1950. Teaching: School of Fine Arts, University of Manitoba, 1960; established the New School, Toronto, 1961. Lived and painted in the Qu'Appelle Valley, Saskatchewan, associated with James Henderson; Vancouver, Montréal, Toronto. Travelled in London, Brussels, Amsterdam, Paris, Barcelona. Worked as stage designer for C.B.C. T.V., Toronto, 1958. First group exhibition, Saskatoon, 1939; first solo exhibition, Regina, 1947. Travelling exhibition covered Western Canada Art Circuit, 1964-65. Regular one-man exhibitions with Gallery Moos, Toronto, 1963-78. Included in *Toronto Painting 1953-1965*, mounted by National Gallery of Canada, 1972, and in *Twentieth Century Canadian Drawings*, Gallery Stratford, Stratford, Ontario, 1979. Lives and works in Toronto.

COMMENTS BY THE ARTIST

What every painter is really painting is a self-portrait. He's trying to find himself all the time...he keeps questioning himself...

> – Mashel Teitelbaum, quoted by Nancy Phillips in ''This Art Trio Scores'', *The Telegram* (Toronto), 10 February 1964.

I would say that the self-portrait for the artist is an autobiographical essay. I have done over the years many self-portraits in various media and differing styles to record different and changing personas.
  Being an artist in Canada is not an easy role, and essaying one's self-image honestly in this role in relation to an indifferent and cold climate is always most difficult...

> – Mashel Teitelbaum, artist's statement, 5 August 1983.

Fig. 1 Mashel Teitelbaum
Self-Portrait 1956
Oil on canvas (159.9 x 124.5 cm)
Signed and dated (l.l.): *Mashel/Teitelbaum/56*
Private collection, Toronto
Photo: Imperial Oil Limited, Toronto

Fig. 2 Mashel Teitelbaum
Two-Gun Teitelbaum, the Terror from Saskatchewan 1983
Oil on canvas (115.6 x 86.4 cm)
Initialled and dated (u.l.): *MT '83*
Collection: the artist, Toronto
Photo: Miklos Legrady

GRAHAM COUGHTRY
(1931-   )

Painter, sculptor, printmaker.

53 Graham Coughtry
Self-Portrait III 1963
Oil and lucite on canvas (119.4 x 92.4 cm)
Carl T. Grant, Q.C., Toronto
Photo: courtesy, Isaacs Gallery, Toronto

Born: St. Lambert, Québec, 1931. Attended children's art classes conducted by Arthur Lismer (*q.v.*) at Montreal Museum of Fine Arts School. Worked in studio of his grandfather, sculptor Hubert Tompkins. Entered commercial course of Montreal School of Art and Design, then switched to Goodridge Roberts' (*q.v.*) painting classes, studying under Jacques de Tonnancour and Gordon Webber, 1948. Family moved to Toronto, 1949. Studied at Ontario College of Art under Jock Macdonald, Harley Parker, Fred Hagan (*q.v.*) and Eric Friefeld (graduated 1953). Won I.O.D.E. prize and T.Eaton Travelling Scholarship, 1953. To Spain, 1953-54, then Paris, 1954. Worked as graphic designer for C.B.C. - T.V., Toronto, 1956-59. Commissions: sculptured walls, Beth David Synogogue, Toronto, 1958; mural, Toronto International Airport, Malton, 1962; sculpture, Yorkdale Plaza, Toronto, 1963. To Ibiza, 1966-71. Returned to Toronto, 1971. Taught at New School of Art, York University, Ontario College of Art. Maintains studios in Toronto and Ibiza. Has exhibited nationally and internationally since first solo show at Greenwich Gallery, Toronto, 1955. Work in major public and corporate collections in Canada and United States, including Museum of Modern Art, New York; Detroit Institute of Arts; Albright-Knox Art Gallery, Buffalo; and Philadelphia Museum. Many prizes and awards, including Canada Council Senior Arts Grants, 1966 and 1973. Travelling retrospective organized by Robert McLaughlin Art Gallery, Oshawa, 1976-77.

COMMENTS BY THE ARTIST

[All of Coughtry's portrait paintings, including those called self-portraits, are intended primarily as attempts] to get something to *sit* there, to have some kind of reality — you're separate from that thing, and you're making a painting of it that tries to get at the reality of the confrontation with it… that *presence.*

– Graham Coughtry, quoted by Barrie Hale in *Graham Coughtry Retrospective* (Oshawa: The Robert McLaughlin Art Gallery, 1976), p.12.

Critics used to say that my pictures were about poignancy and loneliness of the human situation… Actually, they're about *painting itself* — about all the ways it's done and about the tactile wonder of how it works.''

– Graham Coughtry, quoted by Gary Michael Dault in ''Oil's Well that Ends Well'', *Toronto Life* (March 1983), p.83.

Fig.1 Graham Coughtry
Self-Portrait I 1963
Oil and lucite on canvas (129.5 x 99.1 cm)
Private collection
Photo: courtesy, Isaacs Gallery, Toronto

Fig.2 Installation view of *New Perceptions: Portraits*, The Art Gallery at Harbourfront, Toronto, 27 May - 26 June 1983, showing (left to right): Lynn Donoghue, *Mirror Imaged* (1983), Graham Coughtry, *Self-Portrait* (purchased by Art Gallery of Ontario), Joan Krawczyk, *Self-Portrait*, 1983.
Photo: Ihor Holubizky, courtesy, The Art Gallery at Harbourfront, Toronto
Note: dimensions of Coughtry self-portrait: 91.5 x 76 cm.

MAXWELL BATES
(1906-1980)

Painter, printmaker, teacher, architect.

54 Maxwell Bates
Self-Portrait 1965
Oil on canvas with collage (91.2 x 121.2 cm)
Signed and dated (l.r.): *MAXWELL BATES/1965*
Maltwood Art Museum and Gallery,
University of Victoria, Victoria, B.C.
Photo: Barnes Studio, Victoria, B.C.

88

Born: Calgary, Alberta, 14 December 1906. Began work in father's architectural office, 1924. Studied at Provincial Institute of Technology and Art, Calgary, under Lars Haukaness, 1926-27; at Brooklyn Museum School of Art, New York, under Max Beckmann and Abraham Rattner, 1949. To London, England, 1931, joined Lucy Wertheim's Twenties Group. Travelled in Germany, Belgium, France, 1936-37. Enlisted in Territorial Army, 1939, captured in France, 1940, prisoner-of-war, 1940-45. Returned to England, 1945, to Calgary, 1946, working as painter, architect, instructor of evening classes and children's art classes. To New York to study, 1949-50. Began to do lithography, 1953. Worked on St. Mary's Cathedral, Calgary, 1954-57. Travelled in Europe, 1958-59.
Societies: honourary member, Canadian Society of Graphic Art (elected 1947, Western Canada Representative, 1948); Canadian Society of Painters in Water Colour (elected 1951, second vice-president, 1952-53); Federation of Canadian Artists (elected 1947, chairman, Calgary Branch, 1947-48); Alberta Society of Artists (elected associate, 1947, full member, 1950, second vice-president, 1952-53); Royal Architectural Institute of Canada (elected 1951); Canadian Group of Painters (elected 1957); International Institute of Arts and Letters (elected Fellow, 1961); Royal Canadian Academy (elected associate, 1961, full academician, 1971). Honours: LLD., University of Calgary; Order of Canada, 1980. Retrospectives: 1960-61, Norman Mackenzie Art Gallery, Regina; Art Gallery of Great Victoria, 1966; Winnipeg Art Gallery, 1968; Vancouver Art Gallery, 1973; Art Gallery of Greater Victoria, 1982. Died: Victoria, B.C., 14 September 1980.

COMMENTS BY THE ARTIST

Unique, expressive statements interest me more than descriptive statements. I am more taken up by painting than by the subjects I paint. Experience gives me increased ability to transpose what I see. My intention is to transpose meaningfully. This amounts to expressionism, in my opinion... Good painting must offer something meaningful to the spectator, but it may be enigmatic. To convey emotional states of mind is not enough. Painter and spectator collaborate unconsciously.

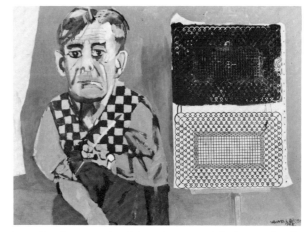

Intentional, prepared collaboration on the part of the painter is treason (he betrays himself), and the sentence is artistic death. But collaboration must take place because, at bottom, the aim is to convey something on one's own terms to the spectator who can respond... It is better to be awkward than facile. The important considerations are ethical. Painting is richly involved with quality and value.

> – Maxwell Bates, "Maxwell Bates on Painting" (reprinted courtesy of the National Gallery of Canada), in *Maxwell Bates: retrospective exhibition* (Regina: Norman Mackenzie Art Gallery, 1960).

The human face has always intrigued me.

> – Maxwell Bates, quoted in *Maxwell Bates in Retrospect: 1921-71* (Vancouver: Vancouver Art Gallery, 1973).

Fig. 1 Maxwell Bates
Self-Portrait 1950
Oil on canvas board (50.3 x 40.5 cm)
Signed and dated (l.r.): *MAXWELL BATES 1950*
Private collection

Fig. 2 Maxwell Bates
Self-Portrait (c. 1956)
Oil on canvas (73 x 52.8 cm)
Private collection, Calgary

HAROLD KLUNDER
(1943-)

Painter, printmaker, sculptor, teacher.

55 Harold Klunder *
Self-Portrait in Four Parts 1980-83
Oil on canvas (152.4 x 365.8 cm)
Signed and dated (*verso*, on panel 4):
Harold Klunder 1980-83
Sable-Castelli Gallery, Toronto
Photo: T.E. Moore, Toronto
Note: Klunder's head and shoulders appear
on the third panel from the right; those of
his companion Catherine appear in panel 1

Born: Deventer, Netherlands, 1943.
Immigrated to Canada, 1952. Studied:
Central Technical School (Art Course),
Toronto (graduated 1964). Worked as
graphic designer, 1964-71, winning
numerous awards. Teaching (design):
part-time instructor at Ontario College
of Art, 1969-70; guest lecturer at
Ontario Gollege of Art, 1971-72. Lived
and worked in Vancouver, 1973. First
solo exhibition, Toronto, 1974;
numerous one-man and group shows
since. Participated in Art Gallery of
Ontario Extension Services' "Artists
with their Work" programme, 1977,
1978, 1979. Works in many public and
corporate collections. Moved to
Flesherton, Ontario, 1983.

COMMENTS BY THE ARTIST

Historically, art is the great leveller, the
last haven for truth good and bad...
...

I'm intelligent enough to make good
shapes and paint pleasing pictures in
the Greenberg convention. But there's
more to painting than that. Painting is
more than an object. It is an
involvement. How can you exclude

ugliness from art when it can't be
excluded from the world?

– Harold Klunder, quoted by James
Purdie in "A painter swims against the
tide to break the ties with New York",
Globe and Mail, 24 September 1977.

In order to make something beautiful
in its totality you're forced to do
certain parts that are quite ugly or
quite grotesque... It's a real easy thing
to say that something has chaos and
has order at the same time, but all of
life has chaos and order. It's a gross

over-simplification of my work, I
think. Any painting, even if it looks
chaotic at first, if you spend any time
with it [, it] becomes extremely calm.
Some paintings are almost Turner-like,
they spin for a while, but then they
become very relaxed, quiet.

– Harold Klunder, quoted by Karyn
Allen in *David Craven/Harold Klunder*
(Winnipeg: The Winnipeg Art Gallery,
1980), p. 30.

Fig. 1 Harold Klunder
Tree, Wheatfield and Mountain (Self-Portrait)
1980-82
Oil on canvas (152.5 x 152.5 cm)
Collection: Art Gallery of Ontario, Toronto
Photo: T.E. Moore, Toronto

Fig. 2 Harold Klunder
Self-Portrait IV 1983
Conté, ink and watercolour on paper
(55.9 x 76.2 cm)
Signed and dated (l.r.): *Klunder/3.28.82*
Signed and dated (*verso*): *H. Klunder/3/28/83*
Inscribed (*verso*): *Self Portrait/IV*
Collection: the artist, Flesherton, Ontario

* *Exhibited at the London Regional Art Gallery
only*

LESLIE POOLE
(1942-   )

Painter and teacher.

56 Leslie Poole
Time Bomb 22 October 1977
Acrylic on canvas (152.5 x 228.5 cm)
Signed (l.r): *leslie poole*
Collection: the artist, Vancouver
Photo: Robert Keziere/The Vancouver Art
Gallery

90 Born: Halifax, Nova Scotia, 3 May 1942. Studied: University of Alberta, Edmonton, 1963-67 (B.F.A. degree, 1967); Yale University, New Haven, Connecticut, 1968-70 (M.F.A. degree, 1970). Teaching: sessional instructor, University of Alberta, Edmonton, 1971-72; instructor of drawing, Banff School of Fine Arts, 1973; painting seminar, Banff School of Fine Arts, 1979; painting seminar, Alberta College of Art, Calgary, 1979; instructor in drawing, Douglas College, Surrey, B.C., 1980; lecturer in drawing and design, Vancouver Community College (Langara Campus), Vancouver 1975-83. First group exhibition, New Haven, 1969; first Canadian solo exhibition, Toronto, 1970. Awards: Queen Elizabeth Scholarship, 1967; Alberta Visual Arts Scholarship, 1968; Yale University Scholarship, 1968; Province of Alberta Grants, 1968 and 1969; Alberta Visual Arts Scholarship, 1969; Yale University Scholarship, 1969; Canada Council Arts Grants, 1972, 1974, 1975, 1980. Elected member of Royal Canadian Academy, 1981. Commissions: portrait, Lieutenant-Governor of Alberta, 1973; Crown Zellerbach, Vancouver, 1978. Represented in numerous public and corporate collections. Lives and works in Vancouver.

COMMENTS BY THE ARTIST

The self-portraits were my first attempts at translating ideas through form into art. My previous paintings were about things that were of interest to me — generally what those things looked like. The portraits were no longer just about me; rather they *were* me.

The self-portraits were begun to deal with my awareness of myself as an angry person. The first lesson of importance was that I could not just be angry on canvas with a loaded brush. The anger had to be translated through form — otherwise one had Susanne Langer's "frozen tantrum". To do this I had to take a step away from anger in order to formalize into art. That one step away was to get a bit "outside" of myself, my anger. That one step out was looking in the mirror — to find the inside by painting the outside. (Since then I have considered all of my works: Man in the Bath, Still Life, Women, Irises, Children, etc., as self-portraits.)

My interest in the self-portraits was to find out about what I was closest to: myself. Then there would be some chance that when that self was expressed in paint, I would know if I was right or not. Regardless of any rules of expression or form which I had

learned, I would know if that piece of art expressed me or not. I often had to break my thoroughly learned rules to get the painting right, but from then on I knew that I was the creator, and I would be the one to decide if my art was art, if it was right or wrong. A critic once said I was "self centered". Thank goodness. Where else should one be centered but in himself/herself? Eventually one who looks deeply enough within himself/herself and learns to translate that information into the language of visual art, will find what he/she has in common with humanity and the self-portraits will be portraits of what it feels to be human. They will be expressions, re-expressions, neo-expressions of the human soul, of its condition.

That is what my art is about. That is why all my painting is self-portraiture.

– Leslie Poole, artist's statement, 11 April 1983.

Fig.1 Leslie Poole
Signal 9 October 1977
Acrylic on canvas (152.4 x 228.6 cm)
Signed (l.r.): *leslie poole*
Collection: the artist, Vancouver
Photo: courtesy, Bau-Xi Gallery, Toronto

Fig. 2 Leslie Poole
Burgundy Portrait 23 December 1978
Acrylic on canvas (152.5 x 228.5 cm)
Collection: the artist, Vancouver
Photo: Russell Keziere/The Vancouver Art
Gallery

GARY OLSON

(1946-   )

Draughtsman, printmaker, teacher.

Born: Minneapolis, Minnesota, January 1946. Became Canadian landed immigrant, 1973. Studied: Minneapolis College of Art and Design, Minnesota (B.A., 1969); Indiana University (M.A., 1973). Teaching: printmaking instructor, University of Alberta, Edmonton, 1973-75; visiting artist, University of Saskatchewan, Saskatoon, summer, 1975; drawing and printmaking instructor, The Alberta College of Art, Calgary, Alberta, 1975-present. First group exhibition, 1967; first solo exhibition, Coon Rapids, Minnesota, 1969; first Canadian one-man show, Edmonton Art Gallery, 1976. Work included in exhibitions in Biella, Italy; Miami, Florida; and Cracow, Poland, 1980. Awarded first place, *4th Miami International Print Biennial Exhibition*, Metropolitan Museum and Art Centre, Miami, 1980. Works in numerous public and corporate collections in Canada and United States. Lives and works in Cochrane, Alberta.

COMMENTS BY THE ARTIST

As with most artists who work with illusion in a representational manner, I want to create an illusion of a three dimensional image existing in a specific space on a flat two dimensional surface. However, I do not consider myself a "realist" in the traditional sense. Both my emotional reactions towards the subject, and the actual drawing process have priority over a camouflaging of the drawing for the sake of a totally illusionistic image.

The self-portrait as subject matter in my work evolved from an early interest with drawing myself which has existed since my days as an art student in Minneapolis.

In 1976 my self-portrait drawings developed into a series of pictures dealing simultaneously with the self-portrait and the concept of the picture plane. My interest in this series developed directly from my experience with teaching drawing to art students, and attempting to instill in the students an awareness of the theoretical existence of the picture plane as an integral part of image making.

My personal approach to the picture plane is to use my image (self-portrait) in a satirical reaction to the serious issue (seriousness) of the integrity of the picture plane. I have taken the concept of the picture plane quite literally and developed an almost caricaturist approach to it. I enjoy satirizing the picture plane both as I confirm and deny it.

In order to establish and define the picture plane I press, push, smash, squeeze, squash or touch my head, various parts of my face (eyes, nose, lips, cheeks, tongue, hair), and occasionally other body parts such as my hands against the imaginary transparent plane of reference. In a sense, I am making fun of art by making fun of myself. My intention is to make fun of Art. My self-portraits represent my personality, while Art is represented by the picture plane. Since I am using my image to satirize the picture plane both the self and the picture plane (Art) are the subject matter of this series. The meaning of my work is conveyed through and by the subject matter, and the manner in which the subject is presented. For me, the subject and the content of my pictures are interrelated, they depend upon each other.

Besides my image I frequently incorporate objects of personal significance from my actual environment to satirize the picture plane. The objects are chosen for their multiple interpretations, varied associations and connotations, their humour when juxtaposed with my image, and the heightened sense of absurdity when they are used in the context of my self-portrait picture plane series...

My deliberate use of fairly explicit and unusually lengthy titles for some of my work in this series grew from my initial self-portrait picture plane drawing entitled "I am Denying and Confirming the Picture Plane" (1976), and has continued throughout the series. All my titles evolve directly from the concept of the individual picture.

I believe my series of self-portrait drawings makes a statement about Art partly as a result of my personality which is contained within my work. However, rather than a self-conscious attempt to make a statement about Art with my work, I allow my personal attitudes regarding Art to surface subconsciously in my work.

Conceptually speaking, my ideas are intellectual but the resultant picture is emotive. My images demand a highly emotional response even though my concepts are intellectually based. I am interested in a strong, dramatic impact upon the viewer in order to solicit an emotional response. Working on a larger-than-life scale forces the viewer to acknowledge the presence of the picture and to establish a relationship with the work.

In my work on the abstract level, I am concerned with investigating and analyzing the subjects' smaller shapes and forms as they relate to and collectively comprise the larger whole, and ultimately their relationship to the

57 Gary Olson
*I am Up Against the Picture Plane
Again* 1977
Graphite on paper (76 x 101.6 cm)
Signed (l.r.): *Gary Olson*
Galerie Dresdnere, Toronto
Photo: T.E.Moore, Toronto

58 Gary Olson
Cataract 1980
Graphite on paper (76 x 101.6 cm)
Galerie Dresdnere, Toronto
Photo: T.E.Moore, Toronto

92 total picture. The large scale and close-up views allow me to select and record the smaller shapes, forms, and surfaces.

I emphasize the differences in topography within the configuraton of the head which enables me to deal with the shapes, forms, textures and values/tones of the subject. I am able to construct the structure and volume of the head through these surface qualities and the effects of light.

In summary, my primary objectives with the self-portrait picture plane drawings are introspective self-examination, and humour, mostly the satirical kind.

– Gary Olson, artist's statement, May 1983.

Recently, I have physically, spiritually, figuratively, emotionally, and literally moved away from the picture plane. The picture plane has temporarily, and maybe permanently, been relegated to a less significant role in my current work. At the moment, I am totally concentrating on the issue of the self-portrait.

My latest self-portrait pictures have travelled in two basic but separate directions. In my initial pictures after the picture plane, I used a magnifying glass which enlarged and distorted parts of my facial anatomy, principally my eyes. The primary idea was two fold. Firstly, I wanted to poke fun at the manner in which people closely examine pictures. Secondly, I was engaging in a type of satirical self-examination by focusing on my left eye which is legally blind and has recently developed a cataract. Obviously this is an in-joke, unperceptable to most people who look at the pictures, and with a brand of humour that will probably have a limited audience.

My current self-portraits incorporate food imagery which is not new, but they do not use the picture plane directly. I am combining more than a single self-portrait image into one picture...I am interested in combining two, three or four images into one picture creating a diptych, tripych, or possibly a ''totem pole'' image...

– Gary Olson, letter to Robert Stacey, 10 May 1983.

57

58

Fig.1 Gary Olson
Self-Portrait 1974
Graphite on paper (76 x 101.6 cm)
Signed and dated (l.r.): *Gary Olson '74*
Inscribed (l.l.): *''Self Portrait August '74''*
Art Gallery of Hamilton, Hamilton, Ontario, Gift of the Hamilton Trust and Savings Corporation, 1975

COLETTE WHITEN
(1945-   )

Sculptor and teacher.

Born: Birmingham, England, 7 February 1945. Emigrated with family to Canada, October 1954. Became Canadian citizen, June 1975. Studied: Ontario College of Art, Toronto, 1968-72, under John Noel Chandler, Hugh Leroy, and Royden Rabinowitch. Teaching: instructor, O.C.A., 1974-present; instructor, Gallery School, Art Gallery of Ontario; resident artist, University of Western Ontario, London, 1978-79. Introduced plaster-mold sculptures at first solo exhibition, Carmen Lamanna Gallery, Toronto, 1973. First use of colour in negative-relief plaster sculptures in *Untitled* (1977). First group exhibition, Toronto, 1972; first solo exhibition, Kingston, 1973. Exhibited at *8e Biennale de Paris*, Paris, 1973. Solo exhibitions, Carmen Lamanna Gallery, Toronto, 1973-75, 1977-81; Scarborough College, Toronto, 1974; London Regional Art Gallery, 1978; McIntosh Gallery, University of Western Ontario, 1979. Included in *Some Canadian Women Artists*, National Gallery of Canada, Ottawa, 1975; *Celebration of the Body*, Agnes Etherington Art Centre, Kingston, 1976; *Realism: Structure and Illusion*,

MacDonald Stewart Art Centre, Guelph, Ontaro, 1981; *Contemporary Figurative Sculpture*, Agnes Etherington Art Centre, Kingston, 1981; *The First Austrialian Sculpture* Triennial, Bundoora, Victoria, Australia, 1981; *"3 + 3 = 9" Sculptors in Exchange: Australia and Canada*, The Art Gallery at Harbourfront, Toronto, 1981. Commissions: sculpture, Art Gallery of Ontario, 1972; Government of Canada Building sculpture, North York, Ontario, 1976; Mental Health Centre sculpture, Toronto, 1978; Sudbury and District Chamber of Commerce Centennial Project, Sudbury, Ontario, 1983. Awards and grants: Governor General's Medal, Ontario College of Art, 1972; Timothy Eaton Travelling Scholarship, O.C.A., 1972; Canada Council grants and bursaries, 1972, '73, '76, '77, '78, '80; Ontario Arts Council grants, 1974 and '77. Work in collections of Art Gallery of Ontario, Toronto; Canada Council Art Bank, Ottawa, and National Gallery of Canada. Lives and works in Bowmanville, Ontario.

COMMENTS BY THE ARTIST

Throughout the working of all my pieces, I am specifically concerned with the total process. The initial concept..., the planning, the building of the structure..., and the actual casting process and documentation. These are all essential factors.

– Colette Whiten, untitled artist's statement, "Colette Whiten", *Eclectic Eve* (Toronto: Women's Educational Press, 1972), unpag.

Earlier work consisted of supporting structures, documentation of the casting process and the end product all centred around particular relationships with people. The confronting structures and the documentation portray the intensity of the casting process and the shared concern of the participants.

My recent work, using negative images, makes this vital aspect more direct. One is aware of the enclosing space that a person occupied and becomes conscious of the person and how the space was defined...

– Colette Whiten, "Colette Whiten", *Artscanada* 34 (May-June 1977): 55.

I don't think of the pieces as sinister at all...When I'm confronted with one of my negative human spaces, I like to fit myself imaginatively into that space. I like to feel the other person's space around me.

Some people think they're a bit spooky, I guess...But on the other hand, one of the visitors to the gallery described them as "familial,"...

– Colette Whiten, quoted by Gary Michael Dault, "Sculptor Colette Whiten builds her work from air", *Toronto Star*, 20 May 1978.

59 Colette Whiten *
Colette (A: front view; B: rear view)
1977-78
Wood, burlap, plaster (215.9 x 254 x
74.9 cm)
Carmen Lamanna Gallery, Toronto
Photo: Henk Visser, Toronto
Note: in background of ''B'': *Patrick*
(1977-78)

94

A

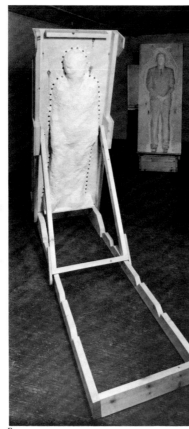

B

Fig. 1 Colette Whiten
September 1975: Unit # 1 1975
Plaster molds, fiberglass, wood, metal, rope,
burlap, paint (203.21 x 148.6 x 84.5 cm)
National Gallery of Canada, Ottawa
Photo: courtesy, Carmen Lamanna Gallery,
Toronto
Note: one of three units.

* *Exhibited at the London Regional Art Gallery
only*

PART IV: "DOUBLE VISIONS, DOUBLE MASKS": QUOTATIONS, APPROPRIATIONS, COLLATIONS

The self-portraits in this section may loosely be characterized as being "about" other art or artists, or "about" the *oeuvres* and/or personae of the individual self-portraitists here represented. Their work in this genre is notable for its inclusion of "quotations" either from their own previous compositions or of personal forms of imagery, stylistic devices, or autobiographical references. It likewise makes frequent allusions to painters or sculptors by whom the artist in question was influenced, or with whom he or she "identifies".

Such referencing, citation, and homage-making are hardly new in art. Sir Joshua Reynolds devoted his sixth Discourse, delivered in 1774, to the subjects of "Imitation" and "Borrowing". "INVENTION", he averred, "is one of the great marks of genius, but if we consult experience, we shall find that it is by being conversant with the inventions of others that we learn to invent: as by reading the thoughts of others we learn to think." Reynolds' admonition to his Royal academy auditors to "Study...the works of the great masters, forever" began to fall on deaf ears with the advents first of European Romanticism, then of international Modernism. Both movements celebrated the individual

Self, exalting "originality" and its spontaneous effusions over careful study and reverent observation. Both arose in necessary revolt against stultifying convention, but both, eventually, lost their *raison d'être* and their energy. Freedom of self-expression was found to be insufficient justification for committing art if the artists had no selves to express.

With the Post-Modernist counter-reformation of the 1970s and '80s, the *open* observance of the fact that most (if not all) art is "imitative", is "about" art, is a reflection of a reflection, has produced a spate of works in every medium and style that explore the terms thrown out to his students by the President of the Royal Academy in 1774: borrowing, gathering, depredation, appropriating, assimilating, submitting to infection (or contagion), being impressed, being fertilized, being impregnated.

Attempts to reduce an infinitude of possibilities to order assume a variety of forms, reflective of the multiplicity of approaches now available to artists who seek release from contemporary alienation through the quotational, parodistic and ironic impulses, rather than through the now-suspect trope of "psychological interpretation". This assimilative compulsion may result

simply in the integrating of elements of past achievements into visual summings-up of an autobiographical or retrospective bent, such as Jean-Paul Lemieux' child-is-father-to-the-manneristic *Autoportrait* of 1974 (See Cat. No. 61), painted in celebration of an international exhibition devoted to his work. Or it may involve a more complex reflection on the tense relationship between imitation and individual talent, such as John Hall's minutely detailed, blown-up airbrush replicas of collages and maquettes and snapshots of his own or his collaborators' construction or taking (see Cat. Nos. 69, 70). What rarely emerges from all these echoings and mirrorings, maskings and unmaskings is a sense of self-critical analysis being applied to the multifarious material being fed on and, in the process, transformed. When does self-referentiality descend into the realm of the reductively incestuous? When is the allusive merely derivative?

In this age of mechanical reproduction and instantaneous electronic communications, the work of art seen by the student and beginning artist is likely to be in second-hand form. The notion of scale and the nature of surfaces tend to get lost in glossy magazine, book and

catalogue reproductions. But from such sources can be constructed a mental museum in scrapbook or collage format, and often such incongruous juxtapositions of past and present as are tacked up on a bulletin-board or studio wall are translated directly to canvas (or to videotape, or into performance).

The result is creative chaos. The plurality of choices now available to artists for adaptation, commentary and parodying are reflected in the synonyms employed by critics to denote the activities of the borrowers, stealers and spenders: quoting, imitating, transposing, echoing, glossing, artistic trespass and repercussion, paraphrasing, excerpting, referencing, anthologizing, appropriating, expropriating...And finally, there is the process of *collating* past and present imagery into a coherent statement to the future about the self and the art produced by the imaginative but also receptive and retentive consciousness, operating on all of art history as well as on the collective unconscious.

THOMAS REID MACDONALD
(1908-1978)

See also Catalogue No. 37 for Biography.

60 T.R. MacDonald
Yorimoto
Oil on canvas (81.5 x 81.5 cm)
Signed and dated (l.r.):
T R MACDONALD 1960
Mrs. T.R. MacDonald, Hamilton
Note: see also Catalogue No. 37

JEAN-PAUL LEMIEUX
(1904-)

Painter and teacher.

Born: Quebec City, 18 November 1904. Began drawing seriously at age thirteen, influenced by American artist named Parnell. Moved with family to Berkeley, California, 1916-17. Studied: Collège Loyola, Montréal; Ecole des Beaux-Arts de Montréal, 1926-29, 1930-34, under Charles Maillard, Edwin Holgate, Maurice Felix, etc. To London, then studied at Grande Chaumière and Académie Colarossi, Paris, 1929; met Clarence Gagnon. Returned to Montréal, 1939; set up commercial art studio with Jean Palardy. Teaching: Ecole des Beaux-Arts de Montréal, 1933-34; professor, painting and drawing, Ecole du Meuble, Montréal, 1935-36; professor of painting, Ecole du Beaux-Arts de Québec, 1937-65; summer school, University of British Columbia, Vancouver, 1958. *Lazare* (1941; Art Gallery of Ontario, Toronto) introduced new allegorical style; turned to new symbolic figure-in-landscape mode, 1956. To France on Canada Council Scholarship, 1954-55. Societies: Royal Canadian Academy (elected associate, 1951, full academician, 1956); Canadian Group of Painters (1950-69). Exhibited with R.C.A., 1934-54. First solo exhibition, Québec, 1953; participated in *Développement de la peinture du Canada*, UNESCO, Paris, 1954; Biennale de São Paulo, Brazil, 1957; Pittsburgh International, 1958; Biennale de Venice, 1960; *Eleven Canadian Artists*, Tate Gallery, London, 1963; *Sept Peintres Canadiens*, Musée Galliéra, Paris, 1963. Retrospective exhibition mounted by Musée des Beaux-Arts de Montréal, 1967. One-man exhibition travelled to Moscow, Leningrad, Prague, Paris, 1974. Awards: Prix Brymner, l'Ecole des Beaux-Arts de Montréal, 1934; premier prix de peinture, for *Les Ursulines* (Musée du Québec), 1951; boursier de la Société Royale pour outremers, 1954-55; Order of Canada, 1968; doctorates *honoris causa*, l'Université Laval de Québec and Bishops University, Lennoxville, Québec, 1971; Prix Philippe Hébert, la Société Saint-Jean-Baptiste de Montréal, 1971. Studio at Ile-aux-Coudres, St. Lawrence River, Québec.

61 Jean-Paul Lemieux
Autoportrait 1974
Oil on canvas (78.7 x 162.6 cm)
Signed and dated (l.r.): *Jean-Paul/Lemieux
'74*
Private Collection, Ile-aux-Courdres,
Quebec
Photo: courtesy, Anne-Sophie Lemieux
Note: canvas with figure in background is
Lemieux's *Le Visiteur du soir* (1956;
National Gallery of Canada, Ottawa)

COMMENTS BY THE ARTIST

I'm not a landscape painter. Don't call me that. I like painting figures too much. When I get tired of landscapes I paint figures. I never use models; I couldn't. I try to convey a remembrance, the feeling of generations. I sometimes see myself as the central figure, but as a child in the continuity of generations.

– Jean-Paul Lemieux, quoted by Patrick Nagle in ''Timeless Painter from Québec'', *Weekend Magazine*, No. 10 (1963): 19

I paint because I love to paint, I guess. I have no theories, and like everyone else who paints, I am never satisfied with my work. I am especially interested in conveying the solitude of man and the ever flowing passing of time. I try to express in my landscapes and my figures this solitude, this silence in which we all move…The physical world around me interests me only because it allows me to picture my inner self.

– Jean-Paul Lemieux, quoted by Clare Bice, ''the enchanted, lonely world of Jean-Paul Lemieux'', *Jean-Paul Lemieux: Retrospective Exhibition* (London: London Regional Art Gallery, 1966), unpag.

I've always loved old yellowed photographs, family albums…and when I'm in my studio, confronted by the empty canvas, something appears in my mind's eye from very far away. People appear, hazily, people from my own inner world. It's through memory that I make them my own…

– Jean-Paul Lemieux, quoted by Gary Michael Dault, ''Lemieux damned by verbose praise'', *Toronto Star*, 20 January 1979.

97

LYNN DONOGHUE
(1953-)

Painter and teacher.

98

Born: Red Lake, Ontario, 1953. Grew up in Meaford, Ontario. Studied at H.B. Beal Secondary School, London, Ontario, under Herbert Ariss (Special Art Diploma, 1972). Canada Council grants 1974, '76, '78, '79-80. Visited Alice Neel in New York, 1976. Taught at London Art Gallery, 1975-76; Three Schools of Art, Toronto, 1976-79; Arts' Sake, Toronto, 1978-79; Laurentian University Museum and Arts Centre, Sudbury, Ontario, 1978-79; Artists in the Schools, York County Board of Education/Ontario Arts Council, York Co., Ontario, 1978. First group exhibition, 1973; first solo show, Richard E. Crouch Resource Centre, London, Ontario, 1977. First visit to Europe, 1979. Numerous solo and group exhibitions nationwide since then. Represented in *Certain Traditions: Recent British and Canadian Art*, Edinburgh Art Gallery, 1978. Commissioned to paint official portrait of Ontario Speaker of the Legislature, the Hon. Jack Stokes, 1978. Did poster for thirtieth anniversary season of Canadian Opera Company, 1980. Represented in Canadian public and corporate collections. Lives and works in Toronto.

COMMENTS BY THE ARTIST

I want to paint people...I always wanted to paint the figure...It's hard to make that decision in Canada...The notion is that to be a good, serious artist you must work in the abstract. There's a leap of faith people have to go through to say, "I'm working with the figure," as though it's something decidedly kinky...I work within a specific art historical context...
...
I'm not dumb enough to exclude art history.

I'm ultimately the complete humanist... Why am I doing figures: Why am I not doing bananas?...I paint people to get something. What I get I'm not sure.

– Lynn Donoghue, quoted by Adele Freedman in "Art: Lynn Donoghue: simply figured portraits", *Toronto Life* (January 1979): 80, 84

Fig. 1 Lynn Donoghue
Mirror Image 1983
Acrylic, oil, mixed media on masonite, charcoal on paper (installation dimensions: 244 x 450 cm)
Collection of the artist, Toronto
Photo: Ihor Holubizky, courtesy, The Art Gallery of Harbourfront, Toronto

Exhibited at the London Regional Art Gallery only

DENNIS BURTON

(1933-)

Painter, teacher, writer, lecturer, musician.

63 (A-E) Dennis Burton

A *Signs/Symbols* I 11 April 1969
Graphite on paper (27.3 x 20.6 cm)
Signed (l.r.): *DENNIS BURTON*
Dated (u.r.): *4/11/69*
Inscribed (u.r.): *NOTEBOOK 8/SIGNS/ SYMBOLS*

B *Signs/Symbols* II 11 April 1969 (*verso of Signs/Symbols* I)
Graphite on paper (27.3 x 20.6 cm)
Signed (l.c.): *DENNIS BURTON*
Dated (u.c.): *4/11/69*
Inscribed (u.c. and u.c.): *NOTEBOOK 8/...SIGNS/SYMBOLS*

C *Self-Portrait* 11 November 1972
Ink on paper (27.3 x 20.6 cm)
Signed and dated (l.r.): *DENNIS BURTON/11.11.72*
Dated (u.r.): *11.11.72*
Inscribed (u.l.): *SELF-PORTRAIT/ NOTEBOOK 38 PAGE 6*

Sequence continued next page.

Born: Lethbridge, Alberta, 6 December 1933; Attended Pickering College, Newmarket, Ontario, 1950-51; studied art under Fred Hagan (*q.v.*). Studied at Ontario College of Art in Painting and Drawing Programmes (four scholarships), under Jock MacDonald and Fred Hagan, 1952-56. Summer studies at University of Southern California with Rico Lebrun and Frances deErdeley, 1955; at Skowhegan School of Painting, Skowhegan, Maine, with Ben Shahn, William Zorach, etc., 1959; and at Fairleigh Dickinson University, Madison, New Jersey, 1967. Many awards, prizes, and fellowships. Worked as a freelance commercial and editorial illustrator, 1957-75, and in Design Department, C.B.C. Television, Toronto, 1957-60. Mural commissioned for Edmonton International Airport, 1963. Seven portrait commissions, 1955-75. Illustrated Jon Whyte's poem, *Homage to Henry Kelsey* (Winnipeg: Turnstone Press, 1981). Teaching positions: York University, Humanities Department, 1966-68; The Artists' Workshop (Three Schools, Toronto), 1965-66; co-founder (1965) and Director (1971-76), The New School of Art, Toronto; Chairman, Drawing and Painting Department, Ontario College of Art, 1970-71;

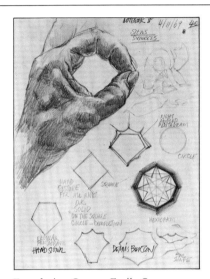

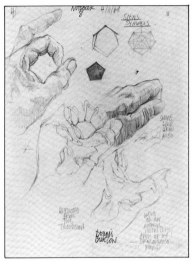

Foundation Course, Emily Carr College of Art, Vancouver, 1979 - present. Numerous one-man and group-exhibitions, beginning 1956. Retrospective exhibition toured by The Robert McLaughlin Art Gallery, Oshawa, Ontario, 1977-79.

COMMENTS BY THE ARTIST

As an artist I am a draughtsman or "line-man", and it is this love of line that is similar to my love of "line" in musical composition.

> – Dennis Burton, "Introduction...", "Special Dennis Burton Issue", *Musicworks*, No. 11 (Spring 1980), p. 3.

"Hmm, portraits?...*You could make a whole show of my portraits*!!"

> – Dennis Burton, letter to Robert Stacey, 23 May 1983.

No, I never did a "large" self-portrait that you could call representational/ recognizeable — but in my drawings...there's at least 4 that are, lifesize — or over. Other than that can't you broaden the category? Isn't everything — every painting — I've done auto-biographical-autofeedback-ical? Especially "Bad Good Friday" [1974-75; Robert McLaughlin Gallery, Oshawa]...and "Suspicion" [1975; Isaacs Gallery, Toronto], and "Before Goldberg", 1961 - 72" x 72" — male eroticism — me...

> – Dennis Burton, letter to Robert Stacey, 13 June 1983, p. 9.

Fig. 1 Albrecht Dürer (1471-1528) *Selbstbildnis* c. 1493 Ink on paper (28 x 20.3 cm) Lehman Collection, New York

Fig. 2 Gordon Rayner and Dennis Burton *D.B. at P.T.* 1964 Mixed media on canvas (180.5 x 122 cm) Canada Council Art Bank, Ottawa *Note:* Burton's contribution is the small inserted self-portrait, upper right.

D *Self-Caricatured Portrait* 19 November 1972
Ink on paper (27.3 x 20.6 cm)
Signed and dated (l.l.): *DENNIS/ BURTON/11.19.72*
Dated (u.l.): *11.19., 72*
Inscribed (u.l.): *SELF-/CARICATURED/ PORTRAIT/...NOTEBOOK 38/PAGE 7*

E *The Left Thumb* 8 February 1974
Ink on paper (27.3 x 20.6 cm)
Signed (l.l.): *DENNIS/BURTON*
Dated (u.c.): *2.8.74*
Inscribed (u.l.): *NOTEBOOK 43*
Inscribed (u.r.): *THE/LEFT/THUMB*
Robert Stacey, Toronto
Photos: T.E. Moore, Toronto

TONY URQUHART
(1934-)

Painter, draughtsman, printmaker, sculptor, teacher.

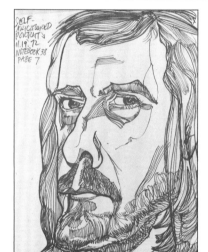

Born: Niagara Falls, Ontario, 9 April, 1934. Studied: Yale-Norfolk University Summer School, 1955; Albright School, Buffalo, New York, 1956-58, under Seymour Drumlevitch, Robert Bruce, Don Nicholls, Larry Calcagno; University of Buffalo, Bachelor of Fine Arts degree, 1958. Painting and studying in Europe, 1959, 1963-64. To Ireland, 1967; Corsica, 1972. Summers in Europe (usually France) since 1970. Teaching: University of Western Ontario, London, artist-in-residence, 1960-63, 1964-65; lecturer, McMaster University, Hamilton, Ontario, 1966-67; assistant professor, University of Western Ontario, 1967-72; professor, University of Waterloo, Waterloo, Ontario, 1972-present (now head of Fine Art Department). Summer school sessions at University of Victoria, University of British Columbia, Vancouver; Banff School of Fine Art; University of Toronto; University of Western Ontario; McMaster University; Queen's University, Kingston; University of Buffalo. Preoccupied with *Lump* series, 1961-62 (influenced by Goya and Francis Bacon). First sculpture: *Germinating Head*, 1964. Began *Box* series, 1965; landscape drawings-in-series, 1971-72; *Floor Piece* series,

1978. First group exhibition, Ontario Society of Artists annual, 1954 (exhibited regularly to 1967); first solo exhibition, Greenwich (Isaacs) Gallery, Toronto, 1956 (exhibited there regularly to 1969). Travelling retrospective, mounted by London Art Gallery, London, Ontario, 1970. One-man exhibitions at Nancy Poole's Studio, Toronto, 1972-77. International group exhibitions include Museum of Modern Art, New York (recent acquisitions); Paris *Biennale*, 1963; Drawing Biennial, Lugano, Switzerland, 1973; *Boîtes*, Musée d'Art Moderne, Paris, and Rennes, Maison de la Culture, 1976-77; 11th International Sculpture Conference, Washington, D.C., 1980. International solo exhibitions at Walker Art Centre, Minneapolis, Minn., 1960; Edinboro State College, Edinboro, Pa., 1974; Richard Demarco Gallery, Edinburgh, Scotland, 1975. Two-artist exhibition

Fig. 3 Dennis Burton
The Three Graces after Rubens 1967
Oil on canvas (152.4 x 152.4 cm)
Dr. R.J. Shroyer, London, Ontario.
Note: Burton introduces himself as a voyeuristic silhouette, extreme left.

with Pat Martin Bates at Centre culturel canadien, Paris, 1975. Twenty-five-year restrospective mounted and circulated by Kitchener-Waterloo Gallery, 1978-80. Awards and Honours: first prize, Western New York Art Annual, 1958; numerous awards, *Winnipeg Show*, 1955-62; special award, *Guggenheim International*, 1958; purchase prize, American Academy of Arts and Letters, 1960; Baxter Award, Ontario Society of Artists, 1961; Canada Council bursaries and grants, 1963, '67, '69, '70, '74, '75, '76, '79, '81, '82; juror, *Spectrum*, Vancouver Art Gallery, 1968; *Editions 1* printmaking competition award, Ontario Arts Council, 1974; University of Waterloo research grant, 1975; commission, Kitchener Court House, 1977. Member: Ontario Society of Artists (1958-69); Royal Canadian Academy (associate, 1961-68); Canadian Society of Painters in Water Colour; Canadian Society of Graphic Art; Canadian Artists' Representation. Publications: *The Urquhart Sketch Book* (Toronto, 1963); *The Broken Ark*, by Michael Ondaatje, illustrated by Urquhart (Ottawa, 1972); *I am Walking in the*

Garden of His Imaginary Palace, by Jane Urquhart, illustrated by Urquhart (winner, certificate of merit, Art Directors' Club of New York, 1983). Works in numerous public and corporate collections in Canada, U.S.A. and Great Britain. Lives and works in Wellesley, Ontario.

COMMENTS BY THE ARTIST

Actually, my grandmother was quite a stong influence throughout my life. She was an artist in the sense that she liked landscaping the grounds of our house which were considerable, given the fact that we lived in the center of the town of Niagara Falls on half an acre. She had ponds made; there was a wood; there was an old barn in the back of the house. It was like an oasis of quiet.

This probably had an influence on making me into a landscape artist which is basically what I would define myself as. I have done very little figurative work; I've never really been interested in the human figure. One reason is that I didn't go to the Ontario College of Art. Drawing the figure was the subject most taught at the College and everyone who went there came to rely heavily on the human figure.

– Tony Urquhart, 'tony about tony', *Tony Urquhart: Twenty-five years: Retrospective* (Kitchener-Waterloo, Ontario: Kitchener-Waterloo Art Gallery, 1978), unpag.

My love of drawing has been the one constant within my work from a very early age right up to the present. During the period from 1964 to 1971 I was concerned with drawing only as a means toward an end, i.e., working sketches for the three-dimensional pieces which occupied all of my time.

Through the period 1967-72 I had investigated with the boxes a great many possible combinations of cutting the doors and hinging them, using various outside textures, even creating cages rather than hiding the interior. This meant that the possibilities for creating entirely new combinations were lessened. There is a lot of "busy" work involved in making a box, much too much to bother working up a box which does not have something new to offer. Therefore, I made fewer boxes after 1972 and consequently had more time to devote to other work, (i.e. drawing).

While in Ireland in 1967 I had discovered a very flexible pen nib which would give me a line ranging from that finer than a steel engraving right up to nearly 1/16'' in width. The nibs turned out to be readily available everywhere; whereas previously I had used quill, brush, twigs, fountain pens, in the early 70's I began to use this pen nib exclusively. I did all my working drawings with it and a sort of 19th c. engraving style began to develop. Also, from 1970 on I have managed to get across the Atlantic at least one a year, if only for a two to three week period. This meant much more access to subject matter than previously and a need to utilize it faster and perhaps differently than building boxes would allow. Consequently, I began drawing in series.

– Tony Urquhart, ''drawings'', *Tony Urquhart: Twenty-five years...*, unpag.

64 Tony Urquhart
Self-Portraits Among Boxes and Flowers I
1976
Ink and watercolour on paper
(64.8 x 94 cm)
Signed and dated (l.r.): *Urquhart 1976*
Inscribed (u.l.): *Self Portraits Among
Flowers and Boxes*
Bau-Xi Gallery, Toronto
Photo: T.E. Moore, Toronto

65 Tony Urquhart
Self-Portraits Among Boxes and Flowers II
1976
Ink and watercolour on paper
(64.8 x 94 cm)
Signed and dated (l.r.): *Urquhart 1976*
Inscribed (l.r.): *Self Portraits Among
Flowers and Boxes*
Bau-Xi Gallery, Toronto
Photo: T.E. Moore, Toronto

IVAN EYRE
(1935-)

Painter, sculptor, printmaker, teacher.

64

65

Born: Tullymet, Saskatchewan, 1935. Moved with family to Saskatoon, 1942. Began drawing lessons at school, 1944, under a former student of Augustus Kenderdine's, and at Saturday morning classes at Saskatoon Arts Centre, under Wynona Mulcaster and George Swinton. Enrolled in after-school art class at Technical Institute, Saskatoon, conducted by Ernest Lindner, 1951-54, and at Eli Bornstein's University of Saskatchewan evening programme. Studied at Winnipeg Art School, 1954-57, under Cecil Richards, George Swinton, etc. To Chicago, end of 1957 term. Taught painting, drawing and design at University of North Dakota, Grand Forks, 1958-59. Returned to Winnipeg, 1959, teaching at University of Manitoba Art School, 1959 to present. Nocturnal urban paintings series, 1962-64. To France, England, Italy, Yugoslavia, Greece, on Canada Council grant, 1966-67. First group exhibition, Winnipeg Art Gallery, 1956; first one-man show, University of Manitoba, 1962. Numerous group and solo exhibitions since in Canada, U.S.A., and Europe, including exhibition at Frankfurter Kunstkabinett, 1973. Represented in numerous corporate and public collections. Exhibits with Equinox Gallery, Vancouver, and Mira Godard Gallery, Toronto. Travelling retrospective exhibition mounted by Robert McLaughlin Art Gallery, Oshawa, 1980-82. Monograph on artist by George Woodcock published in 1981. Awarded University of Manitoba Alumni Jubilee Award, 1982. Lives and works in Winnipeg, Manitoba.

COMMENTS BY THE ARTIST

...being a painter is putting yourself in a state of giving. I feel I'm giving but it's up to the people to decide if I really am; if I'm an artist. I paint. I don't call myself an artist...Really, being called an artist is basically an award for something I do. Painting is part of one's life, like eating, sleeping, loving and all the other things that one does and has to do in order to survive. If I didn't do that, I would feel unhealthy.

– Ivan Eyre, "Leading the Imagination: An Interview with Ivan Eyre by Gary Siemens", *Arts Manitoba*, 1 (Winter 1978): 61

—I see a view back as a view forward. I look into the past and I see that as a view of the future. Or you can turn it the other way around. If one imagines being able to look into the future, you

66 Ivan Eyre
Wrapped Head XIX 1979
Red chalk on paper (33 x 25.4 cm)
Signed (l.r.): *Eyre*
Inscribed (l.r.): *XIX*
Mira Godard Gallery, Toronto
Photo: T.E. Moore, Toronto

67 Ivan Eyre
Birdmen 1981
Acrylic on canvas (162 x 162.4 cm)
Signed (l.r.): *Eyre*
Collection: the artist
Photo: Ernest Mayer, Winnipeg

wouldn't be able to view the future without yourself there. And yourself there involves you and your life, and you are what you've been. So it's all tied up together — views of the past, views of the future, views of now, in one.

– Ivan Eyre, ''Leading the Imagination...'': 62

I have been indifferent to the presence of trends and fads, and perpetually have rejected placement in categories and movements.... Aspects of the great themes and mysteries affecting the human condition are inseparable from the body of my art, and I attempt to deal with them and indicate awareness in as artistic and intriguing a way as possible. On the other hand, it is well to remember that if art connects to life it does so in broad terms, and not in the appearance of things. Underlying the importance of my art is life's continuity, its perpetual cycles and movement, its lasting powers, its mysteries.

– Ivan Eyre, ''Autobiography'', in Joan Murray, *Ivan Eyre: Retrospective* (Oshawa: The Robert McLaughlin Art Gallery, 1980), p. 13

Of all the things that I can imagine doing, painting is still the most enthralling. All I ever had to face in

my professional life was a little intimidation and scorn when certain fashions were popular.

– Ivan Eyre, ''Autobiography'', p. 34

Now, the bearded man figure (as in *Philosopher*) affects me differently from the time when I was working with those formal propositions — I was simply involved and fascinated then. It is more clear now that the image becomes, in varying nuances, statements of power. Of course there will be those who will say they don't see that.

When I was developing that image I was not thinking of Assyrian, Egyptian or the Greeks, hard as that may be to believe. Obviously those old images share some characteristics with my bearded men. However, it would be refreshing to have someone discover, and elaborate on, the differences — some of them are subtle differences, perhaps, but significant to me and, I think, important...

I like the idea of a stylized extension into the past since I feel fluid about past and future. I wouldn't deny such a possibility.

– Ivan Eyre, letter to Robert Stacey, 22 June 1983. *Re* sources of imagery, *cf.* Ivan Eyre, ''Autobiography'', p. 33

Fig. 1 Ivan Eyre
Katepwa 1973
Acrylic on canvas (162 x 142.2 cm)
Private collection, Toronto

Fig. 2 Ivan Eyre
Wrapped Head (Study for Birdmen) 1981
Grease pencil on acetate with acrylic on paper (33 x 25.4 cm)
Singed and dated (l.r.): *Eyre '81*
Nickle Museum, Calgary
Photo: Ernest Mayer, Winnipeg

RON MOPPETT
(1945-)

Painter and sculptor.

68 Ron Moppett
Self-Portrait with Bandaged Ear 1978
Acrylic, oil, photograph, decal, tape, mirror
on plywood (89 x 90 cm)
Initialled (l.r., in pipe cleaners): *RM*
Mira Godard Gallery, Toronto and Calgary
Photo: The Phoebus Communications
Group Ltd., courtesy, Ron Moppett,
Calgary

Born: Woking, Surrey, England, 12 March 1945. Emigrated with family to Canada, 1957; became Canadian citizen, 1978. Studied: Alberta College of Art, 1963-67; Instituto de Allende, Mexico, 1968. First one-man exhibition, Calgary, 1968; first group show, Calgary, 1966. Awards and scholarships: Instituto de Allende Scholarship, Alberta Visual Arts Board Scholarship, 1967; All Alberta, Edmonton Art Gallery, 2nd Prize for Painting, 1969; Canada Council Bursary and travel award, 1971-72; Canada Council Project Grant for *Rose Museum* (with John Hall, *q.v.*), for travelling exhibition; Canada Council Grant and travel award, 1979-80. One-man exhibition, *Ron Moppett*, mounted by Walter Phillips Gallery, Banff, Alberta, 1982. Works in corporate and public collections. Lives and works in Calgary.

COMMENTS BY THE ARTIST

...when we use words we have correspondences so firmly lodged in our brains but the images in a painting have to be much more open. Not meaningless or arbitrary but generous. I think that one of the reasons why artists resort to the coyness of discussing their work in formal terms is that it is what they "know". It can be discussed rather specifically but it doesn't tell you anything. When you employ quite specific images in your work, even though they are so disparate often in their conjunction and stylistic appearance, they beg to be "read". Obviously, I make choices — light bulbs, airplanes, matches, chairs, pipes, etc. I don't paint cars, camels or gnomes. I paint the things around me but they arrive there without me designing them to do so. They are really the only thing that could be there.

Most of the images, I'm aware, are at least double edged — I cultivate ambiguity and worry about contrivance. The work is autobiographical, melancholic, layered and a "slow read" but I hope to God not esoteric. These later pictures of mine look quite "old fashioned" to me and I'm quite encouraged by that.

> — Ron Moppett, letter to Mayo Graham, quoted in *Greg Curnoe/Paterson Ewen/Gathie Falk/Ron Moppett* (Regina: Norman Mackenzie Art Gallery, 1982), p. 58

Early in '76 I did a painting *'FOR ALFRED WALLIS # 2'*...which was triggered by a Tate Gallery flyer [advertising an exhibition of the works of this primitive English marine painter]. Not so much the image

promoting a poster of his works but the words — a pathetic encapsulation of a very trying life. I then did a painting for Van Gogh called *EATING CROW* — another painting for another artist. What interested me was the anecdotal as it relates to a life and content as distinct from what may be painted. They were paintings about Van Gogh only in the sense that I put myself in front of his landscape of images. In many ways that was just a convenience — a way to start working — just like setting up a still life. Also they are not about Van Gogh because they are my paintings as distinct from some notion of didactic of illustrational material. *BLUE STAR PAINTING FOR VINCENT (PIPE)*, 1977, has the (Magritte) disclaimer (dutch)

DIT HEEFT NIETS MET VINCENT TE MAKEN (this is not about Vincent).

Anyway I didn't set about to do a series on Vincent Van Gogh. Only hindsight encapsulates them that neatly. The work gradually turned from Vincent's pipe to my pipe — his chair/my chair etc. etc.

> — Ron Moppett, letter to Robert Stacey, 1 June 1983

Fig. 1 Ron Moppett
Double/Mask 1976-83
Mixed media on canvas and wood (134.6 x 87.6 cm)
Collection: the artist, Calgary
Photo: courtesy, Ron Moppett, Calgary

JOHN HALL
(1943-)

Painter and teacher.

Born: Edmonton, Alberta, 1943. Studied: Alberta College of Art, 1960-65; Instituto Allende, Mexico, 1965-66. Teaching: Ohio Wesleyan University, Delaware, Ohio, 1969-70; Alberta College of Art, Calgary, 1970-71; University of Calgary, 1971-present. Began using acrylic paint, 1964. Influenced by Ron Spickett and Marion Nicholl. Began painting roses, 1965. *The Rose Museum*: a survey of the rose motif in western culture organized by Hall and Ron Moppett (*q.v.*), travelled to four public galleries, 1974-75; key pieces dispersed, 1980. First group exhibition, Calgary, 1966; first one-man show, Calgary, 1970. Received Canada Council Arts Grant A and served on C.C. Advisory Panel, 1978-80. Invited to work at P.S. 1, New York by Institute for Art and Urban Resources, New York, and the Canada Council, 1979-80. Member: Royal Canadian Academy (elected 1975). *John Hall: Paintings and Auxiliary Works 1969-78* shown at National Gallery of Canada, 1979. Lives and works in Calgary, Alberta.

COMMENTS BY THE ARTIST

It's true that *RICOCHET* began its life as a small mixed media work by Ron Moppett for the catalogue cover and poster for my 1978 retrospective exhibition at the ACA Gallery in Calgary. I can't recall if it was tentatively titled *POSTER* in the early stages but it's quite possible, and since it appears on the back of a '79 photo I think we can assume it was. What you're probably seeing on the wall is the original assemblage and either a poster (which, by the way, was deliberately printed off-register in partial homage to Andy Warhol's *INTERVIEW* covers) or catalogue cover. The early work on this painting was done during either the late spring or early summer of 1979, just before my departure for New York. I think I only put a couple of weeks into it. The black and white photos, of which one appears in *COVER*, were taken by Calgary photographer Arthur Nishamura. Copies of these photos were taken to New York in late summer.

COVER was one of eight 44'' paintings completed in New York between September, '79 and April, '80. I think it was done early in the New Year but I can't really remember…In any event, it was done after *SUNSET, LONG ISLAND SUNSET* and *RESORT*, none of which used the figure. The maquette which appears in the photo in *COVER* is for the painting *CALIFORNIA SUMMER* which also has a self portrait in the lower left section. The title of this painting, *COVER*, has many meanings. Some of them are: the idea of covering someone else's work as in the pop music business (both Ron Moppett's and Art Nishimura's), covering as in layering (ribbon on top of photo on top of plywood, etc.), the transferring of Ron's title to my painting…

I returned to *RICOCHET* in late November of '82 and completed it in January of this year [i.e., 1983]. The title, by the way, bounces around in much the same way as *COVER*. The painting is in some respects a self contained retrospective containing, as it does, references to two major paintings done in the seventies.

The *TOURIST* paintings do use, as a unifying element, the small porcelain badge of the tourist (the image is quite similar to the male figure of Duane Hanson's tourist piece). The badge *was not*, however, supplied by Ron [Moppett]. I picked it up in a Christopher Street (Greenwich Village) shop just before returning to Calgary from New York in April, 1980. The self portrait photo in *TOURIST I* is, in fact, a self portrait taken in my New York studio with a tripod and timer. I used both the badge and photo in this painting to introduce myself playing most often: Witness, observer, bystander of the events of our times.

The photo of myself in Ron's assemblage for *RICOCHET* was taken by John Arthur Chenier, an Ottawa political scientist.

TOURIST VII and *VIII* were done primarily from objects given me by Ron Moppett. I, in turn, gave him the maquette to a 1976 painting titled *TANGO* from which he derived some of the imagery for the mixed media work, *DUNCE*. In any event, included in the stuff he gave me was the match box cover bearing the Van Gogh profile.

…

It was the Pop artists who made it possible for me to paint "realistically" in the mid-sixties. In the context of my work realistically simply means descriptively, or recording what the eye sees. To distort seemed to mean to decorate. Now, if one was going to abandon expressive distortion as a belief and replace it with accurate (I'm speaking relatively here) description as one's dominant approach to image making then one way of validating the process was to at least work with traditional drawing skills. There was, I suppose, a fear of "just copying". You

106 must also keep in mind that very few role models existed in the area of photorealism at that time: Bechtle, Estes, Flack, Goings, et al had yet to be discovered. So, one just blundered on making paintings from drawings (pre 1969) and then maquettes (post 1969). It wasn't until 1969 that I first encountered the work of the New Realists in an exhibition titled *Aspects of New Realism*. Every major American New Realist was included and the catalogue essays (one by Sidney Tillim) addressed the question of photography. While respecting, and very much liking, the paintings of many of the photorealists, I found myself siding with the perceptual realists like Pearlstein and Alfred Leslie whose views seemed more likely to parallel my own. In any event, I continued to work without the benefit of the photograph until 1975 or so when I began using a projected slide of the maquette to establish a working contour drawing on the canvas. From this stage I progressed, in 1969, to including actual photographic

information in the maquette for *CALIFORNIA SUMMER*. This was a critical decision in many ways as it not only enabled me to begin working with photographic notation (the way a lens breaks down value areas as in Vermeer) but it also enabled me to open up both the space and time frames because of the information carried by the photos included in the maquette. In New York I continued to work in this manner, which is to say that I worked both from the maquette and from 8 x 10 and 11 x 14 black and white prints. *TWILIGHT*, the last of the New York pictures, was done from its maquette as well as from both black and white and colour prints. Since returning to Calgary I have worked exclusively from 8 x 10 color prints of maquettes destroyed after being photographed. I have no plans to return to working from primary objects.
...

That I seem to eschew the sensuosity of surface should not lead you to conclude that there is a fundamental contradiction between my paintings and my belief in touch as the carrier of meaning. After all, a tour of the Queen Street [Toronto] galleries will certainly lead one to conclude that simply "playing with paint" is no guarantee of either sensuosity or expressivity. One of the most sensuous painters I can think of is Ralph Goings, whose works are both quiet and restrained without being in the least bit "tight". On the other hand, one can think of any number of painters who are overtly painterly as a self conscious way of signalling the presence of meaning in their work. I am not at all interested in "playing with paint", an activity that usually bores me when I see it in the work of others. It is only when paint manipulation deflects attention away from itself and toward some greater content that it is acceptable. There is simply nothing as irrelevant as art that is about nothing but itself... Whether a surface is quiet or noisy is unimportant so as the

picture reveals something of the painter. Anyway, we do seem to move in a pack, and the pack is currently moving in the direction of overt expressivity and sensuosity of surface as a definition of meaning and content... Fads are fun...

I know I didn't really address myself to the imagery in *RICOCHET* as you wanted and I apologize for that. It's partly about appropriation. Anton Ehrenzweig seems to argue, in *THE HIDDEN ORDER OF ART*, that original imagery is less significant than translation as a carrier of meaning in art. *ROSECASE* [1974] and *RICOCHET* are my most direct examinations of that question. Both pictures are problematic too.

– John Hall, letter to Robert Stacey, 28 June 1983.
Note: see Anton Ehrenzweig, *The Hidden Order of Art: A Study in the Psychology of Artistic Imagination* (London: Paladin, 1970).

69 John Hall
Cover 1980
Acrylic on canvas (111.5 x 111.5 cm)
Signed, dated and inscribed (*verso*):
'*COVER*'/completed Feb. 4 '80/acrylic/
New York/JOHN HALL
Art Gallery of Hamilton
Photo: T.E. Moore, Toronto

70 John Hall *
Ricochet 1983
Acrylic on canvas (182.9 x 360.7 cm)
Signed and dated (*verso*): *JOHN HALL
1983*
Art Gallery of Ontario, Toronto
Photo: T.E. Moore, Toronto

Fig. 1 John Hall
Maquette for Cover 1980
Mixed media assemblage (39.1 x 39.1 x 6.7 cm)
Art Gallery of Hamilton
Photo: T.E. Moore, Toronto

Fig. 2 John Hall
Tourist I 1980
Acrylic on canvas (61 x 61 cm)
Wynick/Tuck Gallery, Toronto
Photo: T.E. Moore, Toronto

Fig. 3 John Hall
Studio photograph of John Hall at work on
Ricochet, 1979
Photo: courtesy, Wynick/Tuck Gallery, Toronto
Note: image in background is a collage by Ron
Moppett (*q.v.*) designed for catalogue cover and
poster for John Hall's 1978 Alberta College of Art
one-man exhibition, curated by Moppett.
Richochet is a painted blowup of this printed
assemblage.

* Exhibited at the London Regional Art Gallery
only

Fig. 1

Fig. 2

Fig. 3

ROBERT YOUNG
(1938-)

Painter, printmaker, teacher.

Born: Vancouver, British Columbia, 8 August 1938. Studied: art history, University of British Columbia, 1956-62; The City and Guilds School of Art, London, England, 1962-64; The Vancouver School of Art, 1964-66 (advanced diploma in graphics), under Orville Fisher. Lived in London, England, 1966-76; returned to Vancouver, 1976. Teaching: William Penn School, London, 1967-71; The Dulwich Institute, London, 1967-71; Banff School of Fine Arts, 1973 and '81; Emily Carr College of Art, Vancouver, 1980; University of British Columbia (Extra-Sessional Studies), 1980 and '81; Fine Arts Programme, U.B.C., 1982-present. Visiting artist, Royal College of Art, London, 1975 and Chelsea School of Art, London, 1982. First major group exhibition, Redfern Gallery, London, 1969; first major solo exhibition, Redfern Gallery, London, 1971. Exhibited singly and in group shows at Redfern Gallery and Mira Godard Gallery, Toronto, to 1982; included in *Realism: Emulsion and Omission*, Kingston, Ontario, 1972; *Canadian Canvas*, 1972; *The First British International Drawing Biennale*, Middlesborough, England, 1973; *Bradford Print Biennale*, Bradford, England, 1974; *Realismus und Realitat*, Darmstadt, West Germany, 1975; *From this Point of View*, Vancouver Art Gallery, 1977; *Canadian Video Open*, Calgary, 1978; *Realism: Structure and Illusion*, Guelph, Ontario, 1981; *Canadian Art in Britain*, London, 1982; *Vancouver Art and Artists: 1931 to 1983*, 1983; *The October Show*, Vancouver, 1983; *Contemporary Canadian Printmakers*, Queensland Art Gallery, Australia, 1984. One-man exhibitions at Vancouver Art Gallery, 1974; Centre culturel canadien, Paris, 1976; Glenbow Museum, Calgary, 1978; Canada House Gallery, London, 1979; Art Gallery of Greater Victoria, 1981. Ten-year retrospective mounted by Charles H. Scott Gallery, Calgary, February 1984. Member: Board of Directors, Malaspina Printmakers' Society, Vancouver, 1978-80 (President, 1979-80). Winner, first prize, Malaspina Printmakers' Annual Exhibition, 1976. Represented in numerous public and corporate collections. Lives and works in Vancouver.

COMMENTS BY THE ARTIST

I've been thinking about trying to define my attitude towards portraiture; John Berger's essay on portraiture [in *The Moment of Cubism*]…wasn't far off. Portraiture is difficult in the 20th cent[ury] partly because portraits were historically not concerned with analysis or explications of character or personae so much as authentication of status or role. Certainly, I am suspicious of contemporary portraiture — it seldom seems convincing. As to self-portraiture, it's very difficult to sidestep the Romantic image of the alienated artist with the earnest, searching gaze.
…

I like Francis Bacon's portraits. I like Lucien Freud's portrait of Francis Bacon. Have you seen Stanley Spencer's self-portrait with his second wife — now in the Tate [Gallery, London]? I also like Joe Plaskett's *Self in Camden Town* — now on show at the V[ancouver]A[rt]G[allery] — I remember it from the '50's…

– Robert Young, letter to Robert Stacey, 14 April 1983.

With regard to "psychological interpretation" in self-portraits I wonder if the donning of a mask *is* an evasion of interpretation? Objective truth I don't think we can hope for anywhere.
…

The sequence is called "Juggler" in response (partly) to an article by Fenella Crichton ["A Juggler of Styles", *Art and Artists* (May 1979): 4-10] in which she called me a "juggler of styles". I thought it would be rewarding to consolidate my 10-years-or-so of photograph-based painting and call it quits [to that particular genre] with a piece which would be out-and-out in its ecclecticism, art history refs. and quotes. The painting [*The Juggler*, Fig. 2] is full of generative images; I wanted to use the baby-balancing image again [as in *Down at First Street Bridge*, serigraph, 1972, Fig. 1] but not the pose and information that came with the original snapshot…I wanted to celebrate my family, babies, children, sexuality, intermingling and interrelationships of different characters in an intimate close space. Art and children come from the same source.

– Robert Young, letter to Robert Stacey, undated (May 1983).

71 Robert Young
Study for *The Juggler* 1979
Oil on canvas (90.8 x 61 cm)
Initialled and dated (l.r.): *RY/79*
Ciba-Geigy Canada Limited Art Collection,
Montréal
Photo: T.E. Moore, Toronto

72 Robert Young
The Juggler's Rehearsal 1980
Etching, aquatint, handcolouring on paper
(plate: 60.3 x 69 cm; paper: 74.7 x 93 cm)
Signed (l.l., below platemark): *Robert
Young*
Inscribed (l.c., below platemark): *The
Juggler's Rehearsal*
Mira Godard Gallery, Toronto
Photo: T.E. Moore, Toronto

Fig. 1 *Down at First Street Bridge* 1972
Serigraph on paper (impression: 47.9 x 51.3 cm;
paper: 63.2 x 66.7 cm)
Signed and dated (l.r., below impression): *Robert
Young '72*
Inscribed (l.c., below impression): *Down at First
Street Bridge*
Photo: T.E. Moore, Toronto
Note: background derived from Giotto's *Joachim
and the Shepherd.*

Fig. 2 Robert Young
The Juggler 1980-81
Oil on linen (208.3 x 238.8 cm)
Esso Art Collection, Esso Resources Canada
Limited, Calgary
Photo: courtesy, Mira Godard Gallery, Toronto

PART V: "PHOTO-EXTENDED DIMENSIONS" IN SELF PORTRAITURE

The title of this last section of *"The Hand Holding the Brush"* might be rephrased as *"The Hand Holding the Camera"*. It was derived from the sub-title of a 1979 exhibition catalogue, *Photo/Extended Dimensions*. The curator of this show commented that

Certain artists who have experimented with various media in the past have created works that, while reflecting an awareness of the history of photography as an art form, have stretched the traditional limitations of the medium through the use of large-scale imagery, hand-tinting, and manipulaton in the darkroom.

In her introduction, Karyn Allen more specifically notes that

the artists who are regarded for extending the notions of traditional photography are, in fact, relying on and building from the most classical of art genres—portraiture and narrative/sequential imagery. The recent context of these images is most arresting—the starkness of format, the scale, and the distortion of the elements. There is an aggressive quality to the work, an urgency of statement...

The continual innovations of technology have provided a myriad of tools for the artist. No longer are technical boundaries defined by lack of information and processes.

The ostensibly autobiographical or self-portrait-like photo-constructions in this section of *"The Hand Holding the Brush"* may possess some of the "classic" characteristics of "fine art" portrait photographs but all, through the manifest intervention of their artists, have been extended or liberated from the dimension of images of *subjects* (who happen to be the persons responsible for the existence of the photo-record) and now reside within the realm of *object*.

The manipulation (and indeed, in some cases, deliberate mutilation) of the print-surface, the superaddition of written or typewritten, complementary or integrally related texts, and the mounting of the sequential images on three-dimensional supports, all contribute to the transformation of the pieces into members of a hybrid form that has sculptural as well as visual attributes. It is not as *photographic* self-portraits that we recognize these works, and our terms of reference are more likely to be to those of abstract painting, conceptual and minimalist art, artists' films and videotapes, or performance, installation and "body art", rather than of traditional photography. The convenient (if unpronounceable) coinage, *"camerart"*, serves the purpose of directing us to the reality that the practitioners of this relatively new genre are using the camera as a technical implement, just as a portraitist in oils employs a brush as an intermediary agent between the sitter he portrays and the paint with which the sitter is replicated.

Photography, of course, introduces the time-element even as it captures the actual light-rays reflected off objects, scenery, human bodies and heads. Both time and space are mixed together, not only in the photograph itself but in the composing, exposing, developing, enlarging, printing (and, in some instances, retouching, cutting up and re-composing, or otherwise manipulating) stages. Of course, the photograph is a graphic record of a single instant, but its "time*lessness*" is of a different nature than that of the painting, being compounded and confounded by time*liness*.

A significant common feature of virtually all the artists included in this section is their devotion to multiple or sequential imagery: several contributors are represented by works consisting of a number of photographic (or Xerographic) images of themselves, arranged in what one presumes is chronological order, or else mounted in such a way as to suggest a logical narrative sequence. Instinctively, we scan these compositions from upper left down to the lower right, just as we would if it were words we were reading rather than visual objects being regarded. And frequently, written texts are supplied as a means of providing running commentaries designed to stimulate curiosity in the diaristic or confessional aspect of a series of (in some instances) visually unexceptional self-images. And yet the literary (sometimes sub-literate) content does not distract us from the suspicion that the natural next step for many artists working in this field is to combine the time, space and movement elements with the autobiographical and documentary possibilities of experimental film, video, and performance art. Whether the appearance of the artist in films, tapes or performances constitutes an extension of self-portraiture is a vexed question, to be answered by experts elsewhere than in the context of *"The Hand Holding the Brush"*.

MICHAEL SNOW
(1929-   )

Filmmaker, photographer, sculptor, painter, musician.

Born: Toronto, 11 October 1929. Raised in Chicoutimi, Québec. Studied: Ontario College of Art, Toronto, 1948-53, under John Martin. Began to play music while enrolled at Upper Canada College, Toronto. To Europe as jazz pianist and trumpeter, 1953-54. Returned to Toronto, 1954. Worked in George Dunning's film-animation studio, Graphic Associates, 1954-56. Met artist-filmmaker Joyce Wieland (q.v.), whom he married, 1957. Began making collages, 1955. Became interested in experimental film, 1956. Preoccupied with *Walking Woman* theme (paintings, sculpture, film), 1961-67. Living and working in New York City, 1963-72. Began use of photography as a figurative representational process, 1967. Settled in Toronto, 1972. Teaching: Professor of Advanced Film, Yale University, 1970; visiting artist, Nova Scotia School of Art and Design, Halifax, 1970, '74; visiting artist, Ontario College of Art, 1973, '74; guest lecturer and visiting artist, U.C.L.A., California, 1983. First group exhibition, Toronto, 1952. First solo exhibition, Toronto, 1956. Began to exhibit at Greenwich (Isaacs) Gallery, Toronto, 1957. Retrospective exhibitions mounted by York University, 1965; Art Gallery of Toronto, 1970; Centre for Inter-American Relations, New York, 1972; Cinematheque Québécoise, Montréal, 1975; Museum of Modern Art, New York, 1976; Centre Georges Pompidou, Paris, 1978 (travelled to Lucerne, Rotterdam, Bonn, Munich, 1978-79). First Canadian to be given solo exhibition at Venice Biennale, 1970. One-man exhibition at 49th Parallel Gallery, New York, 1981. Featured in numerous international group exhibitions. Films include: *New York Eye and Ear Control* (1964); *Wavelength* (1966-67); *Back and Forth* (1968-69); *One Second in Montreal* (1969); *La Region Centrale* (1970-71); *Rameau's Nephew by Diderot…* (1972-74) *Two Sides to Every Story* (1974); *Presents* (1981). Publications: *Michael Snow / A Survey* (1970); *Cover to Cover* (1975); *High School* (1979). Solo recording: *Music for Piano,* *Whistling, Microphone and Tape Recorder* (1975). Commissions: mobile, Victoria College Union, University of Toronto, 1954; film based on ''Walking Woman'' theme, Ten Centuries Concerts, Toronto, 1964; major sculpture commission, Ontario Pavilion, Expo '67, Montréal, 1967; ''Video-Photo Environmental Sculpture'', Brock University, St. Catharines, Ontario, 1975; ''Dispersed photo work'', Canadian Government Building, Toronto, 1977; *Flight Stop* mobile, Eaton Centre, Toronto, 1980. Member: Artists' Jazz Band; C.C.M.C. (Canadian Contemporary Music Collective); Royal Canadian Academy (elected 1973). Awards and honours: first prize, *The Winnipeg Show*, 1958; Canada Council grants and fellowships, 1959, '66, '80; Guggenheim Fellowship, 1972; Honourary LL.D. degree, Brock University, 1974; first prize for *Wavelength*, 4th International Experimental Film, Brussels, 1968; award winner for *Wavelength*, *Canadian Artists '68*, Art Gallery of Ontario; award for outstanding film, *Film Culture Magazine*, 1968; Order of Canada, 1981; honourary degree, O.C.A., 1983. Represented in numerous Canadian and American public and corporate collections. Films in film archives in Canada, United States, and Europe.

COMMENTS BY THE ARTIST

…reality was and always is a form of memory even at the moment of perception of perception.

– Michael Snow, ''Passage'', *Artforum* 10 (September 1963): 63.

I'm not at all interested in what's called ''self-expression'. When something is successful it should be like a natural phenomenon. Making the work is itself a clarifying or inventing of itself; to be important to others it has to be important to make it.

My idea of the artist, or the artist that I am, is someone who makes

73 Michael Snow
Venetian Blind (Part I) 1970
24 colour photographs, painted
wood frame, in 4 sections (edition of three)
(127 x 238 cm [overall])
Signed and dated (bottom row,
second photograph from right):
SNOW '70
Canada Council Art Bank/Banque des
oeuvres d'art du Conseil des Arts due
Canada, Ottawa

something or puts something new in the world, something that's never been there before, far more than he or she is commentator or reporter or adjuster of things in the world.

– Michael Snow, quoted by Barrie Hale in ''The Inventions of Michael Snow'', *The Canadian* (1 January 1977): 7.

I like the word ''investigation'' because it sounds as though I'm a scientist or a detective...I work with what's there, with the medium, rearranging all the elements of the world that are meant to be used and showing the process. Basically, I'm a poet of light and space and time.

– Michael Snow, quoted by Meriké Weiler in ''A poet of light and space and time'', *Maclean's Magazine* (11 December 1978) 4.

I'm still interested in what it all means...I'm still interested in all the things that produced us. They can't be explained. It's just the way we are.

– Michael Snow, quoted by Adele Freedman in ''Snow discovers being Canadian is a serious matter'', *The Globe and Mail*, 19 April 1980.

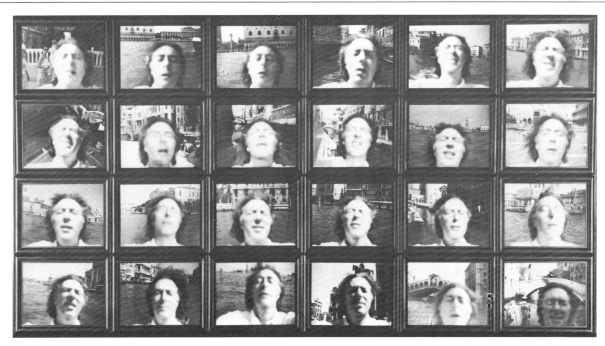

Fig. 1 Michael Snow
Authorization 1969
Black-and-white polaroid photographs, soft
adhesive-cloth tape, mirror and metal (54.6 x 44.5
cm)
Signed (on frame, l.r.): *SNOW 69*
National Gallery of Canada, Ottawa

VINCENT TANGREDI
(1950-   )

Installation artist, sculptor.

74 Vincent Tangredi *
Falling for Her Lightwater 1974
Unit 1: Wooden panel, 6 photographs,
Letraset (69.5 x 241 cm)
Unit 2: Galvanized steel trough with water
and Letraset (8.9 x 20.3 x 241 cm)
Carmen Lamanna Gallery, Toronto

114 Born: Campobasso, Italy, 15 May 1950. To Canada, 1956. Studied: Ontario College of Art, Toronto, 1970-73. First group exhibition, Toronto, 1972; first solo exhibition, Toronto, 1974. Subsequent one-man exhibitions: *Beautiful Blud: Part A for the Production of the Attractive Male*, Carmen Lamanna Gallery, Toronto, 1976; *Transitions: Part Two for the Production of the Attractive Male*, Carmen Lamanna Gallery, December 1976-January 1977; *Breaking a New Record*, Carmen Lamanna Gallery, 1978; *The Whole Course of Art History as MENU*, Carmen Lamanna Gallery, Dec. 1978-Jan. 1979; *Of the Four Considerations*, Carmen Lamanna Gallery, 1980. Presentations: *Beautiful Blud II*, Nova Scotia College of Art and Design, Halifax, 1976; *Breaking a New Record*, Ontario College of Art, 1977; *Of the Four Considerations*, O.C.A., 1983. Included in *Kanadische Künstlers*, Kunsthalle, Basel, June-July 1978. Awards and grants: George A. Reid Scholarship, Ontario College of Art, 1972; Ontario Arts Council grants, 1974, '75, '76, '77, '78, '80; Canada Council grants, 1974, '76, '78, '79, '81, '82, '83; *Editions I* printmaking competition award, Ontario Arts Council, 1974. Represented in the Canada Council Art Bank Collection, Ottawa. Lives and works in Toronto.

Fig. 1 Vincent Tangredi
The Eighth Frame (B) 1975
Part A: Prototype: *The Eighth Frame (B)* Eight black-and-white photographs mounted in cardboard (each: 24.5 x 15.2 cm; overall: 50.8 x 138.4 cm)
Part B: Eight adjacent enlarged black-and-white photographs (each: 50.8 x 34.9 cm) (overall size of work: 105.4 x 280 cm)
Carmen Lamanna Gallery, Toronto

* *Exhibited at the London Regional Art Gallery only*

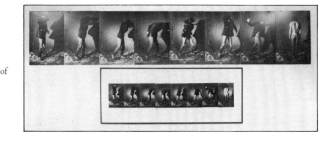

SUZY LAKE

(1947-   )

Camera artist, performance artist,
printmaker, teacher.

75 Suzy Lake
Suzy Lake as Bill Vazan 1974-75
Black and white photographs (76.9 x 91.5
cm each)
Canada Council Art Bank/Banque des
oeuvres d'art du Conseil des Arts du
Canada, Ottawa
Photo: courtesy, Suzy Lake, Toronto

76 Suzy Lake
A Natural Way to Draw* 1975
Colour videotape (25 min)
Print from artist's original tape
London Regional Art Gallery, London,
Ontario.
Photo: courtesy, Suzy Lake, Toronto

Born: Detroit, Michigan, 14 June
1947. Moved to Canada, 1968.
Education: Western Michigan University, Kalamazoo, Michigan, 1965-66;
Wayne State University, Detroit,
1966-68; Concordia University,
Montréal (Master of Fine Art degree),
1978. Teaching: drawing, printmaking,
painting and design, Montreal
Museum of Fine Art School, 1969;
printmaking, Montreal Museum of
Fine Art School, 1975; supervisor
at Loyola University Photography
Workshop, 1975 and '76; printmaking,
Concordia University, 1976. Co-
founded Véhicule Art Gallery,
Montréal, 1971 (publicity chairman
and curator, 1972; secretary and
curator, 1973; president and curator,
1974; active member and curator,
1975). One of ten gallery directors sent
to *Basel International Art Fair*, 1974.
First solo exhibition, Montréal, 1973;
first group exhibition, Montréal, 1972.
Has exhibited widely in Canada and
abroad since. Videotapes: *Box
Concert*, 1973; *A Natural Way to
Draw*, 1975; *The Painter and the
Paintee*, 1976; *Choreographies on the
Dotted Line*, 1976. Performances: *A
Natural Way to Draw*, 1975; *Clouds of
Magellan*, with Ted Dawson, 1977;
Choreographed Puppets, 1976-77;
Choreography with Myself, 1978.
Received Canada Council ''B'' grants,
1974-75, 1978, 1981. Works in
numerous public and corporate
collections in Canada. Lives and works
in Toronto.

COMMENTS BY THE ARTIST

...in a nutshell, I use myself in my
work to represent ''someone''; not
necessarily specifics of my own
identity, but to discuss issues of
identity and its ramifications. I think
that if the image is that of the artist
rather than a model, it lends ''trust''
to the audience (believability?)
concerning the artist's concern with the
more subjective issues in the work.

– Suzy Lake, letter to Robert Stacey, July
1983.

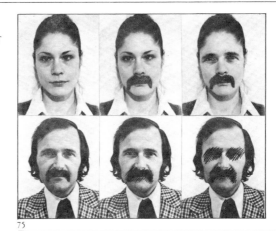

75

76

Fig. 1 Suzy Lake
Storyboard for a Natural Way to Draw 1975
Photographs and drawings on paper (127 x 142.2
cm)
Jared Sable, Toronto
Photo: courtesy, Suzy Lake, Toronto

77 Suzy Lake *
Petrushka's Dance with Abaddon from *Are You Talking to me/* 1979
Black-and-white and tinted photographs
(96.5 x 469.3 cm) (8 sections)
London Regional Art Gallery, Gift of the Allstate Foundation, Canada
Note: photograph reproduced is of Part VI.

BARBARA ASTMAN
(1950-)

Photographer, Xerographer, printmaker, sculptor, teacher and lecturer.

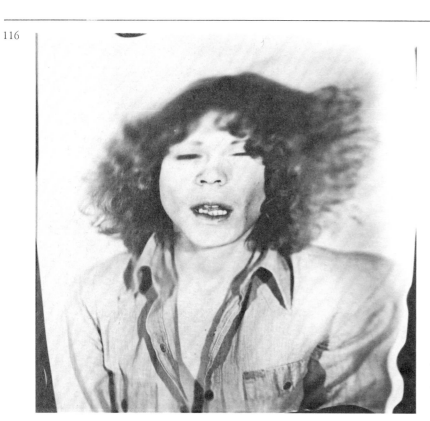

Born: Rochester, New York, 1950. Landed immigrant status, Canada. Educated at Rochester Institute of Technology (Associate Degree, 1970), Ontario College of Art, Toronto (graduated 1973). Teaching experience: Ontario College of Art, 1973-83; York University, Toronto, 1978-80; Co-ordinator, Colour Xerox Artists' Programme, Visual Arts Ontario, Toronto, 1971-83. Has exhibited widely throughout Canada and United States since 1973, and lectured and given demonstrations extensively since 1976. Works in numerous public collections, including the Agnes Etherington Art Centre, Kingston; the National Film Board, Ottawa; the Department of External Affairs, Ottawa; the Ontario Arts Council, Toronto; the Gallery/Stratford, Stratford, Ontario; the Bibliothèque Nationale, Paris; the Winnipeg Art Gallery; the Victoria and Albert Museum, London; the Canada Council Art Bank, Ottawa; and the Art Gallery of Hamilton, as well as in corporate and private collections. Lives and works in Toronto.

COMMENTS BY THE ARTIST

It seems logical to use [one's] self-image to illustrate a concept, by depicting the human situation through my personal frame of reference. This philosophy has been a constant element in my work dating back to 1968. My sense of self extends beyond my physical being and attempts to become an extension of all those within the parameters of my particular social milieu (eg: North American and middle class). Yet, I feel I can extend this desire to encompass those outside of my social realm through the power of communication available within the structure of art. Self-portraiture as an adjunct to autobiographical information allows me to deal with what it is I have learned from my own personal history. I am intrigued by the unravelling of the mysteries of my own life. This helps in my understanding of the actions and thoughts of others. I gain a more universal awareness by an open examination of my particular experience. It is this intrigue that has sustained me creatively over the years, as my quest for self knowledge is unending, much like the creative process itself.

– Barbara Astman, ''Artist's Statement, submitted 24 July, 1983.

Fig. 2 Suzy Lake
Are you talking to me? 1979
Installation photo, Whitby Station Gallery, Whitby, Ontario, January 1981
Photo: courtesy, Sable-Castelli Gallery, Toronto

Fig. 1 Barbara Astman
Barbara Coming, Barbara Going... (c. 1973-74)
Photo-transfer on fabric, with appliqué and clear plastic
National Film Board Photothèque, Ottawa

Fig. 2 Barbara Astman with *Fun in the Sun in Barbados*
(Colour Xerox print, 1976, in the collection of Karl Schantz)
Photo: Art Gallery of Ontario (''Artists With Their Work'' programme)

Fig. 3 Barbara Astman
Untitled (Visual Narrative Series) 1978
Tinted colour photostat (enlarged) of 6 Polaroid SX-70 prints (121.9 x 152.4 cm)
Photo: courtesy, Sable-Castelli Gallery, Toronto

Fig. 4 Barbara Astman
Red 1980
Ektacolour photomural (122 x 122 cm)
Photo: courtesy, Sable-Castelli Gallery

* Exhibited at the London Regional Art Gallery only

78 Barbara Astman
Untitled ('Dear Jared...') 1979
Ektacolour photomural (152.4 x 121.9 cm)
The Robert McLaughlin Gallery, Oshawa,
Ontario

JOYCE WIELAND
(1931-)

Painter, sculptor, filmmaker, quiltmaker.

Born: Toronto, Ontario, 1931.
Studied: Art Programme, Central
Technical School, Toronto, under
Doris McCarthy and Robert Ross;
private lessons with Mrs. Wilson
Patrick (two years). Worked as
package-designer after graduation,
then at Graphic Associates, Toronto, as
film-animator. Married Michael Snow
(*q.v.*), 1957. Made first film, *Tea in
the Garden*, 1958. Living and working
as painter and experimental filmmaker
in New York, 1963-72. Return visits to
Toronto, 1966 and '69. First group
exhibition, Toronto, 1957; first
two-artist show (with Gordon Rayner),
Toronto, 1957; first solo exhibition,
Toronto, 1960. Regular one-woman
exhibitions at Isaacs Gallery, Toronto,
1963-present. Included in group
exhibitions at J.B. Speed Museum,
Louisville, Kentucky, 1962; Albright-
Knox Gallery, Buffalo, N.Y., 1962;
Philadelphia Museum of Art, 1964;
Hudson's Galleries, Detroit, Mich.,
1967; Canadian Government Pavilion,
Expo '67, Montreal, 1967; *Canada:
Art d'Aujourd'hui*, France, Italy,
Netherlands, 1968; *Canada 101*,
Edinburgh Festival, Edinburgh,
Scotland; *Eight Artists from Canada*,
Tel Aviv Museum, Israel, 1970.
Retrospective exhibition, *True Patriot
Love*, mounted by National Gallery,
Ottawa, 1971 (first one-woman
exhibition to be shown at the N.G.C.).
Films include *Patriotism, Parts One
and Two* (1964-65); *Rat Life and Diet
in North America* (1968); *La Raison
avant la passion / Reason over Passion*
(1967-69); *Pierre Vallières* (1972); *The
Far Shore* (1976). Films screened in
United States and Europe as well as
Canada at numerous experimental film
festivals. Retrospective, *The Films of
Joyce Wieland*, held at Pacific Film
Archives, Berkeley, California, 1973;
Joyce Wieland: Retrospective mounted
by Whitney Museum, New York,
1973. Represented in film archives of
Museum of Modern Art, New York;
Royal Belgium Film Archives; Austrian
Film Archives; Farleigh Dickinson
University; Centre Pompidou,
Beaubourg, Paris. Grants and awards:
Canada Council grants, 1966, '68; two
prizes for *Rat Life and Diet in
America*, Third Independent Film-
makers' Festival, New York, 1968;
Victor M. Lynch Award, Canada
Council, 1972. Member: Canadian
Artists' Representation (C.A.R.);
Ontario Filmmakers' Association.
Works in numerous public collections
in Canada and the United States.
Lives and works in Toronto.

Fig. 1

Fig. 2

Fig. 3

Fig. 4

79 Joyce Wieland
Artemis 1-10 1981
Colour photographs of colour photocopies,
framed in two panels (each image: 53.3 x
149.9 cm; overall: 53.3 x 299.7 cm)
Signed and dated (l.r. of No. 10): *JOYCE
WIELAND 1981*
Collection: the artist, Toronto
Photo: T.E. Moore

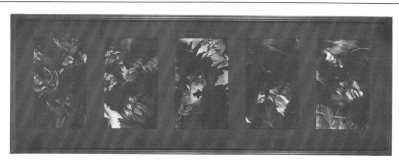 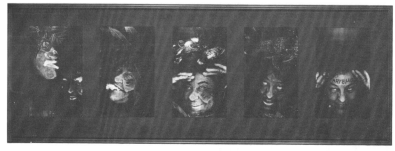

COMMENTS BY THE ARTIST

Drawing has always been with me.
More and more it has become a form of
meditation. My colour drawings are
very sensual and spiritual at the same
time.

My work has always been spiritual
but now I feel I'm allowing a certain
kind of energy to come into me...I'm
now able to embrace my subject
matter, which is animals, people,
landscapes and the history of Canada.
...

I love the image and I want to be as
rich as I can with it. I certainly don't
want to empty it.
...

Painting and film are different
languages to show emotion; thinking
in visual terms to display it. The
rough edges will show the hand or the
mind of the artist at work.
...

I made some self-portraits a couple of
summers back [i.e., in 1978]. They
were painted up very close and when
you get far away, they're a whole
different thing. I really wanted to find
out what I looked like. One is my
Scottish self and one is my English self.
...

Although we're in life, what's
interesting is creating eternals. What
we leave behind us when we die are all
those wonderful forms and sounds for
people to remember us by.

– Joyce Wieland, "Artist Wieland finds
maturity", *Toronto Star*, 27 April 1980.

I used to do portraits when I was a lot
younger...
...

It's a very strange relationship
[between portraitist and sitter]...It's a
chance to really look at somebody. It
starts to make you feel weird. You start
to see the cells, the blood pumping
through the cheeks. You start to
"osmose" the person, absorbing him
so you can put him out again...
...

The skin really says everything — how
the light hits it, what comes through.

– Joyce Wieland, quoted by Adele
Freedman in "Portraits from a daring
artist", *The Globe and Mail*, 4 January
1983.

Fig. 1 Joyce Wieland
Self-Portrait 1978
Oil on canvas (25 x 22 cm)
Collection: the artist, Toronto, courtesy, The
Isaacs Gallery
Photo: T.E. Moore, Toronto

80 Joyce Wieland
Self-Portrait 1978
Oil on canvas (22.5 x 22.2 cm)
Signed and dated (l.r.): *JOYCE WIELAND
'78*
Collection: the artist, Toronto
Photo: T.E. Moore, Toronto

DAVID HLYNSKY
(1947-   )

Photographer, holographer, painter,
editor, writer, lecturer.

Born: 6 May 1947, Bethlehem,
Pennsylvania. Emigrated to Canada,
1970. Studied: Ohio State University
(B.F.A., 1971). Worked as book
designer at Coach House Press,
Toronto, 1970-74. Editor, *Image
Nation*, 1973-82. Teaching: Three
Schools of Art, Toronto, 1976-78.
Founded Fringe Research Hologram
Studio with Michael Sowdon, 1974;
president of Board of Directors,
1974-83. Co-curator with Ben Mark
Holzberg of *Rolling Landscape Show*
in Toronto Transit Corp. subway
system, 1978. First one-man exhibition
at A Space, 1973 (hand-tinted
photographs). Exhibited holograms,
photographs, paintings at Museum of
Holography, New York City, and SAW
Gallery, Ottawa, 1981. *Baggage*
(photographs) and *Salvage* (short
stories and photographs) published by
Coach House Press, Toronto, 1974 and
1981. Articles and photogaphs in *Only
Paper Today, Print Letter, Impulse,
Canadian Forum, Centrefold, File,
Image Nation, Impressions, NOW,
Rampike, Holosphere*. Working as a
freelance photographer and converting
Salvage into film script, 1983. *New

Canadian Holography*, exhibition
co-curated by Hlynsky, on European
tour, 1983-84.

COMMENTS BY THE ARTIST

*FIDGETIST ART, THE FIRST LAW
OF.* This law states that a culture made
hungry for novelty will always adopt
the broadest popular possible
parameters for utility. In this age of
pop rocks, pet rocks, and look-alike
cheeseburgers, a vivid imagination is a
valuable asset. Fidgetism was
discovered by Leonard O. Davinsky
[a.k.a. David Hlynsky] in 1974.

*FIDGETIST ART, THE SECOND
LAW OF.* Art's primary effect is upon
the artist who creates it. Since it is
nearly impossible to separate the
artist's self from the artist's influences,
it is almost impossible to produce an
expression which is either absolutely
relevant or totally irrelevant.
Art-making is simply the higher
perfection of man's basic need to
scribble, mumble, fidget.

*FIDGETISM, THE FIRST AND
SECOND PRINCIPLES OF.* First,
Thou art. Second, Thou shalt not
grumble too much about art.

– David Hlynsky, ''The Fringe Glossary
of Terms'', *Broom 80.* Edited by Flavio
Belli (Hamilton, Ont.: Art Gallery of
Hamilton, 1980), unpag.

I depend a lot on puns as a way of
expressing the density of our
experiences… And I spend a great deal
of time looking for objects that will
symbolize the mundane — and will
still have resonance and generalized
meaning… Actually, I sometimes find
myself sweaty and out of breath trying
to eliminate the extraneous from my
photographs. The purpose of art is to
get off.

– David Hlynsky, quoted by Gary
Michael Dault in ''Photographer doubles
as writer'', *The Globe and Mail*, 7
January 1982.

Clicka click click click…chugga
chugga…bingo! SHAZAM!!!?

– David Hlynsky, ''New(?) Canadian(?)
Photography(?)…!'', *Image Nation* No.
26 (Fall 1982): 7

119

81 David Hlynsky *
Diptych
Part I: *Clone* 1980 Signed and dated (l.l.):
David Hlynsky 1980 Alkyd on canvas (50.8
x 40.6 cm)
Part II: *I've Always Been a Sucker for
Modern Technology* 1983
Hologram in arborite frame (50.8 x 40.6 cm)
No. 2 of an edition of 10
Collection: the artist, Toronto
Photo: T.E. Moore, Toronto

120

Holography is an anomaly, and we have to be careful about exactly how we define it, because it's not an extension of photography, it's a departure…

– David Hlynsky, quoted by Karl Jirgins in "Holography: The 3-dimensional departure", *Toronto Arts News*, (February 1983).

Holography is an advanced optical technique creating highly realistic images which seem three dimensional to the unaided eye. This is accomplished by flooding both the object and an adjacent photographic plate with laser light. Light reflected from the object to the plate interferes with light aimed directly from the source toward the plate and creates a complex pattern which represents the direction, brightness and distance travelled of the object-illuminating light. When placed in a carefully controlled beam of light, this photographically recorded pattern will replicate the optical characteristics of the original object giving the illusion of a solid three-dimensional form hovering at or near the plate surface.

– David Hlynsky, artist's statement, 19 August 1983.

Part I

Part II

Fig. 1 David Hlynsky
Fidgetist Manifesto No. 2 1979
Oil on canvas; easel; paint-rag (canvas: 71.1 x 50.8
cm; easel: 152.4 cm [height])
Signed and dated (l.l.): *David Hlynsky/79*
Collection: the artist, Toronto
Photo: T.E. Moore, Toronto

Fig. 2 David Hlynsky
Untitled photograph (self-portrait) reproduced in
Salvage (1981)

Fig. 3 Michael Sowdon
Untitled ["subject": David Hlynsky] 1980
Image Nation Postcard no. 140

* *Exhibited at the London Regional Art Gallery
only*

Fig. 1   Fig. 2   Fig. 3

Suzy Lake hand-colouring a section of her
photo-sequence, *Are you talking to me,*
1979. Photo: courtesy Suzy Lake.

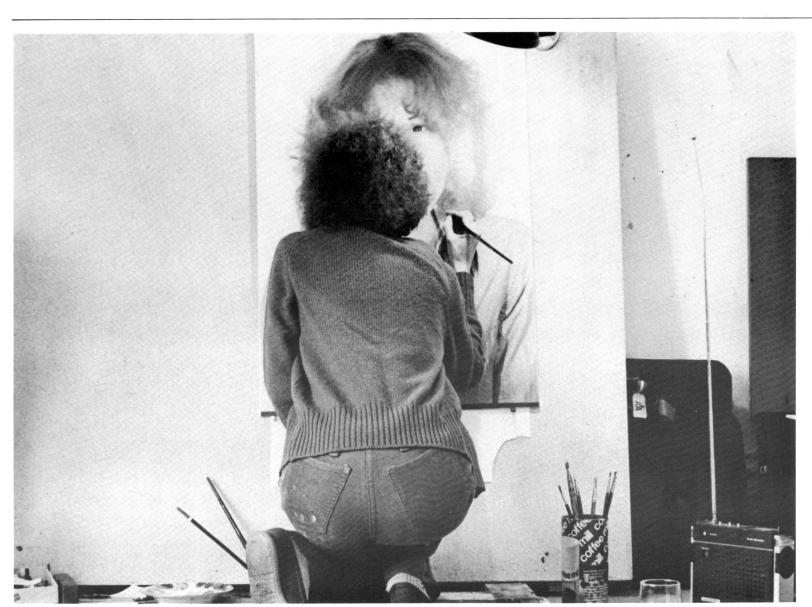

REFERENCES

PART I: Canadian Art: General References

NOTE: Asterisk (*) after entry denotes exhibition catalogue.

Allodi, Mary. *Printmaking in Canada: The Earliest Views and Portraits / Les debuts de l'estampe imprimée au Canada: vues et portraits.* Toronto: Royal Ontario Museum, 1980*

Barbeau, Charles Marius. "Art in French Canada". In *French Canadian Backgrounds: A Symposium,* pp. 64-82. Toronto: Ryerson Press, 1941.

—— *Au Coeur de Québec.* Montréal: Editions du Zodiaque, 1934.

—— *I have seen Quebec.* Toronto: Macmillan, 1957.

—— *Painters of Quebec.* Toronto: Ryerson Press, 1946.

—— *Quebec: Where Ancient France Lingers.* Toronto: Macmillan, 1937.

Bayefsky, Aba, and Milnes, Humphrey N. "Fields of Force in Canadian Art, 1930 to 1980". In *The Arts in Canada: The Last Fifty Years,* pp. 135-45. Edited by W.J. Keith and B.-Z. Shek, Toronto: University of Toronto Press, 1980.

Bell, Michael. *Image of Canada / Visage du Canada.* Ottawa: Information Canada, 1972.*

Bell, Michael. *Painters in a New Land: From Annapolis Royal to the Klondike,* Toronto: McClelland and Stewart, 1973.

Bellerive, George. *Artistes-peintres canadiens-français.* Montréal: Beauchemin, 1927.

—— *Artistes-peintres canadiens-français: les anciens.* 2 vol. in 1. Québec: Garneau, 1925-26.

Bringhurst, Robert; James, Geoffrey; Keziere, Russell; Shadbolt, Doris; editors. *Visions: Contemporary Art in Canada.* Vancouver and Toronto: Douglas and McIntyre, 1983.

Brown, Eric, ed. *A Portfolio of Canadian Art.* Toronto: Rous and Mann, 1926.

Buchanan, Donald W. *Canadian Painters from Paul Kane to the Group of Seven.* London: Phaidon, 1945.

—— *The Growth of Canadian Painting.* Toronto: Collins, 1950.

Burnett, David, and Schiff, Marilyn. *Contemporary Canadian Art.* Edmonton: Hurtig in co-operation with the Art Gallery of Ontario, Toronto, 1983.

Carter, David G. *The Painter and the New World: A Survey of Painting from 1564 to 1867 Marking the Founding of Canadian Confederation.* Montréal: Montreal Museum of Fine Arts, 1967.*

Chauvin, Jean. *Ateliers: A Study of Twenty-two Canadian Painters and Sculptors.* Montréal: Louis Carrier, Les Éditions du Mercure, 1928.

Colgate, William. *Canadian Art: Its Origin and Development.* Foreword by C.W. Jefferys. Toronto: Ryerson Press, 1943, new edition 1967.

—— *The Toronto Art Students' League: 1886-1904.* Toronto: Ryerson Press, 1954.

Dictionary of Canadian Biography. 7 vols. Toronto: University of Toronto Press, 1966-.

Duval, Paul. *Canadian Art: Vital Decades.* Toronto: Clarke, Irwin, 1970.

—— *Four Decades: The Canadian Group of Painters and Their Contemporaries.* Toronto: Clarke, Irwin, 1972.

—— *High Realism in Canada.* Toronto: Clarke, Irwin, 1974.

Farr, Dorothy, and Luckyj, Natalie. *From Women's Eyes: Women Painters in Canada.* Kingston, Ont.: Agnes Etherington Art Centre, Queen's University, 1975.*

Gagen, Robert F. "Ontario Art Chronicle." Typescript in the E.P. Taylor Reference Library, Art Gallery of Ontario, Toronto [ca.1918-1926].

Gagnon, Maurice. *Peinture canadienne.* Montréal: Société des éditions Pascal, 1945.

Godsell, Patricia. *Enjoying Canadian Painting.* Don Mills, Ont.: General Publishing, 1976.

Hammond, M.D. *Painting and Sculpture in Canada.* Toronto: Ryerson Press, 1930.

Harper, J. Russell. *Early Painters and Engravers in Canada.* Toronto: University of Toronto Press, 1970.

——. Ontario Painters 1846-1867. National Gallery of Canada, *Bulletin* 1 (May 1963): 16-31.

—— *Painting in Canada: A History.* Toronto: University of Toronto Press, 1966, new edition 1977.

—— *A People's Art: Primitive, Native, Provincial, and Folk Painting in Canada.* Toronto: University of Toronto Press, 1974.

Harris, Robert. "Art in Quebec and the Maritime Provinces." In *Canada: An Encyclopedia of the Country,* vol. 4, edited by J.C. Hopkins, pp. 353-400. Toronto: Linscott Pub. Co., 1898.

Hill, Charles C. *Canadian Painting in the Thirties.* Ottawa: National Gallery of Canada, 1975.*

Hubbard, Robert H., ed. *An Anthology of Canadian Art.* Toronto: Oxford University Press, 1960.

—— *Catalogue of Paintings and Sculpture. Volume 3: Canadian School.* Ottawa: National Gallery of Canada, 1960.

—— *The Development of Canadian Art.* Ottawa: National Gallery of Canada, 1964.

—— "Primitives with Character: A Quebec School of the Early Nineteenth Centre". *Art Quarterly* 20 (Spring 1957): 17-19.

Hubbard, Robert H., and Ostiguy, Jean-René. *Three Hundred Years of Canadian Art.* Ottawa: National Gallery of Canada, 1967.*

Jefferys, Charles W., comp. *A Catalogue of the Sigmund Samuel Collection, Canadiana and Americana.* Toronto: Ryerson Press, 1948.

Lamy, Laurent et Suzanne. *La renaissance des metiers d'art au Canada français.* Québec: Ministére des Affaires culturelles, 1967.

Landmarks of Canada: A Guide to the J. Ross Robertson Canadian Historical Collection in the Toronto Public Library. 3 vols. in 2. Toronto: Toronto Public Library, 1964-67. Volumes 1 and 2 are illustrated reprints of the 1917 and 1921 editions.

Lavalle, Gérard. *Anciens ornemanistes et imagiers du canada français.* Québec: Ministére des Affaires culturelles, 1968.

Lord, Barry. *The History of Painting in Canada: Towards a People's Art.* Toronto: NC Press, 1974.

—— *Painting in Canada.* Ottawa: Queen's Printer, 1967.*

MacDonald, Colin S. *A Dictionary of Canadian Artists.* 6 vols. Ottawa: Canadian Paperbacks, 1967.

McInnes, Graham. *Canadian Art.* Toronto: Macmillan, 1950.

MacTavish, Newton, *Ars Longa.* Toronto: Ontario Publishing Company, 1938.

—— *The Fine Arts in Canada.* Toronto: Macmillan, 1925, reprinted 1973.

Maurault, Olivier. *Marges d'histoire: l'art au Canada.* Documents historiques, 4. Contribution de la Faculté des lettres de l'Université de Montréal, no. 1. Montréal: Librairie d'Action canadienne-française, 1929.

Mellen, Peter. *The Group of Seven.* Toronto: McClelland and Stewart, 1970.

—— *Landmarks of Canadian Art.* Toronto: McClelland and Stewart, 1978.

Morisset, Gérard. *The Arts in French Canada.* Vancouver: Vancouver Art Gallery, 1959.*

—— *Coup d'oeil sur les arts en Nouvelle-France.* Québec: Charrier et Dugal, 1941.

—— *Peintres et tableaux: les arts au Canada-français.* 2 vols. Québec: Chevalet, 1936-37.

—— *Le peinture traditionelle au Canada-français.* Ottawa: Cercle du livre de France, 1950.

—— *Treasures from Québec.* Ottawa: National Gallery of Canada, 1965.*

Ostiguy, Jean-René. *Un siècle de peinture canadienne, 1870-1970.* Québec: Les Presses du l'Universit Laval, 1971.

—— *Modernism in Québec Art: 1916-1946.* Ottawa: National Gallery of Canada, 1982.*

Reid, Dennis. *A Concise History of Canadian Painting.* Toronto: Oxford University Press, 1973.

—— *The Group of Seven.* Ottawa: National Gallery of Canada, 1970.*

—— *Toronto Painting, 1953-1965.* Ottawa: National Gallery of Canada, 1972.*

Robert, Guy. *L'Art au Québec depuis 1940.* Ottawa: La Presse, 1973.

—— *La Peinture au Québec depuis ses origines.* Ottawa: Iconia, 1978.

Robertson, Heather. *A Terrible Beauty: The Art of Canada at War.* Toronto: James Lorimer, 1977.

Sisler, Rebecca. *Passionate Spirits: A History of the Royal Canadian Academy of Arts, 1880-1980.* Toronto: Clarke, Irwin, 1980.

Spendlove, F. St. George. *The Face of Early Canada.* Toronto: Ryerson Press, 1958.

Toronto. Art Gallery of Ontario. *The Canadian Collection.* Toronto: McGraw Hill, 1970.

Townsend, William, ed. *Canadian Art Today.* London: Studio International; Greenwich, Conn.: New York Graphic Society, 1970.

Trépanier, Jean. *Cent peintres du Québec.* Cahiers du Québec. Collection Beaux-Arts. Ville LaSalle, P.Q.: Hurtubise, 1980.

Trudel, Jean. *Peinture traditionnelle du Québec.* Québec: Ministre des Affaires Culturelles / Musée du Québec, 1967.

Varley, Christopher. *The Contemporary Arts Society: Montréal 1939-1948.* Edmonton: Edmonton Art Gallery, 1980.*

Viau, Guy. *Modern Painting in French Canada.* Québec: Department of Cultural Affairs, 1967.

Victoria, B.C. University. Library. Reference Division. *Creative Canada: A Biographical Dictionary of Twentieth Century Creative and Performing Artists.* 2 vols. Toronto: University of Toronto Press, 1972.

Withrow, William. *Contemporary Canadian Painting.* Toronto: McClelland and Stewart, 1972.

PART II: Portraiture: General References

Alazard, Jean. *The Florentine Portrait.* New York: Schocken Books, 1968.

Altick, Richard. "Faces of the People". *London Review of Books* 4 (19 August-1 September, 1982): 22-24.

American Self-Portraits. New Orleans: Tahir Gallery, 1981.*

Artists' Portraits and Self Portraits Selected from the Permanent Collection, Auckland City Art Gallery. Auckland, N.Z.: Auckland City Art Gallery, 1979.*

Auto-portrait? Exposition organisée par le CARAR avec la collaboration du Musée d'art et d'histoire. Geneva: Muse Rath, 1978.*

Avtoportret na Slovenskem. Ljubljana: Moderna Galerija, 1956.*

Paticle, Jeannine, et Georgel, Pierre. *Technique de la peinture: l'atelier.* Les Dossiers du Départment des Peintures; 12. Paris: Musée du Louvre, Editions des Muses Nationaux, 1976.

Berti, Luciano. "Autoritratti del Novecento per gli Uffizi". *Gli Uffizi* (19 Dicembre 1981): 1-10.

Brophy, John. *The Face in Western Art.* London: George G. Harrap, 1963.

Burroughs, Alan. *Limners and Likenesses: Three Centuries of American Painting.* Cambridge, Mass.: Harvard University Press, 1936.

Catalogue of American Portraits in The New York Historical Society. 2 vols. New Haven, Conn.: Yale University Press, 1974.

The Classical Spirit in American Portraiture. Providence, R.I.: Brown University, Department of Art, 1976.*

Constable, W.G. *The Painter's Workshop.* London: Oxford University Press, 1954.

Dickson, Harold Edward. *Portraits USA, 1776-1976.* University Park, Pa.: Museum of Art, Pennsylvania State University, 1976.*

Dubbelporträt. Rotterdam: Museum Boymans-van Beuningen, 1980.*

Face of America: The History of Portraiture in the United States. Brooklyn: Brooklyn Museum, 1957.*

Fried, Michael. *Absorption and Theatricality: Painting and Beholder in the Age of Diderot.* Berkeley: University of California Press, 1980.

Furst, Herbert. *Portrait Painting: Its Nature and Function.* New York: Frank-Maurice, 1928.

Gasser, Manuel. *Self-Portraits.* London: Weidenfield and Nicolson, 1963.

Goldscheider, Ludwig. *Five Hundred Self Portraits.* London: George Allen and Unwin, 1931.

Gowing, Lawrence. *British Self-Portraits from Sickert to the Present Day.* London: Arts Council, 1962.

Hauser, Arnold. *The Social History of Art.* Vol. 2. London: Routledge and Kegan Paul, 1951.

Hennessey, William J. *The American Portrait: From the Death of Stuart to the Rise of Sargent.* Worcester, Mass.: Worcester Art Museum, 1973.*

Holsten, Siegmar. *Das Bild des Künstlers: Selbstdarstellungen.* Hamburg: Hans Christians, 1978.*

Jenkins, Marianne Duncan. *The State Portrait: Its Origin and Evolution.* New York: College Art Associaton in conjunction with the Art Bulletin, 1947.

Johnson, William McAllister. *French Royal Academy of Painting and Sculpture Engraved Reception Pieces: 1672-1789 / Les morceaux de réception gravés de l'Académie Royale de Peinture et de Sculpture: 1672-1789.* Kingston, Ont.: Agnes Etherington Art Centre, Queen's University, 1982.*

Künstlerbildnesse vom 16. bis 20. Jahrhundert. Köln: Wallraf-Richartz-Museum, 1982.*

Lee, Cuthbert. *Contemporary American Portrait Painters.* New York: W.E. Rudge, 1929.

——— *Early American Portrait Painters: The Fourteen Principal Earliest Native-Born Painters.* New Haven, Conn.: Yale University Press, 1929.

Levey, Michael. *The Painter Depicted: Painters as a Subject in Painting.* London: Thames and Hudson, 1981.

——— *Painting at Court.* London: Weidenfield and Nicolson, 1971.

Lipman, Jean, and Marshall, Richard. *Art About Art.* New York: E.P. Dutton / Whitney Museum of American Art, 1978.*

Maler und Modell. Baden-Baden: Staatliche Kunsthalle, 1969.*

Masciotta, M. *Portraits d'Artistes par eux-mêmes: XIVe-XXe siècle.* Milano: Electa, 1955.

Mayne, Arthur. *British Profile Miniaturists.* London: Faber and Faber, 1970.

Middeldorf, Ulrich und Ugo Procacci. *Die Sammlung der Selbstbildnisse in den Uffizien.* Redigiert von Wolfram Prinz. Berlin: Mann [1971-].

Miles, Ellen, ed. *Portrait Painting in America: The Nineteenth Century.* New York: Main Street Press, 1977.

Modern Portraits: The Self and Others. New York: Wildenstein for the Department of Art History and Achaeology, Columbia University, 1976.*

National Portrait Gallery. *Permanent Collection Illustrated Checklist.* Washington, D.C.: Smithsonian Institution Press, 1978.

Ormond, Richard. *Artists at Work.* London: National Portrait Gallery, 1981.*

Piper, David. *The English Face.* London: Thames and Hudson, 1957.

Pope-Hennessy, John. *The Portrait in the Renaissance.* New York: Bollingen Foundation, 1966.

"Portrait Issue". *Art in America* 63 (January February 1975).

Quick, Michael; Sadik, Marvin; and Gerdts, William H. *American Portraiture in the Grand Manner: 1720-1920.* Los Angeles: Los Angeles County Museum of Art. 1981.*

Reynolds, Graham. *English Portrait Miniatures.* London: Adam and Charles Black, 1952.

Ried, Fitz. *Das Selbstbildnis.* Berlin: Die Bushgemeinde, 1931.

Rose, Barbara. "Self-Portraiture: Theme with a Thousand Faces". *Art in America* 63 (January February 1975): 66-73.

Saissalin, Rémy. *Style, Truth and the Portrait.* New York: Abrams, 1963.

Selbstbildnesse und Künstlerporträts von Lucas van Leyden bis Anton Raphael Mengs. Braunschweig: Herzog Anton Ulrich-Museum, 1980.*

Selbstbildnesse Leipziger Künstler. Leipzig: Museum der bildenden Kunst, 1982.*

Sherman, Frederick Fairchild. *Early American Portraiture.* New York: Privately Printed, 1930.

Sitwell, Sacheverell. *Conversation Pieces: A Survey of English Domestic Portraits and Their Painters.* London: B.T. Batsford, 1936.

Standen, Elizabeth A. *Self-Portraits: The Metropolitan Museum of Art Miniatures.* New York: Metropolitan Museum of Art, 1954.

Thomson, Duncan. *Eye To Eye: A New Look at Old Portraits.* Edinburgh: Scottish National Portrait Gallery, 1980.*

Van Devanter, Ann C., and Frankenstein, Alfred V. *American Self-Portraits 1690-1973.* Washington, D.C.: International Exhibitions Foundation, 1974.*

Walker, John. *The Portrait: 5,000 Years.* New York: Harry M. Abrams, 1983.

Walsh, John Jr. *Portrait of the Artist.* New York: Metropolitan Museum of Art, 1972.*

Wheeler, Monroe. *20th Century Portraits.* New York: Museum of Modern Art, 1942.*

Yung, K.K., comp. *National Portrait Gallery: Complete Illustrated Catalogue 1856-1979.* London: National Portrait Gallery, 1981.

Zakon, Ronnie L. *The Artist and the Studio in the Eighteenth and Nineteenth Centuries.* Cleveland: Cleveland Museum of Art, 1978.*

PART III: Portraiture: Canadian

Aarons, Anita. *New Perceptions: Portraits.* Toronto: Art Gallery at Harbourfront, 1983.*

Allen, Karyn Elizabeth. *Persona.* Calgary: Nickle Arts Museum, University of Calgary, 1982.*

——— *The Winnipeg Pespective 1979: Photo / Extended Dimensions.* Winnipeg: Winnipeg Art Gallery, 1979.*

Allodi, Mary. "Canadian Faces: Some Early Portraits". *Rotunda* 11 (Spring 1978): 18-25.

Artist Paints Artist: The Ontario Society of Artists Seventy-second Annual Spring Exhibition. Toronto: Art Gallery of Toronto, 1944.*

"The artist's image of himself", *Artscanada* 32 (Autumn 1975): 50-56.

Belli, Flavio, ed. *Broom 80.* Hamilton, Ont.: Art Gallery of Hamilton, 1980.*

Belshaw, Linda. *The Figure: A Sensual Response.* Brantford, Ont.: The Art Gallery of Brant, 1976.*

Birnie Danzker, Jo-Anne. *Mannerism: A Theory of Culture.* Vancouver: Vancouver Art Gallery, 1982.

Boyanowski, Christine. *Sight and Insight: Portraits from the Canadian Historical Collection of the Art Gallery of Ontario.* Toronto: Art Gallery of Ontario, 1982.*

Bronson, A.A., and Gale, Peggy, eds. *Performance by Artists.* Toronto: Art Metropole, 1979.

Brown, Elizabeth. *Aspects of Portraiture.* Edmonton: Edmonton Art Gallery, 1978.*

Canada: Face to Face. Sarnia, Ont.: Sarnia Public Library and Art Gallery, 1979.*

Canadian Portraiture: A Continuing Tradition / Le portrait au Canada: continuité d'une tradition. Toronto: Glendon Gallery, York University, 1980.*

Carter, David C. "The Conflict Against Oblivion / Désir de perpetuité," *The Painter and the New World / Le peintre et le Nouveau Monde.* Montréal: Montreal Museum of Fine Arts / Musée des Beaux-Arts de Montréal, 1967.* (Portraiture section of catalogue: plates 64-188.)

Catalogue of an Exhibition of Artists' Portraits by Themselves and Their Friends; Water Colours by American Artists; Little Pictures by Members of the Ontario Society of Artists. Toronto: Art Gallery of Toronto, 1931.*

Dault, Gary Michael. *Barker Fairley Portraits.* Toronto: Methuen, 1981.

Eckhardt, Ferdinand. *Portraits: Mirror of Man.* Winnipeg: Winnipeg Art Gallery, 1956.*

Fairley, Barker. "What is Wrong with Canadian Art?" *Canadian Art* 6 (Autumn 1948):24-29.

Forsey, William C. *The Seven Ages of Man: Inaugural Exhibition.* London: London Regional Art Gallery, 1980.*

Forster, J.W.L. *Sight and Insight.* Toronto: Oxford University Press, 1941.

——— *Under the Studio Light.* Toronto: Macmillan, 1928.

Gale, Peggy. *Video by Artists.* Toronto: Art Metropole, 1976.

Garnet, Eldon, ed. "Auto portrait auto biography self portrait self image" issue, *Im(pul)se* 4-5 (April 1976).

Halifax Portraits. Halifax: Centennial Art Gallery, Nova Scotia Museum of Fine Arts, 1972.*

Here's Looking at You! Hamilton, Ont.: Art Gallery of Hamilton, 1981.*

Hickl-Szabo, H. *Portrait Miniatures in the Royal Ontario Museum.* Toronto: Royal Ontario Museum, 1981.

The Image of Man in Canadian Painting: 1878-1978 / L'image de l'homme dans la peinture canadienne: 1878-1978. London, Ont.: McIntosh Art Gallery, University of Western Ontario, 1978.*

Jarvis, Alan. *Faces of Canada: Portrait Paintings and Sculptures from 1900 to the Present Day.* Stratford, Ontario: Stratford Festival, 1969.*

Katz, John Stuart, ed. *Autobiography: Film/Video/Photography.* Toronto: Art Gallery of Ontario, 1978.*

Kenner, Hugh. "The Case of the Missing Face". *Here and Now* 1 (May 1948): 74-78.

Lennon, Madeline, *Female Archetypes in Art: Madonna/Venus/Eve.* London: McIntosh Art Gallery, 1982.*

Loan Exhibition of Portraits. Montréal: Art Association of Montreal, 1941.*

Loan Portrait Exhibition. Toronto: Women's Art Association of Canada, 1899.*

Lord, J. Barry. "In Search of the Figure in Canadian Painting". *Canadian Art* 21 (July/August 1964): 194-201.

Lowrey, Carol D. "Portrait Sleuthing". *Canadian Collector* 14 (November/December 1979): 42-48.

Mays, John Bentley. "The Snakes in the Garden: The Self and the City in Contemporary Canadian Art". In *Visions: Contemporary Art in Canada,* edited by Robert Bringhurst *et al.* Vancouver: Douglas and McIntyre, 1983, pp. 157-191.

Monk, Philip. "Colony, Commodity and Copyright: Reference and Self-Reference in Canadian Art". *Vanguard* 12 (Summer 1983): 14-17.

—— *Language and Representation.* Toronto: A Space, 1982.*

Morisset, Gérard. *Canadian Portraits of the 18th and 19th Centuries / Portraits canadiens du 18e et 19e siècles.* Ottawa: National Gallery of Canada; Québec: Le Musée de la Province de Québec, 1959.*

Morris, Jerrold. *100 Years of Canadian Drawings.* Toronto: Methuen, 1980.

Plaskett, Joseph. *Joseph Plaskett: Recent Self-Portraits, 1980-1983.* Vancouver: Bau-Xi Gallery.*

Portraits by Canadian Artists. Windsor, Ont.: Willistead Art Gallery, 1950.*

Portraits by Three Photographers. Edited by Shin Sugino and Isaac Applebaum. *Impressions,* No. 13 (March 1975).

Portraits of Painters. Woodstock, Ont.: Woodstock Public Library and Art Gallery, 1973.*

Portraiture in Prints. Kingston, Ont.: Agnes Etherington Art Centre, Queen's University, 1983.*

Ready, Wayne J. *Early Canadian Portraits.* Ottawa: National Gallery of Canada, 1969.*

Rosenberg, Avis Lang. *Mirrorings: Women Artists of the Atlantic Provinces.* Halifax: Art Gallery, Mount Saint Vincent University, 1982.*

Rouleau-Ross, Lucille. *Louise Gadbois, 1936-1955: Le portrait dans la peinture.* Montréal: Musée d'art contemporain, 1979.*

Stacey, Robert. *The Child in Ontario Art.* Toronto: Ontario Ministry of Government Services, 1979.*

Tonnancour, Jacques de. "On Humanity in Canadian Art." *Canadian Art* 7 (October 1949): 6-9.

Town, Elke. *Figures and Portraits in the Thirties and Forties: A Selection of Canadian Paintings and Works on Paper.* Toronto: Art Gallery of Ontario, 1979.*

Treasures fom Québec / Trésors de Québec. Catalogue by J.R. Harper and Dr. R.H. Hubbard. Introduction by Gérard Morisset. Ottawa: National Gallery of Canada / La Galerie nationale du Canada, 1965.

PART IV: Individual Artists in Exhibition

ASTMAN, Barbara

Allen, Karyn. *Barbara Astman: Places.* Calgary: Nickle Arts Museum, University of Calgary, 1983.*

—— *Barbara Astman: Rouge / Red.* Paris: Centre culturel canadien, 1982.*

—— *The Winnipeg Perspective 1979: Photo / Extended Dimensions.* Winnipeg: Winnipeg Art Gallery, 1979.*

Barbara Astman. Peterborough, Ont.: Art Gallery of Peterborough, 1982.*

"Barbara Astman: I Was Thinking About You". *Photo Communiqué* 2 (Fall 1980): 40-41.

Bowen, Lisa Balfour. "Art is Red, Black and Fine". *Toronto Star,* 5 April 1981.

Carroll, Nancy. "Barbara Astman". *Vanguard* 9 (March 1980): 30.

Dault, Gary Michael. "Barbara's Blow-Up..." *Toronto Star,* 12 January 1980.

—— "The Impure Narratives of Barbara Astman". *Saturday Night* (June 1978).

Freedman, Adele. *Barbara Astman: Red.* Lethbridge: Southern Alberta Art Gallery, 1981.*

Pawlenko. Lydia. "Barbara Astman". *Artscanada* 37 (April-May 1980): 39-40.

Sanders, Joyan. *Barbara Astman.* London, Ont.: McIntosh Gallery, University of Western Ontario, 1980.*

ATKINS, Caven

Crawford, Lenore T. "Artist Atkins Claims London as Birthplace" and "Patronage Held vital to Artists." *London* (Ontario) *Free Press,* 9 April 1949.

"Expatriate Artist's Work Returns to Native London". *London Free Press,* 13 February 1982.

Fraser, Ted. *A Retrospective Exhibition of Selected Works by Caven Atkins Spanning Fifty Years of the Artist's Life.* Windsor, Ont.: Art Gallery of Windsor, 1979.*

Murray, Joan. "Caven Atkins: Fifty Years". *Artmagazine* 11 (May-June 1980): 40-44.

BACHINSKI, Walter

Cumming, Glen E.; Plaskett, Joseph; and Tritschler, Tom. *Walter Bachinski: Sculpture and Drawing.* Hamilton, Ont.: Art Gallery of Hamilton, 1981.*

Duval, Paul. *Bachinski: A Decade.* Kitchener, Ont.: Kitchener-Waterloo Art Gallery, 1976.*

Kritzwiser, Kay. "Bachinski's Family a Classical Treat". *Globe and Mail,* 24 April 1981.

Purdie, James. "Bachinski Hurdles the Bronze Barrier". *Globe and Mail,* 10 August 1977.

—— "Luminous Harmony Sealed in Bronze". *Globe and Mail,* 9 October 1979.

Viewpoint: Twenty-Nine by Nine. Hamilton, Ontario: Art Gallery of Hamilton, 1981.*

Weinstein, Alan. *Walter Bachinski.* Introduction by Alan Weinstein. Halifax: Art Gallery and Museum, Mount Saint Vincent University, 1972.*

BATES, Maxwell

Bates, Maxwell, "Native Painting". *Phoebus Calling* (Spring 1934): 20-23.

—— "Visual Art and Photography". *Canadian Art* 17 (March 1960): 76-83.

Graham, Colin. "Maxwell Bates". *Arts West* 1 (1976): 25-28.

Guernsey, Terry. *Maxwell Bates in Retrospect, 1921-1971.* Vancouver: Vancouver Art Gallery, 1972.*

Lowndes, Joan. "Maxwell Bates: In Retrospect 1921-1971". *Artscanada* 30 (May 1973): 59-63.

Maxwell Bates Retrospective Exhibition. Regina: Norman Mackenzie Art Gallery, 1960.*

Page, P.K. "Maxwell Bates". *Artscanada* 27 (April 1970): 62.

Perry, Art. "Maxwell Bates". *Vanguard* 8 (May 1979): 23-25.

Skelton, Robin. "Maxwell Bates: Experience and Reality". *Malahat Review,* No. 20 (October 1971): 57-97.

Thom, Ian M. *Maxwell Bates: A Retrospective.* Victoria, B.C.: Art Gallery of Greater Victoria, 1982.*

BRITTAIN, Miller

Andrus, Donald P. *Drawings and Pastels c. 1930-1967 by Miller Gore Brittain.* Fredericton: Beaverbrook Art Gallery, 1968.*

Costello, Ralph. "Miller Brittain: The Agony and the Ecstasy." *Telegraph-Journal* (Saint John's), 28 November 1981.

Harper, J. Russell. *Miller Brittain: Painter.* Sackville, N.B.: Owens Art Gallery, Mount Allison University, 1981.*

Hume, Christopher. "Art From Thwarted Genius". *Toronto Star,* 20 November 1983.

Miller Brittain (1912-1968). Toronto: Galerie Dresdnere, 1977.*

Miller Brittain (1912-1968). Toronto: Galerie Dresdnere, 1980.*

Mogelon, Alex. *Miller Brittain: In Focus.* Toronto: Simon Dresdnere, 1982.

BURTON, Dennis

Burton, Dennis. "Social Protest and the Heraldic Woman". *Edge* 8 (Fall 1968): 59-79.

—— "Star of David Variations", *Jewish Dialog* (Hanukah 1970): 16-20.

——, and Murray, Joan. *Dennis Burton Retrospective.* Oshawa: Robert McLaughlin Gallery, 1977.*

Dault, Gary Michael. "Dennis Burton Snaps at Garter-Belt Critics". *Toronto Star,* 10 March 1979.

—— "He's Best When True to Himself". *Toronto Star,* 22 July 1978.

Hale, Barrie. "The Wizard of Art". *Canadian Magazine,* 25 June 1977.

Kritzwiser, Kay. "A Well-Earned Retrospective for the Word Painter". *Globe and Mail,* 11 April 1977.

Musicworks. No. 11 (Spring 1980). Special Dennis Burton Issue.

Stacey, Robert. "Dennis Burton - Art Gallery of Hamilton…" *Artscanada* 35 (April-May 1978): 54-55.

Whyte, Jon. *Homage, Henry Kelsey*. Illuminated with eight ink drawings by Dennis Burton, Winnipeg: Turnstone Press, 1981.

CAISERMAN-ROTH, Ghitta

Andrus, Donald F.P. *Ghitta Caiserman-Roth: A Retrospective View 1947-1980 / Ghitta Caiserman-Roth: un aperçu retrospectif 1947-1980*. Montréal: Sir George Williams Art Galleries, Concordia University, 1981.*

Ayre, Robert. "Ghitta Caiserman: An Expanding Vision". *Canadian Art* 9 (Spring 1952): 114-116.

Forsey, Joan. "Paints Figuratively". *Montréal Gazette*, 28 October 1964.

Gladu, Paul. "Une artiste au grand coeur". *Notre Temps* (Montréal), 30 January, 1954.

Golt, Lolly. "Ghitta Caiserman-Roth ou la presence du visible." *Vie des Arts* 27 (décembre-janvier-février 1982-83): 41-43. English original text. p. 78. Traduction par Diane Petit-Pas.

Heviz, Judy. "New Directions for Ghitta Caiserman-Roth", *Artmagazine* 5 (Winter 1974): 35-37.

McCullough, Norah. "Ghitta Caiserman". *Canadian Art* 17 (March 1960): 84-89.

Spurr, Russell. "A Child's Wonderful Make-Believe World". *Weekend Magazine*, 12 March 1960.

Walker, Kathleen. "Works Echo Complex Moods". *Ottawa Citizen*, 3 November 1978.

CARLYLE, Florence

"Carlyle Versatility Shown in Exhibition". *Toronto Star*, 27 May 1925.

Charlesworth, Hector. "Arts and Letters. The late Florence Carlyle, A.R.C.A…." *Canadian Home Journal* (July 1925).

—— "Pictures by Florence Carlyle". *Saturday Night* (6 June 1925).

Farr, Dorothy, and Luckyj, Natalie. *From Women's Eyes: Women Painters in Canada*. Kingston: Agnes Etherington Art Centre, Queen's University, 1975.*

Florence Carlyle. Woodstock, Ontario: Centenial Art Gallery, 1967.*

Hale, Katherine. "A Sympathetic Painter of the Many Phases of Womanhood…" *Star Weekly*, 16 June 1923.

Kritzwiser, Kay. "At Home with Florence Carlyle". *Globe and Mail*, 29 December 1982.

McCausland, Marian. *Florence Carlyle*. Woodstock, Ont.: Woodstock Art Gallery, 1981.*

MacTavish, Newton. "Florence Carlyle and Woodstock." In *Ars Longa*, pp. 106-109. Toronto: Ontario Publishing Company, 1938.

A Memorial Exhibition of the Paintings of the Late Florence Carlyle, A.R.C.A. Toronto: Jenkins' Art Galleries, 1925.*

"Paintings Typify Artist". *Toronto Telegram*, 16 May 1925.

CLARK, Paraskeva

Bell, Andrew. "The Art of Paraskeva Clark." *Canadian Art* 7 (Christmas 1949): 43-46.

Clark, Paraskeva. "Are Painters Being Imposed Upon?" *Canadian Art* 7 (Autumn 1949): 22.

"The Artist Speaks: A Statement by Paraskeva Clark." *Canadian Review of Music and Art* 3 (October-November 1944): 18-19.

Hume, Christopher. "Painting is not a Woman's Job." *Toronto Star*, 29 January 1983.

Kritzwiser, Kay. "Paraskeva in the Looking Glass: Powerful Self-Portraits the Backbone to Her Fiery Body of Work." *Globe and Mail*, 16 February 1983.

McCarthy, Pearl. "Artist Paints Artist." *Globe and Mail*, 11 July 1942.

MacLachan, Mary E. *Paraskeva Clark: Paintings and Drawings*. Halifax: Dalhousie Art Gallery, Dalhousie University, 1982.*

Milroy, Sarah. "Paraskeva Clark." *Canadian Forum* 71 (1983): 38, 40.

Sabbath, Lawrence. "Paraskeva Clark." *Canadian Art* 17 (September 1960): 291-293.

COUGHTRY, Graham

Aarons, Anita. *New Perceptions: Portraits*. Toronto: Art Gallery at Harbourfront, 1983.*

Dault, Gary Michael. "Oil's Well That Ends Well." *Toronto Life* (March 1983): 83-85.

Freedman, Adele. "Romantic Redemption: The Heroic Voyage of Graham Coughtry." *Toronto Life* (October 1978): 48-53.

Hale, Barrie. "Emotion on Canvas: Graham Coughtry Recorded Before a Live Audience." *The Canadian*, 28 February 1976.

—— *Graham Coughtry Retrospective*. Oshawa: Robert McLaughlin Gallery, 1976.*

Kritzwiser, Kay. "Retrospective Unfolds 20 Years of Artist's Life." *Globe and Mail*, 6 March 1976.

CURNOE, Greg

Chandler, John Noel "More Words on Curnoe's Worldly World." *Artscanada* 26 (April 1969): 3-8.

Crawford, Lenore. "'Search' for Portrait Draws Big Gallery." *London Free Press*, 14 December 1962.

Curnoe, Greg, ed. *Region Magazine*, Nos. 1-11 (1961-1968).

FitzGerald, Judith. "Curnoe Memory Paintings: Hospitals, Bicycles, Politics." *Globe and Mail*, 30 July 1983.

Graham, Mayo. *Greg Curnoe / Paterson Ewen / Cathie Falk / Ron Moppett*. Regina: Norman Mackenzie Art Gallery, 1982.*

Hale, Barrie. "Talking Pictures." *Canadian Magazine*, 17 July 1976.

Kidd, Bruce. "Bruce Kidd Interviews Greg Curnoe." *Canadian Forum* 53 (August 1973): 22-30.

Morrison, Ann. "Curnoe: Champion of the Everyday World." *Vanguard* 9 (November 1976): 19.

Nemiroff, Diana. "This is Great Art Because It Wasn't Made by an American." *Vanguard* 10 (October 1981): 24-31.

Reid, Dennis. "Greg Curnoe." In *Canada: Art d'aujourd'hui*. Paris: Musée national d'art moderne, 1968.*

—— *Greg Curnoe: X Biennial Sao Paulo 1969*. Ottawa: National Gallery of Canada, 1969.*

Théberge, Pierre. *Canada: Greg Curnoe: XXXVII Venice Biennale*. Ottawa: National Gallery of Canada, 1976.*

—— intro. *The Great Canadian Sonnet: Drawings by Greg Curnoe*. Ottawa: National Gallery of Canada, 1974.*

—— *Greg Curnoe: retrospective*. Ottawa: National Gallery of Canada, 1982.*

Weiler, Meriké. "London: An Interview with Greg Curnoe - Viewing What Comes Naturally." *Artmagazine* 8 (May-June 1977): 12-14.

Withrow, William J. "Greg Curnoe." In *Contemporary Canadian Painters*. Toronto: McClelland and Stewart, 1972, pp. 185-192.

DALLAIRE, Jean

Beaulieu, Claude. "Dialogue avec mon ami Dallaire." *Vie des Arts*, No. 9 (nöel 1957): 14-22.

Buchanan, Donald W. "The Art of Jean Dallaire." *Canadian Art* 12 (Summer 1955): 143-48.

Dumas, Paul. *Jean Dallaire rétrospective*. Montréal: Musée d'Art contemporain; Québec: Musée du Québec, 1968.*

Morisset, Denys. "Dallaire 1916-1965." *Vie des Arts*, No. 45 (hiver 1967): 32-40.

Robert, Guy. *Daillaire ou l'oeil panique*. Montréal: Éditions France-Amérique, 1980.

Sioui, Anne Marie. *Jean Dallaire*. Montréal: Musée d'Art contemporain, 1979.*

DONOGHUE, Lynn

Freedman, Adele. "Lynn Donoghue: Simply Figured Portraits." *Toronto Life* (January 1979): 80-84.

Mays, John Bentley. "Speaking Quietly of Art's Basics." *Globe and Mail*, 1 March 1980.

Swain, Robert. *Lynn Donoghue: Dancemakers and Other Portraits*. Kingston, Ont.: Agnes Etherington Art Centre, Queen's University, 1982.*

Vane, Harriet. "A Strong Sense of the Person." *CHIMO* 2 (December 1979): 23-26.

White, Peter. "Lynn's World is Peopled by Giants." *Globe and Mail*, 2 April 1977.

DYONNET, Edmond

Ayre, Robert. "Anecdotes of the Late Edmond Dyonnet." *Montreal Star*, 17 July 1954.

Catalogue, Exposition de Edmond Dyonnet, R.C.A..; Ozias Leduc, A.R.C.A.; Joseph Saint-Charles, A.R.C.A.; Elzéar Soucy. Québec: Musée de la Province de Québec, 1945.*

A Century of Canadian Art. London: Tate Gallery, 1938.*

Dyonnet, Edmond. "L'art chez les Canadiens-Français." In *The Year Book of Canadian Art*. pp. 218-229. Toronto: J.M. Dent and Sons, 1913.

—— *Mémoires d'un artiste canadien*. Préface de Jean Ménard. Cahiers du Centre de Recherches en Littérature canadienne-française. Ottawa: Editions de l'Université d'Ottawa, 1968.

—— "Pen and Pencil Club: Portraits des membres, compilés par Edmond Dyonnet, R.C.A." Collection de photos, sans pagination, salle Gagnon, Bibliothèque municipale de Montréal.

—— "Voice from the Academy." *Saturday Night*, 17 December 1938.

"Exposition rétrospective." *Le Soleil*, 12 janvier 1946.

Jones, Hugh G., and Dyonnet, Edmond. "History of the Royal Canadian Academy of Arts." Typescript, 1934.

Morisset, Gérard. *La Peinture traditionelle au Canada Français*. Ottawa: Cercle du livre de France, 1960.

Smith, J. Harry. "Dyonnet and Canadian Art." *Saturday Night*, 18 September 1948.

—— "Edmond Dyonnet, R.C.A.", *The Educational Record of the Province of Québec* (April-June 1955): 102-109.

EYRE, Ivan

Allentuck, Andrew. "Ivan Eyre." *Enroute* (March 1981): 24-28.

Bovey, Patricia. *Ivan Eyre: Drawings 1965-1981*. Victoria, B.C.: Art Gallery of Greater Victoria, 1982.*

Cleroux, Richard. "Ivan Eyre Lets His Haunting Ideas Flow." *Globe and Mail*, 17 November 1981.

Dillow, Nancy E. *Ivan Eyre: Large Paintings (1974-1982)*. Winnipeg: Winnipeg Art Gallery, 1982.*

Eckhardt, Ferdinand. *Ivan Eyre: Recent Paintings and Sculpture*. Winnipeg: Winnipeg Art Gallery, 1974.*

Enright, Robert. "Portrait of the Artist as a Passionate Monk." *Maclean's*, 3 May 1982.

Greenwood, Michael. *Ivan Eyre: New Paintings and Drawings*. Toronto: Mira Godard Gallery, 1978.*

Lord, Barry. "Sundogs in the Sky." *Artscanada* 28 (February/March 1971): 28-35.

Murray, Joan. *Ivan Eyre Exposition*. Oshawa: Robert McLaughlin Gallery, 1980.*

Siemens, Gary. "Leading the Imagination: An Interview with Ivan Eyre." *Arts Manitoba* 1 (Winter 1978): 58-62.

Woodcock, George. *Ivan Eyre*. Toronto: Fitzhenry and Whiteside, 1981.

FITZGERALD, Lionel LeMoine

Ayre, Robert. "Lionel Lemoine FitzGerald, 1890-1956." *Canadian Art* 14 (Autumn 1956): 14-16.

Bovey, Patricia E., ed. *L.L. FitzGerald and Bertram Brooker: Their Drawings*. Winnipeg: Winnipeg Art Gallery, 1975.*

Bovey, Patricia E.; Davies, Ann; and Stewart, Cathy. *Lionel LeMoine FitzGerald (1890-1956): The Development of an Artist*. Winnipeg: Winnipeg Art Gallery, 1978.*

Coy, Helen. *FitzGerald as Printmaker: A Catalogue Raisonné of the First Complete Exhibition of the First Printed Works*. Winnipeg: University of Manitoba Press, 1982.*

—— *L. LeMoine FitzGerald: A Centennial Event*. Winnipeg: Gallery 111, School of Art, University of Manitoba, 1977.*

Eckhardt, Ferdinand. *A New FitzGerald*. Winnipeg: Winnipeg Art Gallery, 1963.*

—— "The Technique of L.L. FitzGerald.": *Canadian Art* 15 (April 1958): 114-118, 149.

FitzGerald, Lionel LeMoine. "FitzGerald on Art." *Canadian Art* 15 (Spring 1958): 118-19.

FitzGerald Memorial Exhibition. Foreword by Alan Jarvis; introduction by Ferdinand Eckhardt. Ottawa: National Gallery of Canada, 1958.*

Harris, Lawren. "FitzGerald's Recent Work." *Canadian Art* 3 (October-November 1945): 10-11.

—— "LeMoine FitzGerald: Western Artist" *Canadian Art* 3 (October-November 1945): 13.

L.L. FitzGerald (1890-1956): Drawings and Watercolours from the Winnipeg Art Gallery. Saint John, N.B.: New Brunswick Museum, 1966.*

Lionel LeMoine FitzGerald: A Memorial Exhibition. Winnipeg: Winnipeg Art Gallery, 1957.*

McDougall, Anne. "La Facture magistrale de FitzGerald." Traduction de Marie-Sylvie Fortier-Rolland. *Vie des Arts* No. 24 (hiver 1979-80): 56-58. Original English text, p. 92.

Memorial Room for LeMoine FitzGerald. Winnipeg: Winnipeg Art Gallery, 1957.*

Nash, Ray. *Drawings of Lionel LeMoine FitzGerald*. Norfolk, N.H.: Norfolk Museum of Arts and Sciences, 1969.*

GRIER, Sir Edmund Wyly

Bridle, Augustus. "E. Wyly Grier, R.C.A." In *Sons of Canada*. Toronto: J.M. Dent & Sons, 1916, pp. 203-206.

Craig, Thelma. "Grier Finds Discomfort in Modernist Painting." *Globe and Mail*, 24 November, 1938.

"Escape Morbid Tendency." *Toronto Telegram*, 26 February 1925.

Exhibition of Canadian Painting by a Group of Selected Artists. Ottawa: National Gallery of Canada, 1935.*

Graham, Jean. "Among Those Present: XLIV-Mr. E. Wyly Grier, P.R.C.A." *Saturday Night*, 19 November 1932.

Grier, C.G.M. "Edmund Wyly Grier." *Upper Canada College Old Times* (Summer 1974): 22-23.

Grier, Sir Wyly. "Canadian Art: A Resumé." In *The Year Book of Canadian Art 1913*. Compiled by The Arts and Letters Club of Toronto. Toronto: J.M. Dent, 1913.

—— "I Have the Grandest Time." *Star Weekly*, 21 January 1939.

Jefferys, C.W. "Portrait Painting." *Canadian Comment* (January 1935): 22.

Miller, Muriel. "Famous Canadian Artists: Sir Wyly Grier, P.R.C.A., D.C.L., Portrait, Figure and Landscape Painter." *Onward*, 27 November 1938.

"Must Study Figure to Develop Art - Grier." *Toronto Star*, 26 February 1925.

"Noted Portrait Painter, Sir Wyly Grier, 95, Dies." *Toronto Star*, 9 December 1957.

Pierce, Lorne. "Sir Wyly Grier, R.C.A., O.S.A., D.C.L." *Educational Record of the Province of Québec* 61 (October-December 1955): 199-203.

"Portrait Painter Needs Joke Book As Well As His Brush and Palette." *Globe and Mail*, 3 February 1930.

HAGAN, Fred

Blackstock, C.R. et al. *Hagan: The Mind and the Hand*. Grimsby, Ont.: Grimsby Public Library and Art Gallery, 1977.*

Burnside, Sharon. "Gallery Show Forces Response." *Owen Sound Sun Times*, 10 January 1978.

Kritzwiser, Kay. "Revealing Exhibition from a Gentle Source." *Globe and Mail*, 24 February 1977.

Littman, Sol. "Hagan: A Relic to Treasure." *Toronto Star*, 12 November 1978.

McKay, Gillian. "Hagan, Artist of Monumental Vision." *Kingston* (Ontario) *Whig Standard*, 29 July 1977.

Purdie, James. "Gallery Reviews." *Globe and Mail*, 26 January 1980.

HALL, John

Balkind, Alvin. "John Hall". In *17 Canadian Artists: A Protean View*. Vancouver: Vancouver Art Gallery, 1976, unpag.*

Bogardi, George. "Art That Goes Pop in the Dark." *CHIMO* (December 1981): 23-25.

Fry, Philip. "John Hall: Paintings and Auxiliary Works, 1969-1978." *Parachute*, No. 18 (printemps, 1980): 9-11.

"John Hall Interview." *Visual Arts Newsletter* 4 (Winter 1982): 8-9.

Madill, Shirley. *Post-Pop Realism: The Winnipeg Prespective 1982*. Winnipeg: Winnipeg Art Gallery, 1982.*

Mays, John Bentley. "Calgary Artist Finds Inspiration in Mass-Produced Miscellany." *Globe and Mail*, 13 April 1981.

Moppett, Ron; Moppett, George; Moppett, Carol; and Hall, John. *John Hall: Paintings and Auxiliary Works 1979-1980*. Saskatoon: Mendel Art Gallery, 1981.*

Moppett, Ron. *John Hall: Paintings and Auxiliary Works 1969-1978*. Calgary: Alberta College of Art Gallery, 1978.*

—— "John Hall: Paintings and Auxiliary Works 1969-1978." *National Gallery of Canada Journal*, No. 35 (5 October 1979).

Nasby, David. *Realism: Structure and Illusion*. Guelph, Ont.: Macdonald Stewart Art Centre, 1981.*

Tousley, Nancy. *John Hall Paintings: Tourist Series / Toy Series*. Lethbridge: Southern Alberta Art Gallery, 1982.*

HARRIS, Robert

Harris, Robert. "Art in Québec and the Maritime Provinces." In *Canada: An Encyclopedia of the Country*. vol. 4, edited by J.C. Hopkins, pp. 353-400. Toronto: Linscott Publishing Company, 1898.

Murray, Joan. *Robert Harris 1849-1919*. Charlottetown, P.E.I.: Confederation Art Gallery and Museum, 1967.*

Percival, Robert M. "Art Department: The Robert Harris Portrait." New Brunswick Museum, *Museum Memo* 3 (March 1971): 4-6.

Sandwell, B.K. "Most Famous Canadian Picture and Its Painter: Robert Harris, R.C.A., and 'The Fathers of Confederation.'" *Saturday Night*, 9 July 1927.

Where are these Works by Robert Harris? Ottawa: National Gallery of Canada, 1973.

Williamson, Moncrieff. "Portraits by Robert Harris (1849-1919): Some Psychological Insights Behind the Great Portraits of Art History." *Artmagazine* 5 (Fall 1973): 7-8.

—— *Robert Harris (1849-1919)*. Ottawa: National Gallery of Canada, 1973.*

—— *Robert Harris 1849-1919: An Unconventional Biography*. Toronto: McClelland and Stewart, 1970.

HÉBERT, Louis-Philippe

Dostaler, Gilles. "Philippe Hébert: sculpteur 'national'." *La Presse* (supp.), 14 décembre 1963.

Dutaud, Gustave. "Hébert the Sculptor." *Canadian Magazine* 33 (May 1909): 49-56.

Gour, Romain. *Philippe Hébert: sculpteur et statuaire*. Montréal: Éditions Eoliennes, 1953.

Hébert, Bruno. *Philippe Hébert sculpteur*. Vies canadiennes. Montréal: Fides, 1973.

Morisset, Gérard. "Le sculpteur Philippe Hébert." *La Patrie* (supp.), 11 juin 1950.

Trépanier, Léon-Z. "A travers les papiers personnels du sculpteur canadien Louis-Philippe Hébert." *La Patrie* (supp.), 13 janvier 1952.

HIND, William G.R.

Harper, J. Russell, *William G.R. Hind*. Canadian Artists Series: 2. Ottawa: National Gallery of Canada, 1976.

—— "William Hind and the Overlanders." *The Beaver* (Winter 1971): 4-15.

Leduc, Joanne. "William G.R. Hind: The Expedition Artist." In *Overland from Canada to British Columbia by Mr. Thomas McMicking of Queenston, Canada West*, pp. xxxi-xxxvi. Edited by Joanne Leduc. Recollections of the Pioneers of British Columbia; v.4. Vancouver: University of British Columbia Press, 1981.

Wm. G.R. Hind (1833-1888): A confederation Painter in Canada. Windsor, Ontario: Willistead Art Gallery, 1967.*

HLYNSKY, David

Dault, Gary Michael. "Art Show Inspired Tomfoolery." *Toronto Star*, 26 May 1979.

—— "Photographer Doubles as Writer." *Globe and Mail*, 7 January 1982.

Hlynsky, David. *Baggage*. Toronto: Coach House Press, 1974.

—— "The Fringe Glossary of Terms." *Broom 80*. Edited by Flavio Belli, Hamilton, Ont.: Art Gallery of Hamilton, 1980, unpag.

—— *Mutilated Photography*. Edited, with introduction, by David Hlynsky. *Image Nation* No. 23 (Spring 1981).

—— *New Canadian Photography / La Nouvelle Photographie Canadienne*. Curated by Jayce Saloum. Designed and edited by David Hlynsky. *Image Nation* No. 26 (Fall 1982). Includes "Middle Word: a conversation between / une conversation entre Jayce Saloum and David Hlynsky'', pp. 5-6, and "New (?) Canadian (?) Photography (?)...!" by David Hlynsky, pp. 7-8.

—— *Salvage*. Toronto: Coach House Press, 1981.

Hollett, Michael. "Renaissance Image Maker." *Now*, 19-25 August 1982.

Wagar, David; Sowdon, Michael; and Hlynsky, David. *Gambling on the Future: Holography, Photography and Painting from Fringe Research Inc*. Winnipeg: Winnipeg Art Gallery, 1979.*

HUMPHREY, Jack Weldon

Abell, Walter, "Jack Humphrey: Painter." *Canadian Forum* 16 (June 1936): 16-18.

Dault, Gary Michael. "Show of Drawings Moving, Disturbing." *Toronto Star*, 7 April 1979.

Duval, Paul. *Jack Humphrey (1901-1967): Oils, Watercolours, Pastels and Drawings 1923-1967*. Toronto: Galerie Dresdnere, 1974.*

Harper, [J.] Russell. *Jack Humphrey*. Fredericton: Beaverbrook Art Gallery, 1966.*

Jack Humphrey: Biographical Data. [Toronto: Galerie Dresdnere, 1973?].

Jack Weldon Humphrey (1901-1967): Early Portraits and Group Paintings and Drawings. Toronto: Galerie Dresdnere, 1980.*

Lumsden, Ian G. *Drawings by Jack Weldon Humphrey*. Fredericton: Beaverbrook Art Gallery, 1977.*

Pfeiffer, Dorothy. "A Visit with Jack Humphrey." *Montreal Gazette*, 1 August 1959.

KLUNDER, Harold

Allen Karyn. *David Craven / Harold Klunder*. Winnipeg: Winnipeg Art Gallery, 1980.*

Dault, Gary Michael. "Klunder Paints Up a Storm." *Toronto Star*, 25 November 1978.

Garlick, Richard. "Human Touch Stressed in Canadian Works." *Winnipeg Free Press*, 6 September 1980.

[Mays, John Bentley]. "Klunder Abandons Acrylics to Find an Oil-Fired Energy." *Globe and Mail*, 13 December, 1980.

Purdie, James. "A Painter Swims Against the Tide to Break the Ties with New York." *Globe and Mail*, 24 September, 1977.

White, Peter. *Harold Klunder*. Stratford, Ontario: The Gallery Stratford, 1977.*

KRIEGHOFF, Cornelius

Barbeau, Marius. *Cornelius Krieghoff*. Toronto: Ryerson, 1948.

——— *Cornelius Krieghoff: Pioneer Painter of North America.* Toronto: Macmillan, 1934.

Guttenberg, A. Ch. de. "Cornelius Krieghoff." *Revue de l'Université d'Ottawa* 24 (1954): 90-108.

Harper, J. Russell. *Krieghoff.* Toronto: University of Toronto Press, 1979.

Jouvancourt, Hugues de. *Cornelius Krieghoff.* Montréal: Editions de la Frégate, 1971.

Robson, Albert H. *Cornelius Krieghoff.* Toronto: Ryerson, 1937.

Soucy, Jean, and Juneau, André. *Cornelius Krieghoff 1815-1872.* Québec: Musée du Québec, 1971.*

Vézina, Raymond. "Attitude esthétique de Cornelius Krieghoff." *RACAR* 1 (1974): 47-69.

——— "Cornelius Krieghoff." *Dictionary of Canadian Biography,* vol. 10. Toronto: University of Toronto Press, 1972, pp. 408-14.

——— *Cornelius Krieghoff: Peintre de moeurs.* Ottawa: Editions du Pélican, 1972.

LAKE, Suzy

Allen, Karyn. *The Winnipeg Perspective 1979 Photo/Extended Dimensions.* Winnipeg: Winnipeg Art Gallery, 1979.*

Barber, Bruce. *Wan/Lake.* Edmonton: SUB Art Gallery, University of Alberta, 1982.*

Cumming, Glen E. *Suzy Lake: Locations and Sites.* Hamilton, Ontario: Art Gallery of Hamilton, 1982.*

Ferguson, Bruce. *Suzy Lake: Are You Talking To Me?* Saskatoon: Mendel Art Gallery, 1980.*

For Suzy Lake, Chris Knudsen, and Robert Walker. Vancouver: Vancouver Art Gallery, 1978.*

Nasgaard, Roald. *Suzy Lake: Impositions.* Toronto: Art Gallery of Ontario, 1978.*

Nemiroff, Diana. "Suzy Lake and Sorel Cohen." *Artscanada* 34 (October/November 1977): 59-60.

——— "Suzy Lake: Impositions." *Parachute,* No. 11 (printemps 1978): 9-11.

Purdie, James. "Lake Stops You In Your Tracks." *Globe and Mail,* 6 October 1979.

LALIBERTÉ, Alfred

Derome, Robert. "Physiognomies de Laliberté." *Vie des Arts* 23 (printemps 1979): 27-29. English translation p. 94.

Déziel, Julien. "Alfred Laliberté, 1878-1953." *Arts et pensée,* No. 14 (novembre-décembre 1953): 42-43.

Laliberté, Alfred. *Légendes Alfred Laliberté: Mes Souvenirs.* Collection Témoins et Témoignages. Montréal: Les Editions du Boréal Express, 1978.

Laurence-Lamontagne, Sophie. "Laliberté et l'ethnologie." *Vie des Arts* 23 (printemps 1979): 30-32.

Légendes: Alfred Laliberté: Collections du Musée du Québec. Foreword by Roger Boulet. Victoria, B.C.: Art Gallery of Greater Victoria, 1976.*

Legendre, Odette. *Alfred Laliberté, 1878-1953.* Montréal: Galerie l'Art Français, 1978.*

Les Bronzes d'Alfred Laliberté du Musée du Québec — Légendes, coutumes, métiers. Québec: Musée du Québec, 1978.*

Montpetit, Raymond. "Alfred Laliberté et la célébration de l'histoire." *Vie des Arts* 23 (printemps 1979): 22-26.

Oxorn, Pearl. "Alfred Laliberté: The Neglected Canadian Sculptor." *Ottawa Journal,* 13 May 1978.

LEDUC, Ozias

Leduc, Ozias. "L'Histoire de S.-Hilaire: on l'entend, on la voit." *Arts et pensée,* no. 18 (juillet-août 1954): 165-68.

Borduas, Paul-Emile. "Paul-Emile Borduas nous écrit au sujet d'Ozias Leduc." *Arts et pensée,* no. 18 (juillet-août 1954): 177-79.

——— "Quelques pensées sur l'oeuvre d'amour et de rêve de Monsieur Ozias Leduc." *Canadian Art* 10 (Summer 1953): 158-61, 168.

Catalogue, Exposition de Edmond Dyonnet, R.C.A.; Ozias Leduc, A.R.C.A.; Joseph Saint-Charles, A.R.C.A.; Elzéar Soucy. Québec: Musée de la Province de Québec, 1945.*

Chauvin, Jean. "Ozias Leduc." In *Ateliers,* pp. 118-126. Montréal: Louis Carrier, Les Éditions du Mercure, 1928.

Corbeil, Gilles. "Ozias Leduc: peinture de natures mortes." *Arts et pensée,* no. 18 (juillet-août 1954): 169-71.

Deligny, Louis. *La chapelle du Sacre-Coeur à l'église du Saint-Enfant-Jésus du Mile-End.* Montréal: Imprimerie du Messager, 1921.

Duffy, Helen. "Leduc's History of Mont Saint-Hilaire." *Artscanada* 35 (October-November 1978): 9-16.

Ethier-Blais, Jean. "Ozias Leduc." In *Autour de Borduas: Assai d'Histoire intellectuelle,* pp. 45-74. Montréal: Les Presses de l'Université de Montréal, 1979.

——— "Ozias Leduc." In *Ozias Leduc et Paul-Emile Borduas,* Conférences J.-A. de Sève 15-16 (1972), pp. 13-56. Montréal: Les Presses de l'Université de Montréal, 1973.

Lacroix, Laurier. "La chapelle de l'évêché de Sherbrooke: quelques dessins préparatoires d'Ozias Leduc." National Gallery of Canada, *Bulletin,* no. 30 (1977): 3-18.

——— "La décoration religieuse d'Ozias Leduc à l'évêché de Sherbrooke." Mémoire de maîtrise, Université de Montréal, 1973.

——— "The Dream Mountain of Ozias Leduc." *Artscanada* 35 (October-November 1978): 9-15.

"Leduc: Undiscovered in His Own Time." *Equinox* 1 (May-June 1982): 72-83.

Montréal. Concordia University. Sir George Williams Art Galleries. *Ozias Leduc, the Draughtsman.* Montréal: Concordia University, Sir George Williams Art Galleries, 1978.*

Ostiguy, Jean-René. "Ozias Leduc: peintre indépendant." *Vie des arts,* no. 29 (hiver 1962-63): 16-21.

——— *Ozias Leduc: peinture symboliste et religieuse / Symbolist and Religious Painting.* Ottawa: National Gallery of Canada, 1974.*

——— "The Preparatory Drawings for the Decoration of the Baptistry of Notre-Dame Church in Montreal." National Gallery of Canada, *Bulletin,* No. 15 (1970): 2-39.

Ostiguy, Jean-René and Corbeil, Gilles. *Ozias Leduc, 1864-1955.* Ottawa: National Gallery of Canada; Québec: Musée de la Province de Québec, 1955.*

Roussan, Jacques de. "Le chant de la Légende d'Ozias Leduc." *Vie des arts* 18 (printemps 1974): 40-42.

Roux, Gilles. "Ozias Leduc: esquisse biographique." *Arts et pensée,* no. 18 (juillet-août): 163-164.

Théberge, Pierre. "De la collection permanente: Leduc et Borduas." *Vie des arts,* no. 58 (printemps 1970): 30-33.

LÉGARÈ, Joseph

Catalogue of the Québec Gallery of Paintings, Engravings, etc. the Property of Jos. Légaré, St. Angele Street, corner of St. Helen Street. Québec: E.R. Frechette, 1852.

Derome, Robert. "Joseph Légaré, 1795-1855." *Canadian Collector* 13 (September-October 1979): 28-31.

Gagnon, François-Marc. "Joseph Légaré, 1795-1855." *Journal of Canadian Art History* 5 (1980): 39-46.

Giroux, Sylvia. *"Le choléra à Québec"* un tableau de Joseph Légaré." National Gallery of Canada, *Bulletin,* No. 20 (1972): 3-12.

Porter, John R. "L'apport de Joseph Légaré (1795-1855) dans le renouveau de la peinture québécoise." *Vie des arts* 23 (automne 1978): 63-66. English translation p. 101.

——— *Joseph Légaré, Painter and Citizen.* National Gallery of Canada. *Journal,* 29 (September 1978).

Porter, John R., Cloutier, Nicole, and Trudel, Jean. *The works of Joseph Légaré, 1795-1855.* Ottawa: National Gallery of Canada for the National Museums of Canada, 1978.* Includes a *catalogue raisonné* of the artist's works.

Tremblay, Claire. "L'oeuvre profane de Joseph Légaré." Mémoire de maîtrise, Université de Montréal, 1973.

LEMIEUX, Jean-Paul

Bice, Clare. *Jean-Paul Lemieux.* London, Ont.: London Art Gallery, 1966.*

Bourget, Jean-Loup. "Lemieux." In *16 Québec Painters in their Milieu.* Montréal: La Vie des Arts Collection: A Survey of Creators, 1978, pp. 97-106.

Corbeil, Gilles. "Jean-Paul Lemieux: Peintre intimiste." *Arts et pensée,* No. 14 (november-décembre 1953): 36-[41].

Dault, Gary Michael. "Lemieux Damned by Verbose Praise." *Toronto Star,* 20 January 1979.

Freedman, Adele. "The Quiet Revolution of Jean Paul Lemieux." *Maclean's,* 27 November 1978.

d'Iberville, Moreau. *Jean Paul Lemieux.* Montréal: Montréal Museum of Fine Arts, 1967.*

Jean-Paul Lemieux. Montréal: Montréal Museum of Fine Arts, 1967.*

Nagle, Patrick. "Timeless Painter from Québec." *Weekend Magazine,* 9 March 1963.

Picher, Claude, and Cadieux, Marcel. "Jean-Paul Lemieux." *Canadian Art* 17 (September 1960): 264-73.

Purdie, James. "Lemieux Has Paid the Price." *Globe and Mail,* 11 November 1978.

Robert, Guy. *Jean-Paul Lemieux: la poétique de la souvenance.* Québec: Garneau, 1968.

——— *Lemieux.* Montréal: Les Editions Internationales Alain Stanke, 1975.

——— *Lemieux.* Toronto: Gage, 1978.

Roy, Gabrielle. "Les Terres Nouvelles de Jean-Paul Lemieux." *Vie des Arts* 7 (hiver 1962): 38-43.

Vézina, Raymond. "Jean-Paul Lemieux: Le Cycle de la vie humaine." *Vie des Arts* 19 (hiver 1974-75): 20-25.

White, Peter. "Getting Away from Stiff Traditions." *Globe and Mail,* 21 July 1977.

LISMER, Arthur

Arthur Lismer: Paintings 1913-1950. Toronto: Art Gallery of Toronto, 1950.*

Ayre, Robert. "Arthur Lismer." *Canadian Geographic Journal* 33 (December 1946): 284-85.

Bridges, Marjorie Lismer. *A Border of Beauty: Arthur Lismer's Pen and Pencil.* Toronto: Red Rock, 1977.

Darroch, Lois. *Bright Land: A Warm Look at Arthur Lismer.* Toronto: Merritt, 1981.

Kelly, Gemey. *Arthur Lismer: Nova Scotia, 1916-1919.* Halifax: Dalhousie Art Gallery, Dalhousie University, 1982.*

McLeish, John. *September Gale: A Study of Arthur Lismer of the Group of Seven.* 2d ed. Toronto: Dent, 1973.

Reid, Dennis. *A Bibliography of the Group of Seven.* Ottawa: National Gallery of Canada, 1971.

LYMAN, John

Biéler, Zoe. "Lyman: Pursuit of Perfection Has Made Him an Outstanding Artist and Critic." *Montreal Standard,* 12 August 1944.

Braide, Janet. "John Lyman: A Bibliography of His Writings." *Journal of Canadian Art History* 4 (1977-1978): 130-40.

Corbeil, Gilles. "John Lyman." *Arts et pensée,* No. 15 (janvier-février 1954): 75-83.

——— *John Lyman.* Montréal: Montréal Museum of Fine Arts, 1963.*

Dumas, Paul. *Lyman.* Collection Art Vivant. Montréal: L'Arbe, 1944.

Duval, Paul. "John Lyman Helps Younger Artists to Experiment." *Saturday Night,* 2 August 1947.

Lyman, John. *Inédits de John Lyman.* Choix des textes et annotations de Hedwidge Asselin. Montréal: Ministère des Affaires culturelles, Bibliothèque nationale de Québec, 1980.

McInnes, G. Campbell. "Contemporary Canadian Artists: No. 5 - John Lyman." *Canadian Forum* 17 (June 1937): 94-95.

Surrey, Philip. "The Paintings of John Lyman." *Weekend Magazine*, 19 November 1966.

MACDONALD, Thomas Reid

Duval, Paul. "Impressive Display by Mac Gallery Director." *Hamilton* (Ontario) *Spectator*, 23 November 1968.

Hubbard, R.H. *Paintings and Drawings by T.R. MacDonald, R.C.A.* Hamilton, Ont.: McMaster University Art Gallery, 1968.*

Inglis, Grace. "MacDonald Deserves More Recognition." *Hamilton* (Ontario) *Spectator*, 1 November 1980.

——— "MacDonald's Paintings Show Rich Colour Harmony." *Hamilton* (Ontario) *Spectator*, 29 October 1980.

Oko, Andrew J. *T.R. MacDonald 1908-1978.* Hamilton, Ont.: Art Gallery of Hamilton, 1980.*

MACKENZIE, Hugh

Duval, Paul. "Hugh Mackenzie." In *High Realism in Canada.* Toronto: Clarke, Irwin, 1974. pp. 122-131.

"Family Portrait." *Time* (Canadian Edition), 26 April 1968.

Hugh Mackenzie. Toronto: Morris Gallery, 1969.*

Hugh Mackenzie. Toronto: Morris Gallery, 1973.*

Hugh Mackenzie. Waterloo, Ont.: Art Gallery, University of Waterloo, 1975.*

Kritzwiser, Kay. "Breaking Free From Magic Realism." *Globe and Mail*, 1 December 1973.

Magic Realism in Canadian Painting. London, Ontario: London Art Gallery, 1966.*

Purdie, James. "Hugh Mackenzie." *Globe and Mail*, 7 August 1976.

Stacey, Robert. "Hugh Mackenzie: Morris Gallery..." *Artscanada* 35 (April-May 1978): 52.

MATTE, Francis

Harper, J. Russell. *Early Painters and Engravers in Canada.* Toronto: University of Toronto Press, 1970, p. 219.

Hubbard, R.H., and Ostiguy, J.R. *Three Hundred Years of Canadian Art.* Ottawa: National Gallery of Canada, 1967.*

Morisset, Gérard. *Coup d'oeil sur les arts en Nouvelle-France.* Québec: Charrier et Dugal, 1941.

——— *La Peinture traditionelle au Canada français.* Ottawa: Le Cercle du Livre de France, 1960.

MOPPETT, Ron

Falk, Lorne; Tousley, Nancy; and Graham, Mayo. *Ron Moppett.* Banff: Walter Phillips Gallery, 1982.*

Graham, Mayo. *Greg Curnoe/Paterson Ewen/Gathie Falk/Ron Moppett.* Regina: Norman Mackenzie Art Gallery, 1982.*

MUHLSTOCK, Louis

[Abell, Walter]. "War Industry Drawings by Muhlstock and Brandtner." *Canadian Art* 1 (October-November 1943): 24-25, 37.

Ayre, Robert. "City Museum Frowns on Muhlstock Nudes." *Montreal Star*, 26 November 1962.

——— "Louis Muhlstock." *Northern Review* 2 (January-February 1949): 15-20.

——— "Muhlstock's Transformation is a Natural Development." *Montreal Star*, 29 March, 1952.

——— "The New Muhlstock." *Canadian Art* 9 (Summer 1952): 140-43.

Forster, Michael. "Art Notes: Artists Lack Support Says Louis Muhlstock." *Montreal Standard*, 8 July 1950.

McInnes, Graham. "Louis Muhlstock: Painter of People." *New World* (March 1941).

Maître, Manuel. "Louis Muhlstock ne renie ni le figuratif, ni l'abstrait." *La Patrie du Dimanche* (Montréal), 6 August 1961.

Muhlstock, Louis. "The Art Forum: Letters to the Editor." *Canadian Art* 4 (May 1947): 134-35.

——— "Letters to the Editor: Lack of Publicity for Art Shows is Criticized by Montreal Artist." *Montreal Standard*, 21 February 1948.

Repentigny, Rodolphe de. "Louis Muhlstock." *Vie de Arts*, No. 16 (automne 1959): 10-15.

Sabbath, Lawrence. "Artists in Action Series: 1 -Louis Muhlstock with Lawrence Sabbath." *Canadian Art* 17 (July 1960): 216-223.

Saint-Denys Garneau, Hector de. "Chronique des beaux-arts: Louis Muhlstock." *La Relève* 2 (January 1936): 158-60. Reprinted in *Saint-Denys Garneau: Oeuvres* (Montréal: Les Presses de l'Université de Montréal, 1971): 281-83, 1120-1122.

NEUMANN, Ernst

Ayre, Robert. "Museum's Memorial Exhibition of Ernst Neumann's Work." *Montreal Standard*, 27 December 1958.

E. Neumann. Hamilton, Ont.: Art Gallery of Hamilton, 1958.

Etchings, Lithographs and Woodcuts by Ernst Neumann. Montréal: Montreal Museum of Fine Arts, 1939.*

Pfeiffer, Dorothy. "Ernst Neumann's Art in Retrospect." *Montréal Gazette*, 20 December 1958.

Roberts, Goodridge. "Ernst Neumann as a Painter." *Canadian Art* 7 (Christmas/New Year 1949/50): 47-50.

Stella Langdale, Ernst Neumann, Jack Nichols, Robert Ross. Toronto: Art Gallery of Toronto, 1941.*

OLSON, Gary

Gary Olson. Edmonton: Edmonton Art Gallery, 1976.*

Madill, Shirley. *Post-Pop Realism: The Winnipeg Perspective 1982.* Winnipeg: Winnipeg Art Gallery, 1982, pp. 20-23.*

Parke-Taylor, Michael. *Gary Olson: Against the Picture Plane.* Regina: Norman Mackenzie Art Gallery, 1980.*

Stacey, Robert. "Six New Realists: Aggregation Gallery..." *Artscanada* 34 (March-April 1977): 58-60.

PEEL, Paul

Armstrong, Isabel C. "Paul Peel and His Art." *Canadian Magazine* 35 (May 1910)

Bice, Clare. *Paul Peel 1860-1892.* London, Ont.: London Art Gallery, 1970.*

Crawford, Lenore. "Peel Paintings Come Home." *London* (Ontario) *Free Press*, 6 June 1959.

Harper, J. Russell. *Early Painters and Engravers in Canada.* Toronto: University of Toronto Press, 1970.

——— *Painting in Canada: A History.* Toronto: University of Toronto Press, 1966, new edition 1977.

Howard, Kirk. *Paul Peel (1860-1892).* Lives and Works of the Canadian Artists. Toronto: Dundurn Press, 1977.

MacDonald, Adrian. "Paul Peel." In *Canadian Portraits.* Toronto: Ryerson, 1925.

PELLAN, Alfred

Alfred Pellan. Ottawa: National Gallery of Canada, 1960.*

Barras, Henri. "Un cinéaste face à un artiste." *Culture vivante*, No. 13 (May 1969): 32-37.

Bédard, Jean. "La sauvagerie apprivoisée de Pellan." *Culture vivante*, No. 26 (septembre 1972): 2-11.

Buchanan, Donald W. *Alfred Pellan.* Gallery of Canadian Art; 4. Toronto: Society for Art Publications, McClelland and Stewart, 1962.

Bulletin du Musée du Québec. No. 14 (mars 1970).

Cassou, Jean. *Alfred Pellan.* Paris: Musée National d'Art Moderne de Paris, 1955.

Daignault, Gilles. "Pellan." *16 Québec Painters in their Milieu.* Montréal: La Vie des Arts Collection: A Survey of Creators, 1978, pp. 127-136.

Drayton, Geoffrey. "Canadian Rebel: Alfred Pellan." *Studio* 142 (August 1951): 54-57.

Duval, Paul. "The Work of Alfred Pellan." *Here and Now* 1 (January 1949): 53-65.

Gagnon, Maurice. *Pellan.* Collection Art Vivant. Montréal: Editions l'Arbre, 1943.

Greenberg, Reesa. *The Drawings of Alfred Pellan.* Ottawa: National Gallery of Canada, 1980.*

——— "Surrealism and Pellan: L'Amour fou." *Journal of Canadian Art History* I (Fall 1974): 1-11.

——— "Surrealist Traits in the Heads of Alfred Pellan." *Journal of Canadian Art History* 3 (Fall 1976): 55-68.

Lefebvre, Germain. *Pellan.* Montréal: Les Editions de l'Homme; Toronto: McClelland and Stewart, 1975.

——— "Saison Pellan." *Vie des arts* 68 (automne 1972): 49-53.

Lefebvre, Germain, and Marchand, André. *Pellan.* Québec: Musée du Québec; Montréal: Montreal Museum of Fine Arts, 1972.*

[Pellan, Alfred.] "La queue de la comète: Alfred Pellan: Témoin du surréalisme. Interview Vie des Arts." *Vie des Arts* 20 (automne 1975): 18-21. English translation, p. 88.

Pellan. Montréal: Editions Yvan Boulerice, 1973.

Robert, Guy. *Pellan: Sa Vie, Son Oeuvre.* Collection Artistes Canadiens. Montréal: Editions du Centre de Psychologie et de Pédagogie, 1963.

Toupin, Paul. "Pellan chez lui." *Vie des Arts* 4 (hiver 1959): 31-36.

Withrow, William J. "Alfred Pellan." In *Contemporary Canadian Painting.* Toronto: McClelland and Stewart, 1972, pp. 33-40.

POOLE, Leslie

Edmonstone, Wayne. "[Leslie Poole]." *Vancouver Star*, 8 July 1977.

Howarth, Glen. "Confessions: Leslie Poole." *Vanguard* 8 (April 1979): 27-29.

——— "Leslie Poole: An ecumenical Intent." *Vanguard* 7 (June-July 1978): 6-8.

Lindberg, Ted. *Leslie Poole: Confessions.* Vancouver: Vancouver Art Gallery, 1979.*

Mertens, Susan. "Artist Immersed in Self-Discovery." *Vancouver Sun*, 23 February 1981.

Purdie, James. "Gallery Reviews." *Globe and Mail*, 12 January 1980.

PRATT, Christopher

Bruce, Harry. "A Rarer Reality: Christopher Pratt Invests Everyday Objects with Mystery." *Canadian Magazine*, 26 November, 1977.

Cook, Michael. "Christopher Pratt: tel qu'en lui-même." *Vie de arts*, No. 22 (eté 1977): 42-44.

Dault, Gary Michael. "Maritimes Artist More than a Realist." *Toronto Star*, 25 October 1976.

Freedman, Adele. "A World Through the Narrows." *Globe and Mail*, 20 March 1982.

Greenwood, Michael, and Bear, Griselda. *Christopher Pratt: Paintings, Prints, Drawings / Tableaux, sérigraphies, dessins.* London: Canadian High Commission for Canada House Cultural Centre Gallery, 1982.*

Hachey, Paul A. *Colville; Pratt; Forestall.* Fredericton: Beaverbrook Art Gallery, 1974.*

Hammock, Virgil G. "Pratt et Pratt." Traduction de Marie-Sylvie Fortier-Rolland. *Vie des Arts*, No. 26 (eté 1981): 45-48. Original English text, p. 78.

Johnston, Ann. "A Brooding Vision." *Maclean's*, 21 September 1981.

Mays, John Bentley. "Pratt's Precise Offerings Reward the Patient Viewer." *Globe and Mail*, 13 December 1980.

Silcox, David, and Weiler, Meriké. *Christopher Pratt.* Toronto: Quintus Press, 1980.

PULFORD, Edward B.

Bentley, E.T. Keilor. *Edward B. Pulford, C.D., B.F.A.* Introduction by Christopher Pratt. Sackville, N.B.: Owens Art Gallery, Mount Allison University, 1980.*

Daley, Hartwell. "Edward B. Pulford — Becoming an Artist." *Arts Atlantic* 3 (Fall 1980): 28-29.

A Tribute to Ted Pulford. Sackville, N.B.: Owens Art Gallery, 1983.*

ROBERTS, Goodridge

Bell, Michael. *William Goodridge Roberts, 1904-1974: Drawings.* Kingston, Ont.: Agnes Etherington Art Centre, Queen's University, 1977.*

Borcoman, James; Ayre, Robert; and Pinsky, Alfred. *Goodridge Roberts: A Retrospective Exhibition.* Ottawa: National Gallery of Canada, 1969.*

Boulanger, Rolland. "Goodridge Roberts." *Arts et pensée* 1 (mai 1951): 74-79.

Jouvancourt, Hugues de. *Goodridge Roberts.* Montréal: Editions La Frigate, 1983.

Sabbath, Lawrence. "Goodridge Roberts comes into perspective." *Montréal Gazette,* 27 August 1983.

Tonnancour, Jacques G. de. *G. Roberts.* Collection Art Vivant, no. 3. Montréal: Editions de l'Arbre, 1944.

Town, Elke. *Goodridge Roberts: Paintings from the 1950s and 1960s.* Toronto: Art Gallery of Ontario, 1980.*

Wilkin, Karen. *Goodridge Roberts: Selected Works / Oeuvres choisies.* Saskatoon: Mendel Art Gallery, 1981.*

Woods, Kay. "The Art of Goodridge Roberts." *Artscanada* 33 (December 1976-January 1977): 52-54.

SAINT-CHARLES, Joseph

Catalogue, Exposition de Edmond Dyonnet, R.C.A.; Ozias Leduc, A.R.C.A.; Joseph Saint-Charles, A.R.C.A.; Elzéar Soucy. Québec: Musée de la Province de Québec, 1945.*

"Joseph Saint-Charles, Esq., Artist." *The Dominion Illustrated,* 8 November 1890.

"Joseph Saint-Charles: un peintre méconnu." *Bulletin de Centre de recherche en civilisation canadienne-française,* Université d'Ottawa, No. 9 (décembre 1974): 13-16.

Laurin, François. "Joseph Saint-Charles, 1868-1956." *RACAR* 1 (1975): 55-64.

"M. Joseph Saint-Charles." *Le Monde Illustré,* 18 octobre 1890.

SAWYER, William

Bell, Michael. *W. Sawyer: Portrait Painter.* Kingston, Ont.: Agnes Etherington Art Centre, Queen's University, 1978.*

Harper, J. Russell. *Early Painters and Engravers in Canada.* Toronto: University of Toronto Press, 1970, p. 280.

SEXTON, Ezekiel

Forsey, William C. *The Ontario Community Collects: A Survey of Canadian Painting from 1766 to the Present.* Toronto: Art Gallery of Ontario, 1975.*

Harper, J. Russell. *Early Painters and Engravers in Canada.* Toronto: University of Toronto Press, 1970, pp. 284-85.

Permanent Collection Catalogue. London, Ontario: London Public Library and Art Museum, 1971.

SHELDON-WILLIAMS, Inglis

Ainslie, Patricia. *Inglis Sheldon-Williams.* Calgary: Glenbow Museum, 1982.*

Dillow, Nancy. "Inglis Sheldon-Williams." *Canadian Antiques Collector* 8 (July/August 1973): 41-44.

Fudge, Paul. "Saskatchewan had Influence on Work of Sheldon-Williams." *Regina Leader Post,* 20 May 1982.

Humphreys, Ruth. "Inglis Sheldon-Williams: Pioneer Artist of the Prairies." *The Beaver,* Outfit 310:3 (Winter 1979): 4-13.

———. "Inglis Sheldon-Williams: Pioneer Artist of the Prairies, Part II." *The Beaver,* Outfit 310:4 (Spring 1980): 24-31.

Irwin, Ted. *Inglis Sheldon-Williams (1870-1940): Paintings and Drawings from the Regina Collections.* Regina: Regina Public Library and Art Gallery, 1969.*

SNOW, Michael

Cornwell, Regina. "Michael Snow: The Decisive Moment Revised." *Artscanada* 37 (April/May 1980): 1-9.

———. *Snow Seen: The Films and Photographs of Michael Snow.* Toronto: Peter Martin Associates, 1980.

Dale, Stephen. "Michael Snow's World." *Now* 1 (May 27-June 2 1982): 7-9.

Field, Simon. "Michael Snow Framed." *Art and Artists* (November 1972): 20-25.

Hale, Barrie. "The Inventions of Michael Snow." *Toronto Star (Canadian Magazine),* 1 January 1977.

Michael Snow: A Survey. Toronto: Art Gallery of Ontario, 1970.*

Michael Snow: Organized [for the] XXV International Biennial Exhibition of Art, Venice. Ottawa: National Gallery of Canada, 1970.*

Michelson, Annette. "About Snow." *October* 8 (Spring 1979): 111-125.

Percival, Jo. "On View: The Many Sides of Michael Snow." *Brick,* No. 5 (Spring 1982): 17-19, 21.

Sayag, Alain; Wacogne, Catherine; and Théberge, Pierre. *Michael Snow.* Paris: Centre Georges Pompidou, 1978; Lucerne: Kunstmuseum; Rotterdam: Museum Boymans-van Beuningen, 1979.*

Snow, Michael. *Cover to Cover.* Nova Scotia Series. Halifax: Nova Scotia College of Art and Design, 1975.

———. *High School.* Impulse Editions; 1. Toronto: Impulse, 1979.

Withrow, William J. "Michael Snow." In *Contemporary Canadian Painters.* Toronto: McClelland and Stewart, 1972, pp. 113-120.

Snow, Michael. "Michael Snow: A letter to Alvin Balkind from Michael Snow, April 1976", quoted in Alvin Balkind, *17 Canadian Artists: A Protean View.* Vancouver: The Vancouver Art Gallery, 1976, unpag.*

TANGREDI, Vincent

Amman, Jean-Christophe. "Vincent Tangredi". In *Kanadische Künstler.* Basel: Kunsthalle, 1978, unpaginated.

Cameron, Eric. "Vincent Tangredi: un Pygmalion à rebours." *Vie des arts* 22 (automne 1977): 75.

Carr-Harris, Ian. "Vincent Tangredi." *Parachute* 30 (March-May 1983): 51.

Klepac, Walter. "Vincent Tangredi..." *Artscanada* 32 (March 1975): 63.

Mays, John Bentley. "Bad news is just fine for Vincent Tangredi." *Globe and Mail,* 6 January 1981.

———. "Vincent Tangredi..." *Vanguard* 12 (March 1983).

Monk, Philip. "Arresting Figures: Vincent Tangredi." *Vanguard* 11 (March 1982): 18-21.

Tangredi, Vincent. "Beautiful Blud." *Impulse* (contributing editor: Vincent Tangredi) 5 (Winter 1977): unpag.

———. "1902." *Impulse* 9 (Spring 1981): 41-42.

———. *Of the Four Considerations.* Toronto: Carmen Lamanna Gallery, 1982.*

———. "Of the Four Considerations." *Impulse* 10 (Spring 1983): 41-43.

TAYLOR, Frederick B.

"Frederick B. Taylor Shows at Dominion." *Montreal Gazette,* 19 November 1955.

Lord, Barry. *The History of Painting in Canada: Towards a People's Art.* Toronto: NC Press, 1974.

"A Painter Turns to the People." *Canadian Tribune* (Toronto), 6 March 1951.

Taylor, Frederick B. "The Arts and Postwar Reconstruction." *National Affairs Monthly* (March 1945): 78-81.

———. "Canadian Artists: Frederick B. Taylor...Painting War Productions." *World Affairs* 8 (January 1943): 17-18.

———. "On Art and Canadian Labor." *Canadian Tribune* (Toronto), 17 November 1945.

TEITELBAUM, Mashel

Fulford, Robert. "An Art Joke on Art Jokes." *Toronto Star,* 21 November 1967.

———. *New Works by Mashel Teitelbaum.* Toronto: Gallery Moos, 1970.

Hale, Barrie. "Almost Snowed Under." *Toronto Telegram,* 27 February 1965.

Hume, Christopher. "Mashel Teitelbaum at Loranger Gallery." *Artmagazine* 10 (May/June 1979): 40.

McPherson, Hugo. "Artist in Opposition." *Canadian Art* 20 (May/June 1963): 168-171.

———. *Mashel Teitelbaum.* Toronto: Greenwich Gallery, 1958.*

Morris, Jerrold. *The Nude in Canadian Painting.* Toronto: New Press, 1972.

———. *100 Years of Canadian Drawings.* Toronto: Methuen, 1980.

———. *On the Enjoyment of Modern Art.* Gallery of Canadian Art; 5. Toronto: McClelland and Stewart, 1965.

Reid, Dennis. *Toronto Painting 1953-65.* Ottawa: National Gallery of Canada, 1972.*

URQUHART, Tony

Cameron, Dorothy. "Reunion with Tony Urquhart." *Artscanada* 28 (April/May 1971): 41-48.

Kritzwiser, Kay. "Retrospective a Divine Revelation." *Globe and Mail,* 16 December 1978.

Littman, Sol. "Tony's Work Deals with Death But He Treats It So Cheerfully." *Toronto Star,* 18 February 1979.

Mays, John Bentley. "Artist Looks Deep Into Symbolic Wells." *Globe and Mail,* 26 March 1981.

Mogelin, Alex, and Laliberté, Norman. *Art in Boxes.* New York: Van Nostrand Reinhold, 1974, pp. 112-13.

Tony Urquhart: Twenty-Five Years. Kitchener, Ont.: Kitchener-Waterloo Art Gallery, 1978.*

Vastokas, Joan. "The Interdimensional Landscape: Archetypal Imagery in the Work of Tony Urquhart." *Artscanada* 30 (May 1973): 30-44.

VARLEY, Frederick H.

Cochrane, Bente Roed. "Entre la lumière et l'ombre: F.H. Varley." Traduction de Diane Petit-Pas. *Vie des Arts* 27 (automne 1982): 46-47. Original English text, p. 91.

Elliot, George. "F.H. Varley: Fifty Years of His Art." *Canadian Art* 12 (Autumn 1954): 3-8.

F.H. Varley: Paintings 1915-1954. Toronto: Art Gallery of Toronto, 1954.*

Mays, John Bentley. "Varley Tortured by the 'Restless and Waking'." *Globe and Mail,* 20 February 1982.

Reid, Dennis. *A Bibliography of the Group of Seven.* Ottawa: National Gallery of Canada, 1971.

Saltmarche, Kenneth. *F.H. Varley Retrospective.* Windsor, Ont.: Willistead Art Gallery, 1964.*

Varley, Christopher. *F.H. Varley.* Canadian Artists Series; 6 Ottawa: National Gallery of Canada, 1979.

———. *F.H. Varley: A Centennial Exhibition.* Edmonton: Edmonton Art Gallery, 1981.*

———. *Varley: The Middle Years.* Burnaby, B.C.: Burnaby Art Gallery, 1974.*

Varley, Peter, and Zemans, Joyce. *F.H. Varley.* Toronto: Key Porter, 1983.

VALENTINE, William

Harper, J. Russell. *Early Painters and Engravers in Canada.* Toronto: University of Toronto Press. 1970, pp. 314-315.

Piers, Harry. "Artists in Nova Scotia." In *Collections of the Nova Scotia Historical Society.* Vol. 18, pp. 101-165. Halifax: Nova Scotia Historical Society, 1914.

WHITEN, Colette

Chandler, John Noel. "Colette Whiten: Her Working and Work." *Artscanada* 29 (Spring 1972): 42-45.

———. "Persona: The Sculpture of Colette Whiten." *Artscanada* 35 (April/May 1978): 4-[14].

Dault, Gary Michael. "Sculptor Colette Whiten Builds Her Works from Air." *Toronto Star*, 20 May 1978.

Freedman, Adele. "Colette Whiten's Humanizing Process: Transforming People into High Art." *Toronto Life* (April 1978): 160-64.

Graham, Mayo. "Colette Whiten" *Some Canadian Women Artists*. Ottawa: National Gallery of Canada. 1975, pp. 80-88.*

Hitzeroth, Connie. "Colette Whiten." *Artscanada* 30 (May 1973): 45-47.

Luckyj, Natalie. *Prince; Prent; Whiten: Figurative Sculpture*. Kingston, Ont.: Agnes Etherington Art Centre, Queen's University, 1981.*

Mays, John Bentley. "Friends are Cast as Artworks in Colette Whiten Sculptures." *Globe and Mail*, 12 April 1980.

Monk, Philip. *Colette Whiten*. London, Ont.: London Regional Art Gallery, 1978.*

Whiten, Colette. Untitled artist's statement, "Colette Whiten", *Eclectic Eve* (Toronto: Women's Educational Press, 1972), unpag.

——— "Colette Whiten." *Artscanada* 34 (May-June 1977): 55.

WIELAND, Joyce

Auchterlonie, Bill. "Joyce Wieland: Filmmaker." *Artmagazine* 7 (December 1975): 6-11.

Balkind, Alvin. "Joyce Wieland", *17 Canadian Artists: A Protean View*. Vancouver: Vancouver Art Gallery, 1976 unpag.*

Cornwell, Regina. "The Film of Joyce Wieland," *True Patriot Love*. Ottawa: National Gallery of Canada, 1971.

Freedman, Adele. "Portraits from a Daring Artist." *Globe and Mail*, 4 January 1983.

McPherson, Hugo, "Wieland: An Epiphany of North." *Artscanada* 28 (August-September 1971): 17-27.

Rabinovitz. Lauren. "An Interview with Joyce Wieland." *Afterimage* 8 (May 1981): 8-12.

Stacey, Robert. *Joyce Wieland*. Lives and Works of the Canadian Artists; 15. Toronto: Dundurn Press, 1978.

Ward, Olivia. "Artist Joyce Wieland: Blossoming at 50." *Toronto Star*, 8 February 1981.

Wieland, Joyce. "Artist Wieland Finds Maturity." *Toronto Star*, 27 April 1980.

——— *True Patriot Love*. Ottawa: National Gallery of Canada, 1971.*

——— Untitled artist's statement, "Joyce Wieland", *Eclectic Eve* (Toronto: Women's Educational Press, 1972), unpag.

Withrow, William J. "Joyce Wieland." In *Contemporary Canadian Painting*. Toronto: McClelland and Stewart, 1972, pp. 121-128.

Wordworth, Anne. "An Interview with Joyce Wieland." *Descant* 8-9 (Spring-Summer 1974): 108-110.

YOUNG, Robert

Allison, Glenn. "Robert Young." *Arts West* 2 (November-December 1977): 17-18.

Crichton, Fenella. "A Juggler of Styles." *Art and Artists* (May 1979): 4, 9-10.

Emery, Tony. "Myth and Style in the Work of Robert Young." *Artscanada* 37 (April-May 1980): 29-32.

Keziere, Russell. "Robert Young." *Vanguard* 8 (April 1979): 21-24.

Mays, John Bentley. "Born Under a Floodlight: How Theatre Inspired Robert Young to Paint His Life." *Globe and Mail*, 23 September 1980.

——— "The show goes on — in paint." *Globe and Mail*, 23 September 1980.

Quantrill, Malcolm. "London Letter." Art International (April 1979): 58-59.

[Shadbolt, Doris]. *Robert Young*. Vancouver: Vancouver Art Gallery, 1974.*

——— "Robert Young, the Implacable Presence." *Vanguard* 6 (May 1977): 9-16.

Taylor, John Russell. "The Arts." *The Times* (London), 9 February 1982.

Thom, Ian M. *Robert Young: Prints/Gravures*. Victoria, B.C.: Art Gallery of Great Victoria, 1981.*

White, Paul. "The Work of Robert Young." *Studio International* 186 (July/August 1973): 22-24.

Yearley, Meredith. "Robert Young: A Dionysian Apollo." *Arts West* 8 (September 1983): 12-15.

Robin Page (b. 1933)
Self-Portrait 1972
Present whereabouts not certain

LENDERS TO THE EXHIBITION

Agnes Etherington Art Centre,
 Kingston
Art Gallery of Hamilton, Hamilton
Art Gallery of Ontario, Toronto
Art Gallery of Windsor, Windsor
Bau-Xi Gallery, Toronto
Canada Council Art Bank, Ottawa
Carl T. Grant Q.C., Toronto
Carmen Lamanna Gallery, Toronto
Catherine Bates, Montréal
Ciba-Geigy Canada Limited Art
 Collection, Montréal
Confederation Centre Art Gallery
 and Museum, Charlottetown
Danny & Paul Bercovitch, Montréal
David Hlynsky, Toronto
Detroit Institute of Arts, Detroit,
 Michigan
Familie Jean Dallaire
Florence Caryle Johnston,
 Woodstock
François Dallaire, L'Acadie
Glenbow Museum, Calgary
Glenn Priestley, Scarborough
Greg Curnoe, London, Ontario
Harold Town, Toronto
Hart House, University of Toronto,
 Toronto
Ivan Eyre, Winnipeg
Joyce Wieland, Toronto
J. Ron Longstaffe (through
 Vancouver Art Gallery),
 Vancouver
Leslie Poole, Vancouver
London Regional Art Gallery,
 London
Louis Muhlstock, Montréal
Louis Painchaud, Sherbrooke

Maltwood Art Museum and Gallery,
 University of Victoria, Victoria
McCord Museum, McGill
 University, Montréal
Mira Godard Gallery, Toronto
Mr. & Mrs. Chen-Chi Ho,
 Moncton, N.B.
Mrs. T. R. MacDonald, Hamilton
Musée des Beaux-Arts de Montréal,
 Montréal
Musée du Québec, Québec
National Gallery of Canada, Ottawa
Owens Art Gallery, Mount Allison
 University, Sackville
Public Archives of Canada, Ottawa
Public Archives of Nova Scotia,
 Halifax
Robert Stacey, Toronto
Sable-Castelli Gallery, Toronto
Simon Dresdnere, Toronto
The McMichael Canadian
 Collection, Kleinburg
The Robert McLaughlin Gallery,
 Oshawa
Walter Bachinski, Guelph
Winnipeg Art Gallery, Winnipeg
Woodstock Art Gallery, Woodstock
and numerous private collections